An Intimate Wilderness

NORMAN HALLENDY

An Intimate Wilderness

Arctic Voices in a Land of Vast Horizons

FOREWORD BY DR. WILLIAM W. FITZHUGH

GREYSTONE BOOKS
Vancouver/Berkeley

Greystone Books Ltd.
www.greystonebooks.com

Cataloguing data available from Library and Archives Canada
ISBN 978-1-77164-230-9 (cloth)
ISBN 978-1-77164-231-6 (epub)

Jacket design by Nayeli Jimenez and Robert Hoselton
Interior design by Robert Hoselton
All photographs by Norman Hallendy
Printed and bound in China by 1010 Printing International Ltd.

We gratefully acknowledge the support of the Canada Council for the Arts, the British Columbia Arts Council, the Province of British Columbia through the Book Publishing Tax Credit, and the Government of Canada through the Canada Book Fund for our publishing activities.

Canada

Greystone Books is committed to reducing the consumption of old-growth forests in the books it publishes. This book is one step towards that goal.

Inuksuliriji, I respect you highly, my friend Norman.
You are a wise man, knowledgeable, and a man of honour.
I am proud to be your friend! You are a friend to all Inuit. We thank you.

Piita Irniq Commissioner of Nunavut 2000–2005.

Osuitok and I at Kinngait (Cape Dorset), 1998.

A PROMISE KEPT
to

Issuhungituk Qiatsuq Pootoogook, Oshutsiak Pudlat,
Pudlo Pudlat, Quvianaqtuliak (Kov) Parr, Ikkuma Parr,
Pauta Saila, Pitaloosie Saila, Eegyvudluk Pootoogook,
Kananginak Pootoogook, Pudlat Pootoogook,
Paulassie Pootoogook, Joanassie Salamonie,
Kiawak Ashoona, Pitseolak Ashoona, Qaqqaq Ashoona,
Majuriaq Ashoona, Kenojuak Ashevak, Pingwartuk,
Ottochie Ottochie, Itidlouie Itidlouie, Kingmeata Itidlouie,
Lukta Qiatsuq, Mannumi Davidee, Munamee Sarko,
Kingwatsiuk, Simeonie Quppapik, and Osuitok Ipeelie

*"I'm telling you these things so that
they are written. Write carefully, you are
carrying the remains of our thoughts."*

isumagijaujut kinguvaariinnuuqattaqtut
Osuitok, 1998

CONTENTS

FOREWORD   18

AUTHOR'S NOTE   22

THE JOURNEY, 1958–2012   24

INTRODUCTION   27
The early years and a time of discovery.

TOUGH GUYS AND GENTLE MEN   31
Growing up in a rough-and-tumble neighborhood
in Toronto and attending the Annual Prospectors'
Convention, a raucous gathering of prospectors and
miners that inspired the author's northern travels.

CONTOURS OF THE LAND   39
The Arctic, its vastness, beauty and a love of the land.

FIRST IMPRESSIONS   41
Arriving in Cape Dorset in 1958, when the Inuit are
moving from traditional camps to settlements created
by the Federal Government. Kananginak Pootoogook,
son of powerful camp boss, talks about how living
in a settlement affected him.

A BIT OF SILVER PAPER   49
Pingwartuk who was the first to take "the Inquisitive One"
out on the land offers the formula for staying alive. The
author travels at sea with Lukta Qiatsuq, who gets them
out of a very serious situation by using the aluminum
foil from a package of cigarettes.

REFLECTIONS 53

Simeonie Quppapik, who was photographed in 1923
by the legendary American filmmaker Robert Flaherty,
talks about his lineage and offers sharp insights
on the importance of words.

BY THE LIGHT OF A SEAL OIL LAMP 57

Kananginak Pootoogook relates his life story. He was
born in a hut lit by a seal oil lamp in a camp reached by dogsled in winter and kayak in summer, at a time when
it was believed that shamans could fly to the moon.
Later in life, he watched men landing on the moon
from the comfort of his home in Cape Dorset,
which was heated by oil from Venezuela.

THE SCENT OF SENSITIVITY 61

The author learns the rules of proper behaviour and
the proper way to ask questions of the elders.

LEGENDS AND REALITIES 65

How to separate myth and legend from reality.

CENTRE OF THE WORLD 67

The author gives a panoramic view of the
remarkable locations all around him: the Foxe Channel, Southampton Island, Igloolik, the ancient camps of
Nurrata and Nuvudjuak, Cape Dorset, and the
Great Plain of the Koukdjuak.

HUNGER, FEAR, AND MAGIC 69

The author and Itulu Itidlouie set off for the small island
of Sarko, and barely return alive.

TABLE D'HÔTE 73

What it's like dining out on walrus, whale skin, eider
duck eggs, ptarmigan, and caribou, while avoiding,
fermented meat or fish, the eyes of animals, and
fully formed chicks still in their eggs.

NUNANNGUAIT, "IMITATIONS OF THE EARTH"   75
The Inuit view of memory, maps and map making.

HOW WE TOOK A GREAT WHALE   83
An elder talks about traditional techniques
for hunting whales.

SILENT MESSENGERS   87
Understanding the complex meanings of inuksuit,
the human made stone figures and markers placed
on the Arctic landscape.

AN INUKSUK UNIVERSE   93
A meditation on the cycle of life growing in the shadow
of a single inuksuk.

MORE REAL THAN YOU COULD IMAGINE   95
An illusion of reality.

THE STONE HUNTER   97
Osutsiak Pudlat talks about how inuksuit were used
as hunters' aids.

INUKSUGALAIT   101
The author travels with Ohito Ashoona and his son
to Inuksugalait where at least 100 inuksuit stand
within an area of three hectares. In this place, one
is overcome with a sense of spirituality and awe.

TUKILIK   107
Travelling by helicopter, Paulassie Pootoogook leads
the author to an ancient site rivaling Inuksugalait. With
careful observation of the entire site and its relation to
the caribou migration, the author unravels its mystery.

LITTLE BEAR AND THE RAVENS   115
Memorable encounters with polar bears and ravens.

WHERE NORTHERN LIGHTS ARE BORN   121
One Inuit legend about how the Northern Lights
came to be.

VISIONS 123
The strange phenomenon of "lightning in the ice."

LUNAR ATTRACTION 125
The author observes a very strange occurrence and
learns from elders about the power of the moon.

GHOSTLY CARIBOU AND PHANTOM DOGS 127
Ethereal sightings when travelling on the land.

TIME OF THE MAGIC LIGHT 129
As the sun sets, a fiery column of light forms and
reaches skyward. Then, a full moon appears to rise
out of the sea, like a great paper lantern floating
heavenward.

A FEARFUL TWILIGHT 131
The author experiences "kayak sickness," a
disorientation so extreme that he did not know
up from down or where he was upon the sea.
An elder talks about dangerous act of gathering
clams below the ice in springtime.

SIGNS FROM HEAVEN 135
Arctic phenomena such as ice blinks, ground drift,
sundogs, diamond dust, and a time when the air
appears to be filled with glittering ice crystals.

ESSENTIAL WOMAN 137
Majuriaq Ashoona talks about the woman's role
in Inuit traditional society.

NEEDLE, THIMBLE, AND ULU 143
Ikkuma Parr and a small group of women share their
stories of camp life, arranged marriages, the status
of women, traditional remedies, and the worst things
that could happen to a woman in camp.

WITCHES AND MERMAIDS 153
Osuitok Ipeelie talks about the difference between what
he believed to be true and what he knew to be true,
and offers a story about a cannibal witch.

WHERE THE SUN DANCES AND THE EARTH SHIMMERS 157
Springtime in the southwest Baffin region, and the land
awakens from a deep sleep.

DREAMS, DREAMING, DREAMERS 159
Osuitok Ipeelie discusses different types of dreams,
some based on what one knows to be real, others that
give a glimpse of the future.

FIVE STATES OF MIND 163
Osuitok Ipeelie on the five states of mind beyond
dreaming.

THE SPIRIT HELPERS 167
There was a time when Inuit believed in the existence
of helpful and evil *tuurngait* (spirits) who were called
upon by shamans to perform all manner of tasks.

PLACE OF POWER, OBJECTS OF VENERATION 169
On the metaphysical landscape of the Eastern Arctic
— places where life was renewed, strict customs
observed, and celebrations staged.

IN THE FIELD, ON THE LAND 173
The difference between woking in the field and living
on the land.

A CHARMED LIFE 177
An elder from Kugluktuk (Coppermine) shares stories
about charms: ones that attract good luck, allow the
owner to perform superhuman feats, or offer a glimpse
of the future.

SPIRITS IN THE STONE 181
The elder from Kugluktuk (Coppermine) continues his
stories about a deadly snowman made by a shaman.
Such an effigy could be used by the shaman to capture
the spirit of the person destined to be either harmed
or killed.

THE STRENGTH OF SPIRITS 183
On the powers of real shamans.

INURLUK   185

The tale of the young girl who was taken as a wife
by the evil spirit Inurluk who transformed her into an
inunnguaq, a stone figure in the likeness of a human.

HAUNTED BY HUNGER   189

The elder Ottochie speaking of desperation and pain
of starvation, and the measures taken to stay alive.

MIRKUT AND THE SHAMAN   195

Two tales of a mysterious fire, the disappearance of
an old man, and an evil female shaman.

LOVE, LIFE, DEATH, AND IMMORTALITY   199

A story about a woman who fell in love with an ijiraq,
a spirit in the form of a caribou. A tale encompassing
love, death, cannibalism, rebirth, and immortality.

FOR THE LOVE OF JESUS   201

Armand Tagoona, the first ordained Anglican deacon
in the eastern Arctic, explains how his traditional beliefs
were affected when he become a minister of the
Christian faith.

ALIGUQ'S WARNING   203

On a solo trip to Mallik, the author has an odd dream
in which he is warned by a woman never to return. The
author would later be told that he was visited in his
dream by the much-loved shaman Aliguq.

BRIDGING WORLDS   211

Deciding to follow Christian beliefs yet saddened at
the same time, a woman and her companions seek
peace by making an offering to Sedna, who lived at
the bottom of the sea.

INCANTATIONS, CURSES, AND THE POWER OF WORDS   215

The author learns about incantations that attract animals,
calm storms, offer protection against evil spirits, and give
thanks for a safe journey or successful hunt.

ETERNITY 219
The author met Issuhungituk Pootoogook during
his first visit to Cape Dorset. The two built a strong
bond, spending hours together at the kitchen table
talking about all manner of things.

QIATSUQ AND THE IMAGINED WINDOW 221
Issuhungituk shares the story of her father, Qiatsuq,
a shaman and artist who depicted traditional life on
the land and scenes of violence and killings.

TUQU: DEATH 229
An elder talks about the rituals and understanding
of death.

ISLAND OF THE DEAD 233
The author learns about a terrible battle between
Attachie's and Kinarnaq's camps. Thirty bodies were
later dumped on a small island known as Iluvirqtuq.

JAYKO AND THE RENDERING VAT 237
In desperation, hunters place the lifeless body of one
of their friends into an iron rendering vat. Several years
later the body is removed and given a Christian burial.

THE OLD WOMAN WHO WAS CARRIED OFF BY WOLVES 239
Fantastic tales about Arctic wolves, real and mythological.

A COWBOY SONG FOR MIKKIGAK 241
The author serenades a old friend on his death bed.

LAMENT FOR AN OLD FRIEND 243
Final words to the elder Joanassie Salamonie.

TRANSFORMATIONS IN TIME 245
An everyday experience as simple as observing the
melting of ice reveals an event of epic proportions.

ADRIFT   249
Pudlo Pudlat watches as his nephew floats out to sea
on an ice floe to face certain death. Miraculously, the
young boy is saved by the turn of the tide.

TEA TIME ON AN ICE FLOE   251
The transcendental part of the world that lies between
the land and the open sea and between different
hunting techniques.

THE PEOPLE WITH THE POINTED SHOES   255
Simeonie Quppapik talks about the Sami reindeer
herders and 600 reindeer who arrived in the Canadian
Arctic in 1921, in a failed experiment to establish
the herd in Canada.

TWO TATTOOS   257
What was the meaning of the tattoos on Charles
Gimpel's arm, Qaqqaq Ashoona wants to know.

DARK SHADOWS   261
Abuse in some camps during traditional times
and repentance.

THREAT AND RECONCILIATION   267
On a trip with a dominant hunter, the author
experiences abuse and humiliation, but in the end
a measure of redemption as he is carried ashore by
his tormentor who becomes a close friend.

THE LAST TRADITIONAL INUIT TRIAL IN SIKUSIILAQ   271
The author comes upon a site where the Great Council
sat in judgement, and offers a unique account of the
Inuit traditional system of justice in action.

THE MYSTERIOUS TUNIIT   283
The author recounts what he has learned about the
Tuniit, the mysterious people who preceded today's Inuit.

CULTURAL THREADS   293
The Inuit understanding of the Tuniit.

WORDS: THE VANISHING ARTIFACTS   297
The importance of gathering names, meanings, and
characteristics of places considered significant to the
elders. For the Inuit, words are carriers of culture,
and their loss is profound.

MEMORIES AND VISIONS   301
Osuitok Ipeelie reveals how Inuit shamans kept alive
ancient words spoken by Tuniit shamans; life in the
early days before the arrival of guns and missionaries;
and how the magnetic North Pole is constantly shifting
its position.

THERE IS GREAT BEAUTY IN FOND MEMORIES   303
The author accompanies Itidlouie on the elder's final
trip to his most beloved places.

EPILOGUE   307
The author shares stories with a niece of one of the
elders, and learns about his Bukovinian roots from
a former Polish cavalryman.

ACKOWLEDGEMENTS   313

AN EXPRESSION OF THANKS   317

WHAT A WONDERFUL THING IT WAS TO KNOW YOU   319

INDEX   324

FOREWORD

When Martin Frobisher arrived in the Canadian Arctic in 1576, searching for the Northwest Passage in three small sailing vessels, the Inuit had lived here for only about 250 years and had already experienced major environmental and social change. They had replaced the previous Dorset inhabitants (known to Inuit as Tuniit), had met Norse and Elizabethan explorers, had acquired iron, and had seen their major subsistence resources — bowhead whales — disappear as the Little Ice Age closed down their summer waterways. This is not exactly the image of the "timeless" Arctic people that emerged from the late 18th and early 19th century ethnographies of Franz Boas and Birket-Smith, and Knud Rasmussen, a folklorist; and it pales before the realization that Inuit predecessors — the Dorsets and/or Tuniit — had been living here four thousand years. Yet, as Norman Hallendy demonstrates, during their relatively brief tenure the Inuit built a world that is richly preserved — not only in artifacts, campsites, and ethnographies — but in the little-investigated field of Inuit language and toponymy.

Norman Hallendy's long-term relationship with the Cape Dorset region of southern Baffin Island brings us closer to understanding the world from an Inuit perspective than any-one since Rasmussen, whose work and publications from the Central Arctic in the 1920s first documented linguistic aspects of Inuit culture. Hallendy did not come to these lands as an anthropologist or explorer. This first generation Canadian immigrant with heritage from Bukovina in Eastern Europe wandered into the Canadian Arctic by chance as a mining prospector's assistant; he became captivated by its people and geography, and for the next forty-five years returned again and again, mesmerized by the vastness of the land, his genial hosts, and the spell of the evocative Inuit language. During seasonal visits to Cape Dorset as a high-ranking Canadian Government housing official he began to explore the meaning of words, concepts, and place-names. Over time his social ties with the Dorset community, particularly elders whose early years had been spent living in camps throughout the year, grew into trustworthy bonds. Visiting homes, travelling far and wide to inspect old camps *(nunalituqaq)*, historic and sacred sites *(saqqijaaringialik)*, and places of power *(itsialangavik)*, he has come closer to seeing through Inuit eyes and thinking in Inuit ways than any previous visitor to the Canadian North. Learning Inuktitut and working closely with translators and knowledgeable elders, he recorded nuanced words for places, states of mind, and relationships, and has made these words and their meanings available in an extensive linguistic database unique to Sikusiilaq (Foxe Peninsula). Hallendy's work in Cape Dorset is likely to stimulate interest in preserving linguistic concepts among Inuit elsewhere.

Hallendy's explorations have made him something of a modern 'Rasmussen' of the Canadian Arctic. Rasmussen was more interested in Inuit mythology, religion, and oral history, whereas Hallendy focuses more on lexical matters like names, meanings, and states of being. Like Rasmussen, he travelled and lived with Inuit, winter and summer, exploring the words Inuit use to describe weather events, ice conditions, or geographic and cultural features. Called by Inuit Apirsuqti "the inquisitive one," Hallendy developed friendships that provided him with access to inner worlds that anthropologists since Rasmussen have ignored or taken for granted. No one before has explored the connections between Inuit conceptions of place, geography, and philosophy in such depth. It is indeed, for the Inuit and for Hallendy, an "intimate wilderness" created through the meaning of words that he reveals in a memoir written as an autobiographical tribute for the Inuit who opened their world to him.

Hallendy is best known through his interviews and lectures and for his documentation of the Inuit stone structures known as *inuksuit* ("acting in the capacity of a human"), whose singular form is inuksuk. His beautiful photography and book, *Inuksuit: Silent Messengers of the Arctic*, illustrate these mysterious rock sculptures, revealing them not only as works of art but as structures with special meaning. Today their most iconic forms have become symbols of Inuit ethnicity and Canadian national identity. In *Intimate Wilderness* we meet more of these creations and learn their meanings and stories as told by Inuit elders.

Because of his previous book *Inuksuit: Silent Messengers of the Arctic,* the once-enigmatic *inuksuit* and their stone relatives are not as mysterious as they once were; they have Inuit names and meanings and tell stories that add to our knowledge of Inuit and Tuniit history.

Intimate Wilderness tells many stories in different ways. It is a memoir, a tribute, a linguistic ethnology, and a story of lives and history in a small part of the Canadian Arctic whose lexical world has never been studied in such depth before. For thousands of years Inuit Paleoeskimo ancestors created a world we know only through abandoned houses, stone tools, food remains, and tiny but beautiful carvings of people and animals.

By eliciting memories of them and their names from the few Inuit still directly familiar with the old Inuit way of life, Hallendy gives us a glimpse of a world that before, was closed to all but the Inuit themselves, a world that may even include some Tuniit history. While we will never fully understand the full significance of their 'silent messengers,' through the narratives and words the Cape Dorset people use to describe their landscape, Norman Hallendy has cracked the door and provided us a glimpse of this land of vast horizons.

William W. Fitzhugh,
Director, Arctic Studies Center,
Smithsonian Institution,
Washington DC.

AUTHOR'S NOTE

The Inuktitut terms and expressions used in this book were given to me by the elders of the Cape Dorset. The terms were transcribed by the Manning sisters — Annie, Nina, and Jeannie as well as Leetia Parr and Pia Pootoogook. Some terms would be considered archaic in one area of the eastern Arctic and common in another. In the Kinngait area, for example, the term Inuksuk is used while in Igloolik the equivalent term is Inuksugaq.

In the early days, I often wrote out words phonetically, as a standard orthography was still in development. Recording the names of people and places presented a challenge and still does because there are variations of their spelling in various documents. For example, is it Ashuna or Ashoona, Kiawak or Kiugak, Itiliarjuk or Itiliardjuk, Nuratta or Nurratta and so forth. After several years accumulating Inuktitut words and expressions and their meanings, I began arranging the information in English and Inuktitut in a simple database using Roman orthography. The database now provides a particularly rich collection of 1,500 Inuktitut terms and expressions many unique to Sikusiilaq (Southwest Baffin).

The database enables one to explore words and expressions arrayed in a semantic field. For example: if one searches the term caribou, 73 different words related to caribou in both English and Inuktitut are displayed. The database has another valuable feature, with the click of a button, it will produce a unique 99 page dictionary containing the Inuktitut word, the English translation of that word and it's meaning. I considered having the entire collection of Inuktitut words and expressions in this manuscript vetted and, where necessary, altered to conform to present-day usage. I was encouraged by my Inuit mentors to leave them be, as the words accurately render the meaning ascribed to them by the Sikusiilaq elders.

I chose to write in a manner that reflected how the stories were told to me. In this way, it was my hope to bring you, the reader, into those moments of intimate conversations and experiences.

Washington

Toronto

New York

Ottawa

Montreal

Kuujjuaraapik
(Great Whale River)

Umiujaq

Sanikiluaq

Hudson Bay

QUEBEC

Inukjuak

Arviat/Arviatjuaq (Eskimo Point)

Puvirniqtuuq
(Povungnituk)

Tikirarjuaq (Whale Cove)

Kangiq&iniq (Rankin Inlet)

Kuujjuaq
(Fort Chimo)

Akulivik

Iguligaarjuk (Chesterfield Inlet)

Ivujivik

Salliq (Coral Harbour)

Kangiqsualujjuaq
(Wakem Bay)

Salluit

Kinngait
(Cape Dorset)

Southampton I

Naujaat/Aivilik
(Repulse Bay)

Hudson Strait

Kimmirut
(Lake Harbour)

Qarmaarjuak
(Amadjuak)

Sikusiilaq
(Foxe Peninsula)

Kugaaruk

Arvilikjuaq
(Pelly Bay)

Sanirajaq
(Hall Beach)

Iqaluit
(Frobisher Bay)

Talurjuaq/
Taloyoak
(Spence Bay)

Nettilling
Lake

NUNAVUT

Iglulik
(Igloolik)

Pangnirtuuq
(Pangnirtung)

Baffin Island

Ikpiarjuk/
Tununirusiq
(Arctic Bay)

Qikiqtarjuaq
(Broughton Island)

Qausuittu
(Resolute Ba

Kangiq&ugaapik
(Clyde River)

Mittimatalik/
Tununiq
(Pond Inlet)

Ausuittuq
(Grise Fiord)

KALAALLIT NUNAAT
(GREENLAND)

Ellesmere
Island

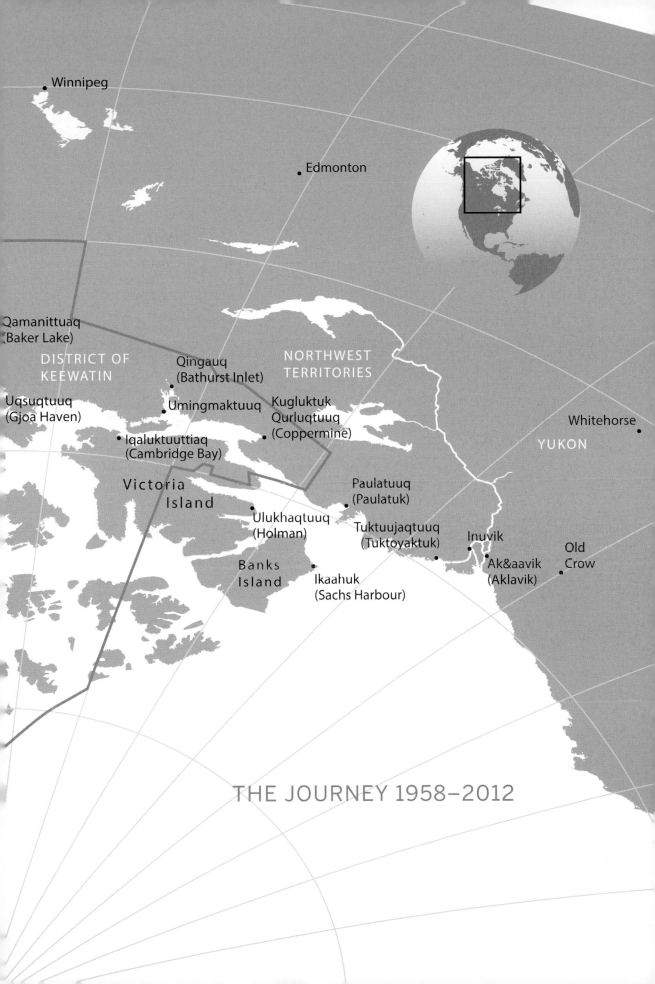

Winnipeg

Edmonton

Qamanittuaq
(Baker Lake)

DISTRICT OF
KEEWATIN

NORTHWEST
TERRITORIES

Qingauq
(Bathurst Inlet)

Uqsuqtuuq
(Gjoa Haven)

Umingmaktuuq

Kugluktuk
Qurluqtuuq
(Coppermine)

Whitehorse

YUKON

Iqaluktuuttiaq
(Cambridge Bay)

Victoria
Island

Paulatuuq
(Paulatuk)

Ulukhaqtuuq
(Holman)

Tuktuujaqtuuq
(Tuktoyaktuk)

Inuvik

Old
Crow

Ak&aavik
(Aklavik)

Banks
Island

Ikaahuk
(Sachs Harbour)

THE JOURNEY 1958–2012

Reflections of the few weeks of summer.

AN INTIMATE WILDERNESS

INTRODUCTION

I am visited by a gentle sadness, for soon, like the geese, I will leave this place and fly south where summer lingers. *Sekkinek*, the sun, rises later each day while darkness arrives ever earlier. It is late August, a time when caribou shed the soft brown velvet from their antlers. Among the shards of summer scattered across the tundra, little grey spiders dart in and out of silken tunnels spun below the now pale gold leaves of Arctic willow. The women and children have picked the berries. White tufts of Arctic cotton have been carried away on the wind. Early morning frost has transformed the grey-green tundra into a vibrant landscape of red, orange, yellow, and gold. My footsteps on the dry lichen sound as if I am walking on crisp snow. Soon, another sound is heard, the moaning of the sea.

There is a place on a hill that opens to the vast horizon. Here we can sit and reminisce upon the sweet thoughts of life and wonder what lies beyond the horizon of our dreams. We can journey along a trail of memories to places so hauntingly beautiful they have to be seen to be believed, and to places so powerful that they have to be believed to be seen. I will shake the dust off my notes that tell of shamans and a world inhabited by spirits, and share with you all that was given me by men and women who lived at the very edge of existence in one of the most demanding places on Earth. They were people who had the genius of knowing how to create an entire material culture from skin, sinew, ivory, bone, stone, snow, and ice. They spoke to me of hardship, love, wonder, and all that defines the human spirit. *Sargarittukuurgunga*, a word as old as their culture, suggests travels across a land of vast horizons.

An Intimate Wilderness is an account spanning 45 years of journeys in Canada's Arctic. Travelling in the company of Inuit

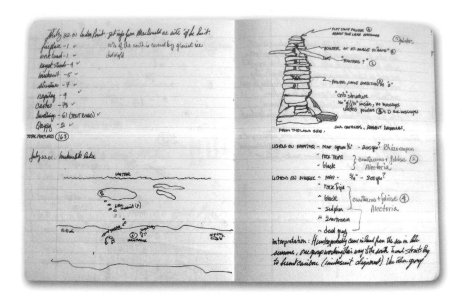

One of many notebooks filled with observations while in the field.

elders, I learned about *unganatuq nuna*, the deep love of the land often expressed in spiritual terms. Other journeys were inward, across the last great wilderness within ourselves. There were times, when travelling on the sea ice to a distant camp, that we ached with cold, and there were times when we snuggled in an igloo beneath warm, soft caribou skins.

In a real sense, these journeys made it possible for me to live in two different worlds in a single lifetime. The familiar world was the one defined by the daily requirement to make a living. I spent my career in various capacities within the federal public service; eventually, I became a senior vice-president of one of Canada's Crown corporations. I married, and my wife and I had two daughters, but our marriage suffered and ended while I worked gruelling twelve-hour days.

The other world was one in which I was free to traverse a place of endless wonder and where, for a brief time, I could become the person I had always wanted to be. Being in the company of elders exposed me in an intimate way to the land and to a way of life I had never known. They referred to themselves as "*Inuit,*" which means, simply, "the people." From the very beginning, I saw myself as a student, continually seeking help from the Inuit elders to feed an insatiable curiosity. They helped me to understand why I was so moved by the landscape, the environment, and the insights of those who knew and experienced their surroundings so intimately. Whether living in a settlement or camp or travelling on the land, I assumed my correct place in the pecking order, which was inevitably at the bottom and in need of being "looked after."

Over the years, I found myself becoming attached to certain individuals and families as their *ilisaqtaulaurpunga innarnut*, their student, relationships that lasted throughout our lives. I realize now that certain experiences gave coherence and a larger meaning to the individual things learned from day to day. The most important of these "learnings" was the attempt to understand what it meant to travel in one's mind from a world believed to be filled with a multitude of spirits to an existence underlined by the promise of something better after death. So began a line of inquiry that will close at the end of my own earthly journey.

It was my *akaunaaruliniapiga*, great fortune, that these Inuit elders shared with me their perceptions, along with their words and expressions now seldom used and in some cases no longer understood. I learned that to be moved by the touch, the smell, and the sounds of the land was not unmanly. This sensual communion, this *unqanatuq*, is a "deep and total attachment to the land" often expressed in spiritual terms. I am unable to forget how an old woman spoke quietly to me of *nuna* the land's fearsome, deadly, and divine qualities with equal reverence.

From time to time, I wondered why the elders with whom I travelled gave so freely of their thoughts and assistance. They could see me capturing their words and putting them on paper, and with their permission, I made their words available for others to read. On rare occasions, I would be told not to disclose a certain event or fact for personal reasons. As time went on, I found that many elders in Cape Dorset actually looked forward to my visits, when I would record what was said over tea, bannock, and goodies. The range of names I was given reflects the different ways I was known to the Sikusiilaq elders: Apirsuqti, the inquisitive one; Angakuluk, the respected one; Inuksuksiuqti, the one who seeks out inuksuit; Innupak, Big Foot; Ittutiavak, a respected elder; and Uqausitsapuq, the word collector.

My Great Aunt Marie, centre, and our relatives in Bukovina, 1955.

TOUGH GUYS AND GENTLE MEN

I first became conscious of manhood in 1948 at the Annual Prospectors' Convention in Toronto. I was sixteen years old. As I remember it, the convention was a spirited gathering of men and women who worked in the mining industry in the North. The majority who attended the convention were, of course, prospectors. This was when they came together from all parts of the North to celebrate the coming field season, renew old friendships, scout the territory for new jobs, swap yarns, and enjoy a moment of nirvana before setting out on their lonely trails in search of El Dorado.

My parents came to Toronto in 1917 from Bukovina, a region in central Europe. At the time, kissing the holy icon on Sunday and being on the lookout for the evil eye on all other days was quite normal. I have hardly any recollection of my grandparents beyond the fact that they were quite superstitious. My father's family were like serfs whose struggle to eke out a living left no time or reason to fashion a family tree. Like countless other immigrants, they came to the promised land not because they believed the streets were paved with gold but to escape the endless brutality that seemed to be their birthright.

Like most immigrant and first-generation kids, my friends and I formed tribes, developed secret signs, held clandestine meetings, and swore to uphold the honour of our group. None of us had any idea that our respective parents were plotting to have us committed to institutions where we would forsake our roots and undergo the process of learning. We would acquire the instruments of success; our success would be their success; and so our parents would acquire status for the first time in their lives. To our parents, the sound of the wind rustling through the beech trees in Bukovina was only a distant dream.

As a youth, I learned important life lessons by working odd jobs. Even at a tender age, I learned that diversity of experience was the pathway to success. At age fourteen, I landed a summer job at a doll factory as a gofer and floor sweeper before progressing to the production line, making Baby Wett'em dolls. I also worked in a graveyard raking leaves and filling in groundhog holes. The giant leap forward was becoming head boy in the fresh produce department of Canada's largest grocery chain.

To my parents, these early jobs were all fine, but having sent me to private school, they were of the opinion that I would surely become a doctor, a lawyer, or, at worst, an engineer. They were utterly dismayed when I blithely announced that I had decided to study art. The decision seemed perfectly natural to me. I had always had a strong instinct for curiosity and a means of expressing it at a very early age. Art appealed to me because it had a magical quality that defied scientific explanation. But when my father, who clearly thought that studying art was a cop-out from the real world, asked me to explain this direction, I fumbled. He told me then that my future was in my own hands and I best put them to work as soon as possible.

I quickly discovered that in order to earn enough money to pay for school, buy books and supplies, and have a little pocket change, I would need to work up north for the entire period I was not attending school. "Working up north" was a euphemism for having a job in either the mining or forestry industry.

To the family of Alexei,

Sending you my photo for your children and mine to remember. Giving you many hugs and kisses forever.

Until we see each other again,

Frozina
2 November 1958

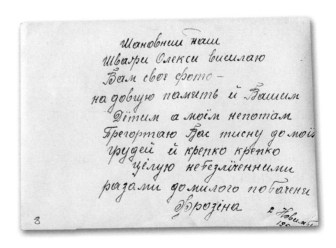

AN INTIMATE WILDERNESS

The Moldavian side of the family, 1954.

Natural resources companies offered the relatively well-paying seasonal jobs that appealed to students like me. I had no romantic notions about the North — I was going there out of necessity. Getting there would not be difficult. The real problem was convincing an employer to hire a sixteen year old kid with no experience in the field. I caught a break when I came across a notice in the *Toronto Daily Star* announcing that the Annual Prospector's Convention would take place at the Royal York Hotel. Dressed as

A sixteen year old packing a box of high explosives
unaware it's leaking nitro glycerine.

neatly as possible, with two dollars and a ten-cent streetcar fare in
my pocket, I was off to the most important convention of my life.

Amid the raucous gathering of those tough miners, I felt a
sense of belonging. I knew I was in good company. I met Eddy
the Swede, Johnny B., Louis Four Toes, and the unforgettable
Big Biff Breakey, who once said to me gruffly, "I'm gonna hire you
kid, but if you ever let me down, you're out'n your arse."

That spring, before I headed into the bush, my father gave
me a .22 rifle and a piece of advice: "Never work," he said, "for
anyone stupider than yourself." The next day, I boarded the train
to Lake of the Woods on behalf of the Northern Canada Mining
Company to locate and re-examine an abandoned gold mine.
That evening, under the spell of the clickety clack of the coach's
wheels, I fell into a deep sleep. The next morning, I awoke to a
sight that astonished me. Entering the boreal forest, I saw a sea
of trees flashing by my window. I had seen forests and woodlands
but never such a powerful living thing as this. The forest evoked
in me a sense of wonder and imagination I had never known.

AN INTIMATE WILDERNESS

I would experience dwelling within this great living thing. Each night, the forest seemed to pulse with a mysterious presence. The sounds coming from deep within were those of owls, loons, foxes, wolves, and the clacking of hooves. Occasionally, my heart skipped a beat as a branch broke loudly and sharply somewhere in the darkness. Some nights in the boreal forest were filled with wonder, when the very air seemed to crackle beneath a blanket of stars showering the Earth with their brilliance. Under a rising full moon, I felt as if I were being drawn into an ancient spell.

One starry night while watching the silhouettes of geese flying south, I experienced the most beautiful event in these northern latitudes, the aurora borealis. It was unlike any display of the northern lights I had ever seen. At first, a faint wisp of light drifted between the stars, a hint of a heavenly event. Then this faint wisp appeared to grow in strength. It became ever brighter, gathering colours from some unseen source. Like some great luminous curtain, it began to unfold across the sky as if set in motion by a celestial wind, its hues changing each moment. The once darkened sky was transformed by this mysterious expanding radiance. Next, as mysteriously as the aurora had arrived in the night sky, she began to fade and the stars, once pale, now regained their original brightness. Having seen such beauty, having stood beneath a moon wrapped in a blanket of stars while listening to the haunting voices of wolves, I entered a wilderness of one, where each footstep led to some new thought.

My life in the forest was filled with many happy experiences. I worked with rough and tough son-of-a-gun men who were never unkind and who would look out for one another. They didn't write poetry or read the writings of Antoine de Saint-Exupéry. They worked hard and from time to time sought out their own private spaces. If some knew that I saw them enjoying a sunset or standing with outstretched arms in a howling wind, I am sure they would have growled in embarrassment and told me to bugger off. In a notebook that I kept under my bunk, filled with observations, expressions of feelings, and random thoughts, I wrote, "I feel a sense of belonging here, yet I don't know why. I'm almost afraid I've been lured into some strange chimera."

One evening, I began to write the words and expressions I was learning in Ojibwa from a Native elder who lived in a nearby camp. The elder came into our camp looking to buy tobacco, paper, and matches. He had taken a shine to me, as I was about the same age as his son. I had asked him if he would teach me a few words in Ojibwa. When I had repeated them to him, he was astonished that my accent sounded perfect. I put this down to the fact that my first language was a Slavic one (a Bukovinian dialect of Ukrainian), in which the phonetics were quite similar.

The elder's camp was only a few kilometres from ours, and on each of his visits, I would ask to be taught a few words, which I would write out phonetically. I learned the names of familiar things — birds, animals, the method of making a fire. I learned evocative expressions such as "the sun which shines in darkness" (referring to the moon) or "the place of talking waters" (referring to a nearby set of rapids). The Ojibwa elder talked of once travelling in a great *schkoodayodabah*, meaning the great fire sleigh or railway train. He talked of forest spirits, leaving gifts to the land, and the importance of showing respect. The one thing he never told me was his name. He simply referred to himself as *neweecheewahgun*, meaning "a friend."

Each year, I returned to the North, leaving behind the amenities of the city, the pleasures of school life and good friends, and began to discover an awareness of the eternal beauty of the wilderness. I would see some new place, gain valued experience, and think about things only they could evoke. Each year, I found myself moving ever northward. No longer doing the bull work of my earlier days, I was now a partner in a reconnaissance team. We moved quickly on foot across the landscape, mapping hundreds of square kilometres in a single season. That sense of self-reliance learned while working under the eye of experienced old-timers became more important than ever. Now I often travelled alone. With only a one-day supply of food, a knife, matches, map, compass, and notebook, I ventured out each morning, with the expectation of a safe return each evening to a little tent somewhere in a vast wilderness. Often at night before falling asleep, I would conjure a fond memory; in reliving it, I

In Ungava now called Nunavik
(Arctic Quebec) at the age of seventeen.

would soften the sharp edge of loneliness. I would fall into a deep sleep, often visited by dreams too ethereal to remember. Upon awakening to the smell of spruce needles and sunlight entering the tent, I found that the lure of distant hills replaced the sense of loneliness.

In the early summer of 1949, I was no longer in the forest. The only trees I encountered were no higher than the length of my hand. I was now in the Arctic, where the earth remained permanently frozen. I was surrounded by a vast horizon, a sight I could never have imagined. Until that day, the Arctic of my imagination had been only a barren and icebound landscape. It was the most forbidding place, shaped in the mind's eye by heroic tales and films that dramatized the land and its people. Even the numerous and often startling photographs I had seen merely confirmed my impression of a frightfully beautiful, frozen corner of the planet. In the years to follow, the Arctic I would come to know extended far beyond the boundaries of my imagination.

The powerful landscape of the Pangnirtung Pass (Pangnirtuuq), Baffin Island.

AN INTIMATE WILDERNESS

CONTOURS OF THE LAND

Arctic. The very word conjures an image of a frozen landscape in the grip of an icy sea. A place of icebergs and polar bears, where winter is cloaked in darkness and summer is an endless moment under the midnight sun. The stereotypical image we southerners have of the polar region emerged from early accounts of whalers and the few survivors of doomed expeditions. These words, written in the golden age of Arctic exploration, reflected what many souls endured at that time: "We seem to be dwelling in some haunted house filled with unearthly and mysterious noises," wrote Charles Edward Smith, the surgeon aboard the icebound whaler *Diana* in 1886. "We sit like hares, startled and alarmed at the slightest sound dreading and fearing we know not what."

Woodcuts and copperplate engravings often illustrated a fantastic world in which life and death teetered on the sharp edge of chance. All the while, somewhere out there lived a people who had adapted perfectly to their environment. They beheld their place as *nunatsiaq*, the beautiful land. To those who lived in favoured locations, it was *nunatiavaluk*, a very fine land rich in food and beautiful to behold. *Nunarrak*, the land, sea, and sky, was regarded as great living thing. Upon and within her dwelled the *tuurngait*, the spirits, and all things were temporarily imbued with *inua*, the life force.

The Arctic is often described as a cold desert where precipitation, including melting snow, averages a mere 14 to 26 centimetres annually. Imagine a place with so little precipitation, where winter temperatures average -34° Celsius and can plummet to -60° Celsius; where just below its surface, the earth can be frozen solid for hundreds of metres; where whatever soil thaws in summer is poor in nutrients, and anything that can grow must do so within 50 days.

When you stand upon the Arctic landscape for the first time, you are overwhelmed by its vastness, power, and sheer beauty. Whether you are at the foot of a glacier, on the crest of a mountain, or on the great plains of the central Arctic, you are surrounded by evidence of the unimaginable forces that shape mountains, melt glaciers, move oceans, and drive winds as far as the Gulf of Mexico.

No general profile of the Arctic landscape exists. The shape of the land varies from the great delta plain of the Mackenzie in the west to the imposing mountains of Ellesmere and Baffin in the east. Travelling by airplane from Inuvik to Iqaluit, you can appreciate the grandeur of the Canadian North. You begin the journey in the far west, gazing upon the sinuous delta landscape, an endless maze of twisting rivers and lakes — a surrealistic view of the planet where the infinite number of lakes and twisting rivers reflects images of clouds, as if the Earth were a giant perforated leaf floating on a calm, glassy sea.

As you travel eastward, the landscape changes from the water world of the delta to vast lowlands sweeping toward the coast. They pass in sombre tones of grey and brown, stretching to infinity. Here and there, last year's snowdrifts lie in the protection of shadows, waiting for the arrival of winter. Below, you see the shadow of your plane continually changing shape as you pass over countless eskers, rivers, and lakes.

Flying over the west coast of Hudson Bay, you note the landscape lies flat, shaved by the glacier that scoured this place a mere 9,500 years ago. You are about to be astonished. There it is: You now behold an Arctic shaped by mountains, snowfields, glaciers, and icebergs. This is the Arctic described in heroic accounts, stories, songs, dreams, and nightmares. At first, you are spellbound. Then inwardly, you come face to face with your utter insignificance. You are exposed to the terrible realization of your vulnerability; everything you have ever learned is irrelevant because, unequipped with the knowledge and skill of how to survive on the land, you are likely to die here in a matter of days if left alone.

FIRST IMPRESSIONS

For my generation, getting up to the Arctic was easy. Weather permitting, I could fly to the most remote regions in a day or two. Yet just a single generation before mine, those hearty souls who ventured north were resigned to the prospect that it might take them at least a year or longer, depending on the weather, to reach their destination. At that time, getting to the Arctic was by way of train to the end of the line, then a stomach-churning voyage on a small supply ship, often followed by walking and sledding enormous distances. There was no food supply from the outside world, no global positioning system, no sideband radio. The essentials were simple: Learn from the Inuit how to survive, make no mistakes, and regard hardship, no matter how severe, as a natural occurrence to overcome. Savour a sense of personal triumph, however small. In those early days, grants, steady wages, or sponsors were rarely available to those travelling to the Arctic. Many paid the costs of doing their fieldwork out of their own pocket.

I arrived in Cape Dorset — or Kinngait as it is also referred to — in 1958, when I was 26 years old. At the time, I was working with the Department of Northern Affairs as an industrial designer. The department did groundbreaking work, such as developing the Arctic char fishery, a lumber operation on the George River, and, most important, a network of Inuit cooperatives across the Arctic.

When I arrived, Cape Dorset was a pleasant community of about 700 people, many living in flimsy shelters known as "matchboxes." The town faced the sea and was blessed with good hunting in the surrounding area. A few people were still living in permanent camps along the coast and came into Dorset to trade with the Hudson's Bay Company. At the time, probably fewer than 100 *qallunaat*, white people, lived in the entire eastern Arctic (excluding military personnel). This number would swell each summer when a few dozen scientists arrived just in time to feed our little *leituriaraluit*, voracious mosquitoes.

In those days, many Inuit of southwest Baffin Island, historically known as *Sikusiilaq*, were still living on the land. Though they were equipped with rifles and an increasing number of articles obtained from the *qallunaat*, staying alive still meant securing enough food to keep from starving, fashioning one's own clothing and shelter to keep from dying of exposure, and rearing children who were expected to be future providers. Such was the *taimaigiakaman*, "the great necessity."

It was with these people of Cape Dorset that I would develop a lasting friendship. Many had recently started living in settlements. They left behind articles designed for living entirely off the land. They brought to Cape Dorset few material goods — perhaps a harpoon for seal hunting, a stone lamp handed down from mother to daughter, and other assorted articles of sentimental value. They also brought vivid memories of their traditional way of life and enduring perceptions of both the physical and metaphysical world that continued to exist just beyond the visible limits of their new settlement.

The familiar expression "going out on the land" meant leaving the often mundane life in the settlement. Going out on the land also meant journeys upon the sea or ice to locations dear to the heart: returning to the places of one's childhood and family life, to favoured locations on the tundra where caribou grazed, or fishing spots where, during twilight hours, one could listen to the haunting cry of red-throated loons.

Upon my arrival in Dorset that first year, one of the people I met was Kananginak Pootoogook. The son of one of the most powerful camp bosses on Baffin Island, Kananginak represented the generation of Inuit who had been born on the land and lived long enough in traditional camps to learn many traditional skills. Kananginak and his contemporaries later moved into settlements with their elders and became the first generation of Inuit exposed to a *qallunaat* way of life.

Kananginak was a sturdy man as a result of years of hunting and tending his father's traplines which extended for hundreds of kilometres throughout the Foxe Peninsula. Though he had come to live in Cape Dorset as a young man, Kananginak retained a strong attachment to the land. His remarkable drawings of wildlife, traditional camp scenes, and contemporary themes are well known to Inuit art curators and collectors in North America and Europe. One of Kananginak's last drawings is a small map he did for me documenting his family's immediate hunting area in Kangisurituq (Andrew Gordon Bay).

Though Kananginak and I had known each other since 1958, in the early years we never sat down for a good chat. We would often just trade good-natured insults, shake hands, and be on our way. Only in the later years of his life when we finally came together did he make known there were things he would like me to record. In these conversations, Kananginak spoke movingly about how he had perceived life when living on the land and how living in a settlement had affected him.

What I'm about to tell you is how I remember life as it was on the land when we lived at Ikirasaq. Our entire life was spent looking for food. Just think about that! Staying alive depended on knowing where to look and when to look at places where the animals would be. We were always on the move. We travelled by boat, sled, and most often we walked.

Entire families would take everything that was needed for the journey. We carried everything on our backs. Some of us were lucky enough to have a few dogs who would carry things on their backs as well. The man and the eldest son would carry the hunting equipment and the heaviest things. We would carry the tent, bird catcher, throwing stick, fish spear, antler knife, bow drill, a special rock to make fire, and bows and arrows. It was necessary to carry sinew, pieces of ivory and bone and other materials so you could repair things along the way.

It was important to make extra arrowheads before setting out. Especially beautiful and accurate arrowheads could be made only during one day in the year. They were made by using the last rib of an udjuk *(square-flipper seal). Of course, arrowheads were made at other times but lacked real importance. All kinds of other things were brought along, but the most important was the harpoon. You see, the harpoon has many functions. It is used for hunting seal, walrus, and whales. But even when travelling inland, it has many uses. It can be quickly converted to a spear by changing its tip. It can be used as an ice chisel, a snow probe, a rod to help someone in need, and other useful things, but most importantly, as a weapon to defend yourself.*

The wife and daughter had much to carry on their backs. They carried pieces of scraped skins to repair clothing and caribou skins to lie upon. They brought needles, sinew, thimbles all placed inside a bag made from a loon skin. The woman carried a stone ulu *(women's knife) skin stretchers, one made from stone, another from the scapula of a seal, and a special one from the shin bone of a caribou. They carried the extra clothing, the* qulliq *or* kudlik *(soapstone lamp), a small bag of moss for the lamp wick, soapstone pot, and a skin bucket and dipper made from sealskin. She brought dried seal meat and blubber to burn in the lamp, as well as to eat along the way until the men got fresh food. Because the women must keep clean, they brought seagull skins to clean their hands and rabbit skins for when they had their period. Rabbit skins are also good for wiping the baby's bum and the skins from the rabbit's legs are carefully peeled off to be used as finger bandages. The woman brought a scraping board for cleaning skins, together with tent poles and a drying rack.*

With all this, she would probably be carrying a baby in her amaut *(parka hood). She knew how to carefully remove the skin from small birds and turn the skins inside out. They become nice warm booties for babies. Women had to keep up with the men while carrying all these things. If a woman gave birth along the way, by late the* same day she put the baby in her amaut, picked up her belongings, and continued on with the rest.

Our journey inland would begin in the season when the caribou have short hair (toward the end of August). Different families lived in different places all the way from Nuvudjuak to Sugba. There were 14 main camps in our region and many seasonal camps all along the coast. The people in our region who lived the furthest away were from Nuvudjuak and Nurrata, and so their journeys were across land and began in the northwest. The families who lived below Tikiraaqjuk, the great finger, would meet at a few traditional gathering places at the Sugba. It was important to know the whereabouts of the katittarvit sinaani nunaqpagiarnialiqtunut (gathering places on the shore in preparation of going inland). It was here where families gathered checked everything and discussed their plans before setting out for the great walk. It was a place and time of excitement. It was here that we left some things behind, carefully cached for our return just before the sea began to freeze in early November. We would pick up all our belongings put them on our backs and begin the great walk inland.

We all would start walking as soon as there was light and each day walk as far as we could. Some parents were careful to watch their small children during these long periods of walking because the young children could suffer a painful dislocation we call azalujuk, which is the same expression used when the runners of a sled start to splay outward. The men hunted along the way, thankful that fresh food was had to replace the dwindling supply of blubber and dried meat.

The older men would point out landmarks to their young sons. The boys were learning about the meaning of life... survival. They would memorize the shapes of distant hills. They were taught how to observe all the things around them. The angaituq (the specialist) was our teacher.

In those days our people had very strong ways to describe things, especially the landscape. The expression *tauuunguatitsiniq means creating a picture of a thing in another person's mind. Our maps were in our mind. We knew the places where one had to be very cautious. We had pictures in our head where animals would likely be at certain times of the year. We knew the favoured locations of caribou and where they would cross rivers. We knew where we could cross rivers in search of them. And when the crossings were too deep, we would take a caribou skin, shape it into a bag, stuff it with dry moss, and paddle safely to the other side. One of our most important maps we had in our mind was a map of all the shallows, the ikaniigiik. Without it, travelling over long distances would be very difficult.*

We gathered together before starting out, as I explained, and often would start out going inland as a group. Later we would separate into small family groups, each going to its preferred locations along a familiar route. By the time we reached the places where the caribou were plentiful, their coats were in the very best condition. Understand that though seals were our main food supply, caribou were vital for our survival in winter. From their back came the sinew to sew their skins needed to make the winter clothing that kept us from freezing to death. The meat and the marrow from their bones nourished us. We used portions of their antlers to make tools. We dressed in their skins. We slept on their soft skins in a warm tent made of their skins. It was as if for part of a year we lived inside a fat, warm caribou.

Sometimes we would agree to meet again at certain places along the way but, most certainly, we would agree to meet as a group at the end of our journey inland north of Natsilik (Nettilling Lake). It would take at least a month to reach it. By then our journey was only half-completed. We began our return home at the time when days and nights were of equal length (late September). If a certain family did not show up within a few days of our agreed departure time it was no big worry; they may have had some reason to stay awhile or take a different route

AN INTIMATE WILDERNESS

for part of the way. The time we began to show some concern is when we got back to our main camp and there was still no sign of them. Some people would decide to winter over at Natsilik, especially if there was a lot of food around.

By the time the caribou had mated, the sea ice was becoming thick enough to travel upon (mid-November). If one was fortunate to have a good dog team, we would make the journey all over again to Natsilik, but this time it was easier, for we travelled by sled. Because the conditions of snow and ice could change from day to day, one had to know how to get to a desired place by many different routes We not only hunted we also trapped white foxes. Now it was important to know which lakes and rivers had treacherous places where the ice was always thin even during the coldest time of the year. It may surprise you, but we sometimes met Igloolikmiut *(people who had travelled all the way from Igloolik) at Natsilik. We would hunt and trap during the winter and once more return to our camps at Sikusiilaq about the time when the ringed seals were born (late March).*

When you were young it was important to be on the land with an angusuitug, *a good hunter, a very competent person. Your mother and father gave you life but it was from an* angusuitug *that you learned how to stay alive.*

Pingwartuk who gave me the secret of staying alive.

Opposite: Lukta, son of Qiatsuk, brother of my beloved Issuhungituk.

AN INTIMATE WILDERNESS

A BIT OF SILVER PAPER

Pingwartuk was the first Inuit elder I met in Cape Dorset and the first to take me out on the land, which often meant going out to sea. Compact and deceptively strong, Ping, as we called him, had hands that were as gnarled as ancient Arctic willows yet as dexterous as those of any artist. His face looked like well-tanned leather, for he was out on his boat as often as weather permitted. At the end of the season, his skin was the same hue as a *Portugee*, the term Cape Dorset Inuit used to refer to black-skinned people.

Ping's name means a gentle and friendly plaything and in fact he was well known for his jovial manner and delightful countenance — he was like a smile on two feet — qualities that obscured the fact he was a serious and competent hunter and trapper. His laughter, especially following some antic that caused him injury, was infectious. "Laughter," he once said, "is very good when things are bad."

But his laughter was not reserved for hard times. As I wrote in *Silent Messengers*, Ping was completely at ease with the *qallunaat*, the white men, who often sought him out for help, guidance, and the use of his boat. One day we were out hunting seal with a well-known writer from New York City. Unfortunately for the writer, no seals were to be had. As the day wore on, one finally surfaced near the boat, dove back into the water, and then returned to the surface where it was met by our hail of bullets. The seal seemed to elude us for quite some time until it finally swam away. I don't believe our guest from New York City ever realized that our elusive prey was, in fact, a stone-cold seal animated by a mischievous Ping. He had rigged the animal with fishing lines and was playing it like a puppet.

Of all our trips together, one stands out. The August day began with the two of us lying on a hilltop watching a great flock of sea pigeons. Their singing caused us to abandon hunting. We lay down on the rocks, inhaled the sweet scent of Arctic heather, and gazed out into the icy blue of the Hudson Strait. We watched icebergs sail in the distance and made out the pale mirages of ghostly islands looming on the horizon. The Earth shimmered. After a long while, I turned to my old mentor and asked him: "If we were never to see each other again, *Angak* (Uncle), what words would you choose to leave with me to remember you?"

"I would tell you," he replied, "always place yourself in a position to take advantage of that which is about to happen."

This formula for staying alive meant doing those things required to improve one's chances of success and those things required to lessen one's chances of disaster. Nothing was more directly related to staying alive out on the land than the chanciest thing of all — *sila*, the weather. *Sila*'s unpredictable behaviour affected all living things. Neither astute observation nor magical incantation could remove all risk.

The power and influence of weather is reflected in the vast number of words and expressions describing it in the Inuit language. Words enabled the intelligent person to carry out a multitude of observations, classify them, and assess the nature of the prevailing conditions. The particular colour of the landscape, the structure of snow and ice, the pattern and formation of clouds, the direction of the tide and wind, ice crystals, the behaviour of the sun, aurora, mirages, sound, and most important, the relationships among all these required a highly specialized vocabulary. If you could choose an example where science and magic came together, it would have to be in the language of weather. *Sila* also means intelligent thought and wisdom.

On one memorable occasion, I was travelling with Lukta, the son of the *angakok* (shaman) Qiatsuq, who was taking me to his father's old camp. I wanted to visit Qiatsuq's now abandoned camp because I was curious to learn why some people were afraid to go there. Heading off by boat with neither map nor compass, Lukta and I navigated safely through a dangerous narrows and across the yawning bay to reach the camp. After I had

AN INTIMATE WILDERNESS

finished documenting the area, we got back into our boat and began crossing the bay.

We were not far into our return trip when I noticed a white line quickly approaching us. I thought it was ice, but it turned out to be a very dense fog that overtook us within half an hour. The fog was so thick that I could barely make out the other end of the motorized canoe seven metres away. Sharing my concern, Lukta shut down the motor and listened carefully. It was what he could not hear — the sounds of waves lapping on the shore — that troubled him. He thought back to the time we had set off, when the sun was shoulder high, and estimated we had been travelling roughly an hour.

He took out a package of cigarettes, removed the silver foil, and folded it into a tiny boat with a sail. He placed it on the water, where it quickly drifted off. From its direction, and taking into account the time of day and season, Lukta knew that the tide was going out into Hudson Strait, which was definitely not where we wanted to be.

Lukta restarted the motor and continued in the direction opposite to the drifting silver paper. We would go along slowly, stop, listen, then continue. Listening was the most important thing. Then, suddenly, we bumped into an outcrop, something not indicated on the map I had. In the middle of the still dense fog, we quickly got out of the canoe, and Lukta looked around. He could tell by the presence of lichens that the outcrop was not covered at high tide. Aware that it would be all too easy to slip off the rock and fall into the icy water, we carefully sat down facing where we thought the land would be and waited.

It took a few hours and then, sure enough, the fog dissipated and we could see the land facing us. The first thing Lukta did was to pick up some loose rocks and build an inuksuk that pointed toward the land. In his mind, he recorded the image of precisely what the outcrop looked like.

When we finally returned safely to Cape Dorset, Lukta told his fellow hunters all that had happened; that if ever they came upon the outcrop out in the bay and saw an inuksuk in the shape of a pointer, it indicated the direction toward the land.

And so a new image was added to the cognitive maps carried in the minds of the hunters of Sikusiilaq.

Simeonie Quppapik my mentor for over 40 years.

AN INTIMATE WILDERNESS

REFLECTIONS

By the time I met him in 1958, Simeonie Quppapik was a respected elder. Simeonie, claimed he had been born twice: first when his mother's midwife brought him into the world, when whalers still visited the area, and second when the Canadian government said he was born, which a bureaucrat determined to have been in 1909, duly written on what looked like an important piece of paper. In either case, Simeonie was adopted as a young child.

I remember clearly one of my visits with Simeonie. I watched him watching something in the distance but, try as I might, I could not detect what he was looking at. Was he dreaming or was there something moving out there? I scanned every inch of the horizon looking for clues that might lead me to the object that had captured his attention. There was nothing floating on the sea. No sign of bad weather approaching. No movement on the land. My curiosity got the better of me. "What are you looking at, *Atatasiak* (Grandfather)?" I asked.

"I am looking toward the place of my childhood," he replied in a whisper.

"Where is it, Grandfather?"

Simeonie took a piece of paper and a stub of a pencil, and drew the entire coastline from Kinngait (Cape Dorset) to Qarmaar-juak (Amadjuak) on south Baffin Island, a distance of about 300 kilometres. "There," he pointed, "that's where I was born and had my childhood captured, put into a box and attached to a piece of paper forever."

In 1923, when Simeonie was fourteen, the legendary American filmmaker Robert Flaherty captured his likeness on film. At the time, the Inuit with whom Flaherty lived had given him the name White Swan. One of Simeonie's relatives, the beautiful Glass Nose, was White Swan's girlfriend and likely influenced him to photograph members of her family before he headed back south. I've often looked at that sweet photograph, then looked at one taken when Simeonie was a strong and handsome hunter. In later years, I would turn and see a small and delicate man who had not wielded a harpoon for some time. But until the end, Simeonie possessed a remarkable memory. He could still sing the songs he had learned many years ago when he lived in skin tents and snow houses while growing up at Qarmaarjuak, the land of the ancient sod houses.

Bright and inquisitive, Simeonie often offered sharp insights into the importance of words. I remember one story about how some *qallunaat* (white people) came to Sikusiilaq many years ago to make *nunannguait*, "imitations of the Earth," or maps. Just off the end of Itiliardjuk is a small island that was the traditional summer camp of the *Kinngnarmiut*, the people living in the Dorset area. When the *qallunaat* arrived, their maps made in the South showed that the island had no name, so they asked their guide, "What's the name of the island?" The guide's son made a slight misinterpretation by telling his father that the *qallunaat* wanted to know who was living on the island, to which the guide replied, *"Alariaq."* So the place that the locals referred to as *Shaqu* or *Sarku* or *Saarru* (the armpit), named for its pleasant little bay, was inadvertently given the place name *Alariaq*, the name belonging to one of the most influential *angakkuit* (shamans) in all of Sikusiilaq.

I had assumed that all the people living in southwest Baffin referred to themselves and were referred to by Inuit living in other distant places as *Sikusiilarmiut*, meaning the people of Sikusiilaq. Yet when Simeonie referred to himself as once having belonged to the *Qarmaaqjummiut*, people of the sod houses, and not to the *Sikusiilarmiut*, I thought it prudent to have a little ethnogeography lesson.

One Sunday in July my interpreter, Jeannie Manning, and I visited Simeonie after church armed with the usual paper, pens, pencils, and his favourite snack, a garlicky sausage I had brought north from my home in Carp, Ontario.

Simeonie began by explaining that the place where you were born and lived most of your life denoted the general name given to all who lived in that place. For example: Pauta was born in Nurrata, and therefore he belonged to the *Nurrattamlut*. The general area, however, was known as Qaumarvik (the land that is in brightness), which included the ancient camp Nuvujuaq, as well as several small camps whose people were known as *Nuvujjuaqmmiut*. Therefore, the *Nurattamiut* and the *Nuvujjuaqmmiut* would be regarded as the regional group the *Qaumainnasuuqmiut*, the people from where the land is bright.

Who, then, were the *Sikusiilarmiut*? I asked Simeonie. He explained that the name of the people from where the land is bright began to change from the *Qaumainnasuuqmiut* to the *Sikusiilarmiut* as they vastly expanded their hunting territory due to the introduction of fox trapping by the Hudson's Bay Company in 1913. Just when I was beginning to grasp Simeonie's teachings, I learned that the *Qaumainnasuuqmiut*, later regarded by other Baffin Islanders as the *Sikusiilarmiut*, had yet another name. Their relatives in Nunavik, Arctic Quebec, referred to them as "the people of the other half."

Simeonie went on to explain the meaning of the name by offering the analogy of a pair of mitts. One mitt represented the people of the Arctic Quebec coast and the other the people of southwest Baffin to whom they were related. Just as I was beginning to understand the lesson, I asked Simeonie to tell me what the *Sikusiilarmiut* called their relatives in Arctic Quebec. "They called them *Akianimiut* (those on the other side)," replied Simeonie.

Almost afraid to go any further, I asked him the origin of the *Kinngnarmiut*, people now living in Cape Dorset. Without any outward sign of impatience, Simeonie explained the following: When people from along the coast became settled in Kinngait, whatever they were called before, changed. They referred to themselves (in the present tense) as *Kinngnarmiut*. Having noticed me constantly revising my notes, he drew a small diagram revealing the names of the groups who lived throughout the Foxe Peninsula from Nuvujuak to Iqaluit. Later, he would draw an extraordinary map for me, which was exhibited in art galleries in Canada and elsewhere and at UNESCO in Paris.

The kudlik, *It gave us light and warmth for over a thousand years.*

BY THE LIGHT OF A SEAL OIL LAMP

I shared too brief a time with Kananginak, one of the few people with whom I never had the opportunity to go out on the land. Yet he was a close friend for more than 45 years, a confidant who, without hesitation, shared his thoughts, concerns, and perspectives on life with me. Kananginak represented that generation of Inuit in southwest Baffin who had been born on the land and were exposed briefly to the traditional way of life. Missionaries were still strangers, the *angakkuit* (shamans) were still to be respected, and outboard motors and snow machines were things of the future. Settlements and nursing stations had yet to be created, and no radio links existed from village to village.

Kananginak was born in a hut lit by a seal oil lamp in a camp reached by dogsled in winter and kayak or canoe in summer. He was born at a time when it was believed that shamans could fly to the moon; later in life, he watched men landing on the moon from the comfort of his home in Cape Dorset, which was heated by oil from Venezuela.

Kananginak's father, Pootoogook, was the most respected man throughout the Baffin Island region. From the earliest times, *qallunaat* (white people), including officials travelling along the Sikusiilaq (southwest Baffin) coast, would stay at Pootoogook's camp. Kananginak once told me, "All *qallunaat* were big and scary to me."

I was baptized by a missionary and learned how to smile and be very pleasant to the big men (RCMP) who were sent here to keep us good. They always seemed to know about any wrongdoings, so we smiled a lot. There were some grumpy qallunaat, *but they were not scary because their behaviour was predictable. The scary ones were those who showed no expression.*

In the early days Inuit working for the qallunaat *were not paid money. They were given about two days worth of food for six days of work. When country food was scarce, they had to make two days of food last a week. Once you started working, you could no longer go hunting like in the old days. More and more people became dependent on having flour, lard, sugar, baking soda, tea, and other goods from The Bay (Hudson's Bay Company). No work, no food. You couldn't buy much when you only got 50 cents for a seal skin.*

Things were so tough in the early days that some people returning to their camp with goods from The Bay would pass by other camps in the middle of the night so as not to be noticed. Some people came to our camp at Ikirasaq to get food rather than go to The Bay. Country food was much healthier. My older brothers would work at ship time to be able to get the things we could not make, like bullets, needles, and other special things from the South.

I experienced difficulty when it came time to support myself. It was the time when the dogs were being killed. It was the beginning of my adult life and yet I could not raise my own dogs, I could not have a strong dog team. The best dogs were the most aggressive dogs and they were the first to be destroyed. We were told it was because they were a threat to humans. Then the others were destroyed because we were told that they were diseased. The destruction of the "real" dogs was the destruction of a strong breed that helped us to survive for generations. When you think of it, the destruction of the dogs and the replacement of sleds with snowmobiles took away our strength forever. We lost our endurance. I can remember when we walked great distances, when we could lift huge stones or haul sleds loaded with food for days and my brothers and I did such things long ago.

The year before you came to Kinngait (1957), I was living permanently in settlement. I was quickly losing the strength in my body and in my way of thinking.

The small kudlik that can be carried on long journeys.

My thoughts were no longer shaped by living on the land but by a ready made lifestyle. Because we began to live like you, we began to behave like you, and in many ways we have become like you. You asked me what would have happened to our lives if the qallunaat had never come north. The answer is simple: We would have continued to live the only life we knew.

When I think about the future I also think about the past. I remember when giving thanks at feasts, we faced each other. Now when we pray, we look at the back of another person's head. We are losing things along the way. We're losing traditional knowledge about a world known to our ancestors. We seem to be losing our ability to live in harmony with one another. Perhaps if we're not careful, we'll even lose those adopted beliefs that have replaced our traditional ones.

I think that living in the future will be so different from the past that it is beyond our imagination. Perhaps the future is that time when the present, yours and mine, is thought of as just another fairy tale.

Pitaloosie Saila, my "little sister", a wonderful artist from Kinngait (Cape Dorset).

AN INTIMATE WILDERNESS

THE SCENT OF SENSITIVITY

My southern colleagues have marvelled at how fortunate I was to develop a remarkably close and lasting relationship with the Inuit of Sikusiilaq. This relationship took a long time to grow. Three different families often refer to me as "our relative from the South," which makes me feel at home whenever I return to Cape Dorset. In my experience, lasting relationships include admonishments such as the time when Osuitok Ipeelie impatiently said "It's time you started to learn to call things by their proper names." There are other times when one faces occasional disagreement, anger, and in some cases, hostility. In any case, my relationship with the Inuit elders was based on my respect for them rather than any judgment.

It helped also to learn the elements of proper behaviour. I recall with amusement the time Simeonie Quppapik roundly chastised me: "You have been visiting me long enough. Stop knocking on my door when you come! Only *qallunaat* and police knock on doors. Stop scaring me!"

One of the most important gestures of decent behaviour was to be thoughtful. When a younger person was visiting an elder, bringing food was considerate. I simply left it on the table and learned that no thanks was necessary or expected.

From time to time, I was scolded and brought down a peg or two without rancour. I remember the time I was out on the land with Pitaloosie Saila and her family. Pitaloosie told me to go out and put up the pole that acted a mast for the two-way radio. What seemed like a simple task turned out to be embarrassing. I tried valiantly to put a thin two-metre high pole upright between small round boulders.

"What's the matter?" Pitaloosie yelled. "You went to university and you can't even stick a pole up in the air?"

"I forgot how about five thousand years ago," I lashed out at her.

"Too bad," she retorted. "Anyway, you *qallunaat* descended from monkeys, we didn't. Everyone knows that there were no monkeys in the Arctic."

I couldn't stop laughing. The next morning, the pole was standing straight, no doubt put there in a couple of minutes by one of the kids.

Shortly after my first visit to southwest Baffin in 1958, many of the old Inuit who had been born and grown up in hunting camps were reaching the end of their lives. While some of their legends, songs, and stories would live on, the way they thought and felt about things and the way they viewed their world grew dimmer with each elder's death. Leetia Parr and Pia Pootoogook, along with the sisters Annie, Jeannie, and Nina Manning, helped me gain insight into some of the thoughts and experiences of the old people in Cape Dorset. I could never have gathered some of the stories and many other accounts without their help. It was important for my helper to understand not only what I was trying to learn from the elders, but also why I was interested in such things. The old adage "Ask the right question and you will get the right answer" is not necessarily true. Quite often, the answer is a response to questions in the storyteller's mind: "What is it that he or she would like to hear?"

I was careful to ensure that whoever accompanied me was socially acceptable to the various people with whom I wanted to speak. Even the best interpreter in the community would be severely handicapped if, for example, the person I was meeting had a history of animosity with a member of the interpreter's family. I almost blundered into a situation where I was about to have a conversation with an old man who, as a youth, was a camp slave (the polite term is *servant*) to the father of the interpreter with me at the time.

Knowing or having a feeling about when to back off from a line of inquiry was important. The approach to conversations was critical to what transpired during them. I began by explaining what I was seeking and why I was interested in the subject. At times I said to the person, I have heard such-and-such from so-and-so and would like to know more about the subject, and I asked the person if he could help me. I was often asked, "What will you do with what I tell you?" To this I replied, "I will never repeat the things you want me to keep to myself. The things that can be repeated to others will be written down as I understand them, and that is why I ask you to be patient with me during our conversation."

I explained to my interpreter and the person with whom we spoke that we would not interrupt each other's thoughts with translation. I would say whatever I had to say, and the interpreter would then say to me, "That is what I understand you to mean." Any further articulation was made at that time, before the question or thoughts were transmitted to the elder.

The same held true for the elder speaking to me. Often, we would speak for long periods without breaks in the conversation for translation. The thing we would frequently say to one another was, "I understand you to mean... Is that so?" The reply was either, "Yes, that is so," or "No, you don't really understand what I have said, and I will try to explain it in a different way." Before leaving the community, if necessary, I would meet once more with the elder who had spoken to me, along with my companion interpreter. We would recount our understanding of the conversation we'd had, and only when the elder was satisfied would the notes we'd taken be considered complete.

My desire to show respect extended to how I carried out field research. When examining a location of significance, I consciously avoided touching any object or disturbing, in any manner, anything at a site. Partly, this was due to superstitions handed down from my own family. I remember Simeonie smiling approvingly when he noticed me whistling softly while passing nearby a grave. On the other hand, I often made copious notes, took general measurements, and captured many photographs at the sites I was taken to. I gave my records back to the community and deposited them in the local schools where, from time to time, Inuit teachers invited me to share my stories with their students.

Every major site I observed and documented in southwest Baffin was revealed to me by an elder who often accompanied me. When I planned to travel extensively photographing the landscape or revisiting sites with elders, I'd write to the Community Council of Cape Dorset to seek permission, and I received a formal letter signed by the mayor of the community.

When I had the opportunity to travel by helicopter throughout the Sikusiilaq region, I made it a priority to take elders back to the camps were they had been born and to areas where they had hunted. Such helicopter trips were useful to the community as well because it was possible to survey the freshwater supply, waste lagoons, road construction, and potential sources of gravel. Strange as it may seem, gravel is often a scarce commodity near most communities in the Arctic. Gravel is needed for constructing pads for houses and repairing roads and landing strips. Often very old sites are located on gravel beds and, unless protected, bits of artifacts can be scooped up and find their way into road and runway surfaces or house pads.

LEGENDS AND REALITIES

As I gathered and recorded accounts from elders about their beliefs and experiences, I wondered how best to separate myths and legends from realities. Did I really need to know what was real or not real? After all, one person's myth could be another's reality. And why would I want to separate these perceptions in the first place? Was the monster that hid under my bed as a child as real as the elders' belief in *Qugalugaki*, that wee imp that lives at the back of the sleeping platform?

The question of what is true and what is not true was posed to various elders. In response, they offered ten words and expressions that ranged from things known not to be true to things believed to be absolutely true. The expression I found most enlightening was *ukpirijaujut*, things which are believed.

The first of many storytelling sessions that I experienced occurred in a tent, lit by the warm glow of a Coleman lantern. It was at Sapujuaq, where entire families go to fish for Arctic char. Sapujuaq is an ancient site where you can see the signatures of many generations on the landscape: old tent rings, caches for storing food, the faint outlines of sleeping platforms, and *nappariat*, the little inuksuk-like figures that were used to dry filleted fish. Like all who came here before us, we gathered sometime toward dusk to eat and drink strong tea made fragrant by the smoke of an open fire.

Eventually, someone began by telling a story of some personal adventure on the land or of a folly and others soon followed, at times drawing gasps of wonder or gales of laughter. Stories told about life on the land were often brief and without embellishment. Some had no conclusion, which left the listener stranded as it were on the story's edge.

Simeonie Quppapik shared one such account. "When I was still a boy, my father and his hunting companions came back to the camp with walrus meat. We were joyful. But no one in our family ate any meat; we were full. The next day, those who had eaten the meat were sick, dying, or dead. In a rage, my father took up his rifle and shot each lump of meat... and each piece began to move!"

The storyteller elders expected me to collect their tales and so they were written as told and retold without embellishment.

CENTRE OF THE WORLD

About 100 metres off my left shoulder lies that part of the Arctic Ocean known as the Foxe Channel, named for Luke Foxe, who sailed into these treacherous waters in 1631. Some believe that ships shaped like seagoing monsters sailed these very waters 400 years before Luke Foxe. As I look toward the sea it is difficult to comprehend how anyone could entrust his life to a small wooden ship, sail across an ocean, then enter a sea choked with ice that never ceases moving. Here, tides rise and fall anywhere from six to nine metres, causing riptides and whirlpools and changing the profile of the entire coastline every six hours. This is where the Inuit elders I knew took to the waters in little boats made of seal-skin and driftwood to hunt walrus that could destroy their kayaks with a single lunge. Buried in the Inuit legends of Sikusiilaq are accounts of huge and fearsome creatures that plied these very waters long before the arrival of the *qallunaat*.

Across from me and hidden below the horizon lies Southampton Island, known to the Inuit as Salliit or Shugliaq. If I look carefully in that direction, I can make out a faint and distant cloud that behaves as if tethered to some invisible body. Its unmoving presence tells us that below the horizon and within its very shadow lies Salliit.

Looking north, I face into the prevailing wind. It drives down the length of the Foxe Basin, moving enormous slabs of ice around in the sea as if they were mere snowflakes. Far beyond my line of sight lies the ancient settlement of Igloolik. Inuit have lived there long before the coming of wooden ships, some people believe as far back in time as 4,000 years.

Turning slightly to my right, I look straight along the western edge of the Foxe Peninsula. Here I see a powerful landscape.

It is a virtual desert of rolling hills, frost- shattered rock, count-less small inland lakes, and tiny pockets of the most delicate wildflowers trembling in the incessant Arctic wind. Far beyond lie the two ancient camps of Nurrata and Nuvudjuak. The ancestors of many of the elders I knew lived here for countless genera-tions. Many of the legends, stories, and personal accounts of extraordinary happenings divulged to me relate to this strangely beautiful region.

Now I turn slightly to the northeast. Far in the distance can be seen an inuksuk. It points the way to one of the most extraordinary places in the entire Arctic, the Great Plain of the Koukdjuak. An eerie landscape, it is a vast plain, part of the sea bottom that rose when the great mantle of ice receded from here nine thousand years ago. Here I see small, perfectly round lakes, some filled with azure water. In the middle of this vast plain lies a huge freshwater lake called Nettilling. It is connected to the sea by the Koukdjuak, which means a Great River. It is indeed great, in some places over two kilometres wide as it winds its way to the sea. But unlike other great rivers, it traverses a land so flat that it has carved no banks. Upon the Great Plain of the Koukdjuak, geese in the tens of thousands come to nest each brief season.

I now turn once more, this time facing south and notice the rugged landscape unfolding in the distance. I am looking along the inland route stretching across the west end of the Foxe Peninsula. The landscape is exceptionally beautiful with its valleys, hills, gorges, small plains, and hidden places. Because the dominant features of this landscape are oriented in a north-south direction, sun and shadow create an astonishing effect. The landscape never looks quite the same; there are times when even the passage of clouds casts moving shadows that make mountains look as if they are moving and valleys disappear. Still further in the same direction is Kinngait (Cape Dorset), meaning high mountains or hills, the place from which this journey began.

Where I stand at this moment is at the centre of all these re-markable places. I catch my breath, not wanting to speak. Finally, I sit in the windless shadow of yet another circle of experience.

HUNGER, FEAR, AND MAGIC

On a bright, beautiful day in mid-July, a group of us set out for Sarko (Shaqu), a small island just off the tip of Itiliardjuk. Sarko lies about three hours east of Cape Dorset by boat. The island, mistakenly called Alariaq Island, is rather featureless with its bare rock, a few rain ponds, and some very old inuksuit placed on a low ridge near the gap between the island and Itiliardjuk. When you see the gap at dusk or when mist rises from the sea, the inuksuit standing on the ridge appear as dark, shrouded figures. The landscape is both gloomy and forbidding.

Yet the Sarko area provides a favoured location for hunting ring seal, bearded seal, occasionally walrus, and beluga whales off its rocky shores. Despite the powerful current at the gap, the occasional caribou swims across it to browse the lichen that grow in abundance between the rocks on the island.

No caribou were on the island when we went there on a summertime trip. And no rabbits or wildfowl were to be seen that late in the summer. The weather had become sullen by the time we landed. We set up our camp, had a small meal of bannock, some caribou that we had brought with us, and tea.

Itulu Itidlouie and I left the others and went out to have a look at the weather conditions. Itulu was definitely a person you would want by your side during a challenging trip. He was skilled in all aspects of living on the land. He and his brother Udjualuk were remarkably strong. I was told that on one occasion when loading a canoe, Itulu, losing patience, brushed aside two fellows trying to load a fifty-gallon drum of gasoline. He seized the drum of gas, pushed it down into the water, and, upon its rebound, heaved it into the boat. Itulu was a rather serious man whose sensitive side only came out when he sang songs and played his guitar.

On this occasion, I looked to Itulu for guidance. The sea was becoming rough as the wind from the northwest began bearing down on us. During the night the wind had gathered so much strength that we had to haul the canoe further up onto the shore and secure it with rope tied to the boulders. We placed more than the usual amount of rocks around the base of the tent, which billowed in and out from time to time as if it were gasping for breath in the rising storm.

The storm assaulted us relentlessly for three days . Though the wind had ceased its howling, the sea continued to be too dangerous for travel. We had little to eat with only a few fish heads and some rock-hard pilot biscuits. On the fourth day, we boiled the remaining fish heads, drank the broth, and ate everything — and I mean everything — except the few remaining bones.

It was then Itulu determined that we had to go out on the water regardless of how rough it was to hunt for food on nearby islands. I had no choice but to accompany him. The thought of going out on the rough sea in a twenty-two-foot canoe powered by a fitful 25 horsepower outboard, frightened the hell out of me. We struck out toward the islands in Andrew Gordon Bay. It was a terrifying trip. Each time the bow of the canoe rose and then smashed down, I feared the force would split open the vessel. A tragic event a few years before was fresh in my mind. Hunters returning to Cape Dorset with a load of walrus had got caught in similar weather conditions. Pounding waves cracked their canoe, and they drowned. One whose body has not been recovered to this day is said to be walking the hills that rise from the sea where he vanished.

Soaked to our skins by sea spray, we arrived at a small island. Carefully securing the canoe, we headed inland. I can remember seeing several walrus skulls and numerous other bones sticking up from the moss. There were no signs of shelters or caches having been built in the area. As we approached a low ridge, Itulu motioned me to lie down. About thirty metres in front was a scrawny looking caribou pawing away at lichens. Itulu handed me the rifle, but I refused to take it. He took careful aim and the caribou fell like a stone. We approached it gingerly, and I remember the look in the caribou's eyes. Rather than celebrating the kill, Itulu carefully observed the dying animal, then put it out of its misery by thrusting his knife where the spine connects to the skull. He looked about, picked up a small stone, and began to tap the caribou's body while listening to the sound his tapping made. Finally, he bent down and near the caribou's head said in a voice just above a whisper, "I'm sorry." Itulu explained to me that the caribou was sick and could not be eaten. So it was back in the canoe and out to sea to another island.

We came upon the second island a short time later. I was beginning to suffer spasms of shivering and dull pain from the cold. We landed, went ashore, and within a short time saw a caribou feeding in the distance. This time Itulu made no offer of the rifle. He took careful aim and brought the caribou down with a single shot. Approaching it carefully, we could see that the animal was in its prime. We jumped up and down like kids in a playground, hugging each other and laughing.

I helped Itulu remove the caribou's hide, which caused a thin veil of vapour to rise. We slipped our hands inside the caribou and felt life flowing back into our hands that were numb with cold. Without a word to each other, we took out our knives and cut a piece of meat that tasted warm and sweet. At that moment, with warm blood on my hands and in my mouth, I realized I had just experienced an event that would have been part of the daily life of my earliest ancestors who hunted from the Carpathian Mountains to the shores of the Black Sea.

Itulu's sharp voice shattered those thoughts. "Move the canoe!" he shouted. The tide was quickly receding, which could leave us stranded on this island until the following day. The canoe was loaded and, though the sea had hardly calmed, I felt secure in Itulu's company. Upon reaching Sarko, we were greeted with much enthusiasm, as was to be expected. The caribou was divided among the other three families. We filled our bellies with fresh caribou and fat. Itulu went on to crack bones as southerners would crack walnuts at Christmas, scooping out the nourishing and sweet- tasting marrow. That evening, we snuggled beneath our sleeping robes warm and content, and when I looked upward, I discovered a marvellous thing.

While we were gone, Leetia had taken those few discarded fishbones and performed a wonderful transformation. Using only the fishbones, she had fashioned a bumblebee, butterfly, gull, and murre, and with a few remnants, had also made a little mosquito. These she had hung from the ceiling of the tent on threads. As darkness fell, our small naphtha lamp provided them with shadows that flew silently about our tent like dreams.

The "aunt" who wanted to adopt me as long as I looked after her for the rest of her life

Opposite: The pleasure of feasting

AN INTIMATE WILDERNESS

TABLE D'HÔTE

I'm often asked what I eat when travelling with elders in the North. The simple answer is that I eat whatever is edible and available. When I'm with other *qallunaat*, I eat southern food. When I'm out on the land, I eat what the Inuit eat. I must admit I was pleased to discover from the onset that I could eat raw meat without the consequences suffered by some *qallunaat*. There are only a few things I avoid if possible without offending my host: fermented meat or fermented fish, the eyes of animals, and fully formed chicks still in their eggs. I have tried those delicacies and, while they taste fine, I've found that they don't agree with me. Eyes taste somewhat sweet but have no texture. Fermented (rotten) meat or fish has a taste and smell similar to very ripe Stilton cheese and works through me within minutes of its consumption.

The elders I knew favoured caribou — raw, boiled, dried, or cooked — above all other food. I asked a few elders to categorize their preferences in food, resulting in the following list: walrus, caribou, ringed seal, bearded seal (square flipper), beluga whale, Arctic char, goose and ptarmigan, various bird eggs, and when available, berries and edible seaweed. Once while travelling with Kiawak Ashoona, I discovered a chunk of dried caribou in the bottom of my parka that must have been at least two years old. Having deftly picked off the debris that had accumulated on the meat over the years, Kiawak and I proceeded to have a delicious and well-seasoned snack.

It can be amusing to watch a *qallunaq* eating country food for the first time. They tend to take a small piece of meat, pinch it between the fingers, and display an exaggerated chewing motion as if they were really enjoying the food. Even more amusing is seeing a person trying to eat *maktaaq*, whale skin, for the first time. Though the taste is similar to that of walnuts, *maktaaq* tends to have the consistency of Indian

rubber, leaving the unsuspecting *qallunaq* desperately trying to find a place to hide it while no one is watching.

I remember the time I met Joanassie Salamonie coming in from hunting at Kiaktuq. He carried a brace of ptarmigans and asked me to come and join him for a meal. After plucking the entire bird, the Inuit eat it raw, innards and all, except for the beak and claws. "You can taste the season of spring," Joanassie said. He went on to describe how the taste of an animal in its prime allows you to "taste the season" in which it was taken. I reminded Joanassie about the time he visited me in Carp, Ontario brought me a snow goose from the Arctic. Upon examining the bird, I discovered that it was half-eaten. "It was dinnertime," Joanassie said with a shrug and smile. "I got hungry waiting for you."

I found that eating country food when travelling or out on the land is both nourishing and satisfying. Even a single boiled eider duck egg kept me going for a long time. There is, however, one dish that makes my mouth water whenever I think of it. First you make a small *iga* (fireplace) with three rocks and place a fourth flat rock on top to act as a griddle. Then you gather an armful of Arctic heather and, if available, dried Arctic willow twigs. Place the heather and twigs beneath the flat rock on the fireplace, light it, and allow the griddle to become very hot. Then place strips of fresh caribou on top of the griddle, feeding the fire with heather until the meat is cooked to a golden brown. The sweet smoke of the heather infuses the meat with an exquisite flavour. It is not the taste of a season; it is the taste of paradise.

NUNANNGUAQ,
"AN IMITATION OF THE EARTH"

Travels with Inuit companions inland, on the open sea, or on the ice without a map or compass never ceased to amaze me. This was especially true when we kept moving while enveloped in dense fog at sea or wrapped in a blizzard.

"Maps" were registered in memory as a series of images illustrating features, places, and related objects located in a temporal and spiritual landscape. Each one of these entities had names. I was able to document 230 different geographical terms in Sikusiilaq alone, ranging from the simple *nuna*, the land, to *laumajurniavissagalaaluit*, areas that can support life, to *najuratsaungittuq*, places forbidden to ordinary human beings, places where evil things were practiced. Inuktitut terms for hills, rivers, lakes, eskers, and mountains were familiar to people living in widely separated regions. I found that topographical names collected in Arviat are almost identical to those throughout the Foxe Peninsula.

The names of places and objects, however, often reflected how they appeared to the eye and thus how they were imagined. The images they evoked were multi-dimensional, recognizing that their appearance varied depending on the relative position of the traveller, season, or position of the sun. Because the Arctic landscape changed about every hundred days, these cognitive maps were dynamic, reflecting the prevailing conditions of the seasons, weather, and tides.

Nurrata, on the east coast of the Foxe Peninsula, is an example of an ephemeral landscape whose character is reflected in the name of an ancient site. The name *Nurrata* implies, "where the land and the sea appear as one in winter." Nurrata lies in the region of Qaumarvik, which is the region beyond *Tikiraaqjuk*, the

"Great Finger," or the peninsula pointing to Southampton Island. Thus one could construct a vivid mental image as follows: beyond the place of the great finger where the land is in brightness lies the place where there is no boundary between land and sea in winter.

Some places had more than one name. They would have a common name known to most in the region and an arcane name not disclosed to outsiders. An example of such a place is Igaqjuaq near Cape Dorset, southwest Baffin Island. Igaqjuaq is described as "the overturned kettle" because of its appearance, but its name implies a great fireplace, suggesting a place of feasting. Its archaic name is Qujaligiaqtubic, according to the elders in Dorset, a name so old that its exact meaning is no longer known. An elder interpreted *Qujaligiaqtubic* as, "the place from which one returns to Earth refreshed". Qujaligiaqtubic was where the people of Sikusiilaq had gathered once each year for generations to celebrate the ancient fertility ritual of *siiliitut*.

There were places, essentially retreats, known only to women, who referred to them as *arnainnarnut qaujimajaujuq*. Men could merely speculate about what occurred there and ascribed little importance to such places except to acknowledge that they existed.

If you examine a contemporary map of the Foxe Peninsula and superimpose the traditional travel routes of the Sikusiilarmiut, it is difficult to comprehend how entire families travelling on foot, laden with children and gear and confronted by countless bogs, rivers, and lakes, could find their way there and back on their annual journey of well over nine hundred kilometres. During these journeys, the most important consideration was where one could safely cross rivers; the complex geography was one of shallows that could vary in depth depending on the prevailing conditions. The vital element that the families added to the visible landscape is where they could find food along the way. It was essential to know the locations for intercepting caribou, finding geese, and, if need be, catching fish. There were no paper maps, no way-finding tools, only memory providing a sense of direction. Occasionally they would encounter an inuksuk known as a *nalunaikkutaq*, literally "a deconfuser," placed in a strategic location during some forgotten time to help the traveller.

AN INTIMATE WILDERNESS

These mental maps could be translated to sand, snow, or even paper if need be. There are several accounts of Arctic whalers and explorers who engaged Inuit as pilots and map makers. One such account can be found in Robert Huish's book on the travels of Captain Beechey along the coast of the Bering Strait in 1826.

On the first visit to this party, they (the Eskimos) constructed a chart of the coast upon the sand, of which, however, Captain Beechey at first took very little notice. They, however, renewed their labour and performed their work upon the sandy beach in a very ingenious and intelligible manner. The coast line was first marked out with a stick, and the distances regulated by the day's journey. The hills and the ranges of mountains were next shown by elevations of sand or stone, and the islands represented by heaps of pebbles, their proportions being duly attended to. As the work proceeded, some of the bystanders occasionally suggested alterations, and Captain Beechey removed one of the Diomede Islands, which was misplaced. This at first was objected to by the hydrographer, but one of the party recollecting that the islands were seen in one from Cape Prince of Wales, confirmed its new position and made the mistake quite evident to the others, who were much surprised that Captain Beechey should have any knowledge on the subject. When the mountains and islands were erected, the villages and fishing stations were marked by a number of sticks placed upright, in imitation of those, which are put up on the coast, wherever these people fix their abode. In time, a complete hydrographical plan was drawn from Point Darby to Cape Krusenstern.

That remarkable map depicted the entire coastline of the Seward Peninsula of Alaska, approximately 1,000 kilometres in length.

In my collection of over 100 maps there are three kept among my treasured objects. They are *nunannguait*, imitations of the earth, drawn by Kananginak Pootoogook, Simeonie Quppapik and Ruth Qaulluaryak.

Kananginak Pootoogook's Nunannguaq

Shortly before Kananginak died in November 2010, we spent a quiet afternoon reminiscing about the old days. I had been to Ikirisaq, the famous and now abandoned Pootoogook camp on the east side of Kangisurituq (Andrew Gordon Bay). I expressed the regret that we had never travelled to all the favoured locations around Ikirisaq together. In my heart I knew we would never make that journey because Kananginak had only a short time to live. On the last day we would see each other alive, he handed me a a small sheet of paper, it was his *nunannguaq* (above) depicting all the favoured locations around Ikirisaq that we had hoped someday to visit together. Perhaps we will.

Simeonie Quppapik's Nunannguaq

Simeonie drew two maps for me. The first shown here (opposite) drawn in 1990 depicts the coast of southwest Baffin Island, from Cape Dorset (far left) to Simeonie's birthplace near Qarmaarjuak (Amadjuak), some 300 kilometers distant. He identifies the location of whales, square-flipper seals, walrus, small seals, fish,

AN INTIMATE WILDERNESS

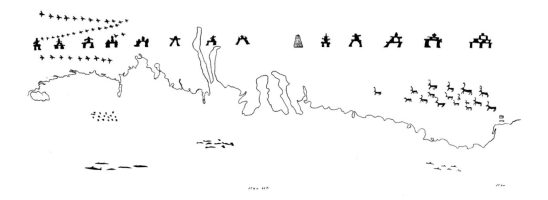

birds, etc. He shows the migration path of geese and the reindeer herd once tended by the Sami Laplanders, (see the chapter on The People With the Pointed Shoes) at Qarmaarjuak (HBC Amadjuak Trading Post).

The inuksuit he illustrates across the top of the drawing are those he describes as the "important ones" that relate to major sites of ancient ceremonial centres, fish weirs, where Tuniit once lived as well as other significant places. He is careful not to relate an inuksuk to a specific place thus revealing the location of what we would interpret as a "sacred site."

Interestingly, he hints of such a place by including a figure which is not an inuksuk. The sixth figure from the left is in fact a *tupqujak*, a shaman's doorway located at Kangla (Kungla). This wonderful map has been exhibited in numerous exhibitions and publications in Canada and abroad.

Ruth Qaulluaryak's Nunannguaq

Many years ago a delightful young lady gave me a little tapestry (see page 80) which has hung in my bedroom all these years. I was told that Ruth Qaulluaryak who lived in Qamani'tuaq (Baker Lake) in Nunavut, made the tapestry. Though I had been in Baker Lake for short visits on three occasions, I had never met Ruth. I learned a little bit about her early life through a friend who lived in Baker Lake. Ruth was born and grew up in Haningayok the back river area of Kivalliq, the Keewatin region in Nunavut. She was born the same year (1932) as I though our childhood experience could not be further apart.

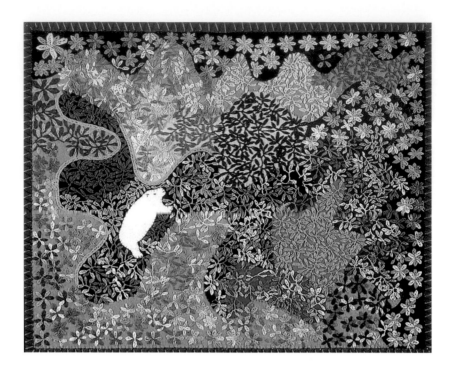

Tapistry, 17"x21", by Ruth Qaulluaryak,
Baker Lake (Qamanittuaq), 1969.
A depiction of her universe.

Her family and her people lived a life governed by the movement of caribou. Periods of starvation were not uncommon in the region. I was informed by elders in Arviat that they knew of families starving to death in the interior as late as 1958. It was only in 1970's that the Qaulluaryak family reluctantly left the land they knew, and moved to Baker Lake.

The landscape familiar to Ruth was a somber one unlike the often spectacular vistas found in the eastern Arctic. It is a landscape which is relatively flat, covered by snow for much of the year only to emerge for a very short time draped in somber shades of grey and brown. For a few weeks there is a patchwork of various shades of green with pockets of Arctic wild flowers whose beauty lasts for a number of days rather than weeks.

It should come as no surprise that a child growing up in a land that often provided such hardship would behold it, as a painful memory of a forsaken place. With this brief narrative as our backdrop, let's look at Ruth's tapestry. At first we see a small polar bear amongst a field of various coloured flowers. Her tapestry appears to be a charming little decorative wall hanging. However, look more closely.

The landscape, the sea and the sky are defined by a myriad of flowers. They vary in shape and colour denoting those that live on the land or grow by the seashore including the plants that live in the sea. The only two figures not defined by flowers are the polar bear that moves about the land and in the sea and the thin yellow ocher line that defines the sea from the land. Just above the polar bear's head, we see a white patch of early spring snow on the ground. Some "flowers" appear monochromatic suggesting shrubs, lichens and grasses while others are brightly coloured illustrating the great variety of flowering plants that carpet the tundra each brief summer. If you look at the top left side of the tapestry, you notice flowers placed on a midnight blue background. The background represents the night sky and the flowers represent the stars. Notice the flower in the top left corner of the sky. It is larger than all others. It represents *Nikkisuitok*, the pole star we call Polaris. Ruth's *nunannguaq* of the earth, sea and sky is portrayed by flowers symbolizing a great living thing, of beauty and renewal.

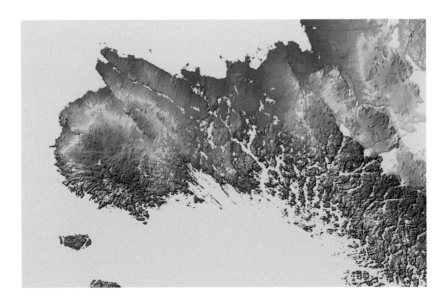

Satellite image of the entire Foxe Peninsula (Seekuseelak or Sikusiiliq).

Ivory and bone carving of a whale hunt, artist unknown.

AN INTIMATE WILDERNESS

HOW WE TOOK A GREAT WHALE

You had to stoop to enter old Jimmy Killabuck's house. It was a replica of a Hudson's Bay Company house, but scaled down to one little room with small sleeping quarters that were reached by climbing a ladder.

The place was filled with pieces of this, bits of that, and parts of things, all lodged in their proper places. There was the sweet smell of woodsmoke from the stove and the sound of the kettle as the water for our tea came to a boil. The skins of Canada geese covered the chairs. We drank tea, ate biscuits, and felt very good in each other's company.

For a moment, the old man was lost in thought as he gazed out the window toward the sea. Then he looked toward me, lit a cigarette, and said,

I will tell you how we hunted great whales in the old days. I am an old man, I think I am 85 years old, and what I am about to tell you was told to me by my father when I was a very young boy.

In the old days we hunted not only belugas and narwhals but the big whales as well. Some Inuit may have hunted whales from umian *(large skin boats) but we hunted them from* qajait *(kayaks). A man in a* qajaq *in the water is no threat to a whale. She thinks that the* qajaq *is nothing more than a peaceful little animal seeking her company. The* qajaq *is silent, moves quickly, and is much better to handle than any* umiak. Umian *are for women, children, and dogs, not for hunting.*

When the hunters saw the spout from a whale, they came together. They took their panar *(bone knife) and lashed it to their* qajaq *paddle, so as to make a spear. In the old days it took a long time to make our weapons and tools because we had no saws or metal tools. We cut bone and ivory with pieces of "glass." We found that special glass that looked like icicles growing from certain rocks. We would take a sliver of that glass and set it into a piece of caribou bone so as to give it a handle. That was our saw. We would then scratch a line over and over again on both sides of the bone or ivory until we could break the piece exactly in the right way. We could do other things with that glass, like make holes, grooves, and decorations.*

Now I will tell you how we killed great whales. You must understand that the great whale is a peaceful animal. It doesn't kill other animals, nor is it afraid of any animal except arluk *(killer whale). When we saw whales, we could move among them and they were not afraid of our little* qajait. *They moved slowly, feeding on things that lived on the top of the ocean. There was no fear of trying to kill a great whale if you knew how to do it. My father was such a man. He was the one who knew the right place to stick in the spear. He would paddle beside the whale, carefully looking at her body. There is a place below her spine where you can see a movement.*

At this point the old man put his left thumb under the flap of skin between the thumb and forefinger of his right hand and began to make a pulsing motion.

You see, there is a place on the whale that moves just the way I am showing you. That's where the kidney is, and that's the only place where it is safe to stick in the spear.
This was done carefully and quietly, and you may be surprised to know that the whale did not even know that she was being killed. There was no fight. She kept swimming on and began to bleed to death.

We would follow her sometimes for a very long time until she died. As soon as she was dead, we would come to her side and fasten lines to her body. Our lines were made from walrus hide, and the hooks on the end of the line that were stuck into the whale were made from polar bear claws.

Each hunter fastened a line to the whale and together we paddled toward the shore. There was much hard work and much rejoicing because she gave us food and oil and everything else that we needed in the making of things, even a new panar *(snow knife).*

The old man looked into his empty teacup and quietly said, *They were such peaceful things, such beautiful and peaceful things.* I left Pangnirtung (Pangniqtuuq) the following day with many fond memories.

Various forms of inuksuit.

SILENT MESSENGERS

There are places across the circumpolar world where the Inuit and their predecessors have left traces of their presence on the land reaching back thousands of years. The most enduring signatures of the Inuit are stone figures known as inuksuit — objects that act in the capacity of a human.

My interest in inuksuit began in 1958, on my first visit to Cape Dorset. Inuksuit could be seen in many places along the entire southwest Baffin coast. I photographed each inuksuk from at least three perspectives, wrote short notes about its location and orientation, and any other details that seemed relevant. During two summers travelling along the coast, I had produced more than 100 images and decided that it was time to seriously study these remarkable and puzzling figures. I wrote a polite letter of inquiry to most universities and other institutions in North America with an interest in Arctic studies. Of the five responses I received, four stated that they had no information on inuksuit in their holdings, and the fifth letter from a well-known Arctic archaeologist advised that the purposes attributed to "those cairns" were often exaggerated and serious study of them would be a waste of time. Instinct caused me to think otherwise.

At first, I attempted to classify inuksuit into obvious groups. I noted their morphology, size, the type of rock used, and a number of other physical traits associated with each inuksuk. What little written information I could find was included in my ever increasing pile of data and notes. That gave me a feeling of making headway, but the Inuktitut expression "he hides its meaning within words" gnawed away at me. I realized that by arranging and rearranging facts, I was merely conjuring an illusion of progress. In real terms, this seemingly logical approach had done little to increase my understanding of what had been revealed to me about inuksuit. Once again, I reviewed all the information I had collected: interviews, pages of field notes, and hundreds of photographs. No matter how I arranged and rearranged the data, insight was nowhere to be found.

Then one evening, while idly shuffling papers, I noticed that a single expression, *utirnigiit*, referring to traces of coming and going, appeared often in my notes. That word prompted me to examine my data in a new way. By grouping Inuktitut words and expressions related to *utirnigiit*, I created what I later learned to recognize as a semantic field. What emerged was a totally different way of perceiving the meaning of the things I struggled to understand.

It was through the Inuktitut meanings attributed to physical and non-physical entities that I was able to understand what the elders described when they lived on the land: when it was vital to know the nature, character, quality, and behaviour of everything around them; when the essence of what we call traditional knowledge was focused on one purpose, the *taimagiakaman*, the great necessity of staying alive.

Try to imagine how to describe your environment, define your reality, or understand the essentials to sustain life without knowing the existence of science, art, literature, or mathematics. The Inuit with whom I've travelled for more than forty-five years developed, sustained, and communicated a highly specialized body of knowledge handed down from their ancestors that enabled them to stay alive in what southerners describe as one of the most hostile environments on Earth. They developed a material culture based on the ingenious use of bits of wood, skin, stone, ivory, and bone: hunting devices, food caches, graves, shelters, objects of veneration such as healing arches, dancing rings, initiation sites, and, most important, inuksuit. These remarkable stone constructions acted like message centres and formed an essential part of a life-support system for a people who lived at the edge of life for more than four thousand years.

Inuksuit can be found in countless forms, shapes, and sizes. They can be large, small, slender, or squat. Some are taller than the height of two men combined, one standing upon the shoulders of the other, and some are no higher than a one-metre slab of stone known as a *turaaq*, an inuksuk acting as a pointer indicating the best route home. Inuksuit tend to be about 120 centimetres high, roughly corresponding to the height to which an average person can lift a fair-sized stone while keeping his arms close to the sides of his body. Inuksuit taller than a human appear to be quite rare. The elders claim that such an *inuksullarik*, referring to a very important inuksuk, would have been constructed by the efforts of several men often working from temporary platforms of stone found nearby.

I learned that three factors determine the shapes of inuksuit. First and most important, the shape of the stone used to construct the inuksuk largely determines its size and general appearance. Generally, loose stone is found in the shape of rounded boulders or in flat slabs of varying thickness or, more often, in irregular broken and angular material of all shapes and sizes.

Rounded boulders offer the least possibility of variation in shaping an inuksuk because about the only thing you can do with boulders is stack them into a pyramid. Inuksuit constructed of boulders tend to be massive because of their base-to-height ratio. Often built to serve as important direction markers, they are referred to as an *inuksummarik* or an *inuksukjuaq*.

Large slabs of stone can be arranged in a number of ways beyond just stacking. They can be stood on end to form supports for a lintel and thus become a structure rather than just a heap. Some structures were quite elaborate, while others were in the distinctive shape of a *niungvalirulult*, "window" that often acted as a sightline to distant places of great importance.

Irregular, angular, and broken rock offered the widest possible variety of forms in the construction of an inuksuk. Carefully balancing one rock upon another required care. I've often watched an elder carefully looking at a seeming jumble of broken rock and, without so much as touching a single stone, visualize how one piece would fit with another. Only then would his helper bring the selected stone to where the inuksuk would be built. The shape of the figure that emerged was as much determined by the shape of the stones selected as by how the inuksuk builder finally arranged them.

A typical large inunnguaq at Aupaluqtuq.

Even a casual observer can easily recognize five general shapes of inuksuit. The first is the *inunnguaq*; though technically not an inuksuk, its distinctive human-like form is familiar to many.

The second group is the *tikkuuti*; they are clearly pointers of different sizes and shapes. The predominant variation is the straight, post-shaped pointer. They can also be in the form of a triangular-shaped rock usually lying flat upon the ground or appear as a simple but useful arrangement of rocks in a straight line on the ground, with the largest rock at one end and the smallest at the other, denoting the direction to be taken.

The third type of easily recognized inuksuk is an *inuksummarik* or an *inuksukjuaq*, which is noted for its larger-than-average size that enables it to be seen from a distance. These large inuksuit act as major coordination points.

Then we have the distinctive *niungvaliruluit*, the window-shaped inuksuit that may form a sightline or frame the view of an important place or object.

Finally are the inuksuit that have clearly been used as message centres in addition to their original purpose. One can find an arrangement of stones at their base left by a hunter for a follower. The arrangement of stones could signify a change of direction from an intended course, a precaution, or a sign for the follower to go to an alternative location or to the camp of a relative. The configurations that shaped these messages were known to hunting partners and often to members of their family.

Unique types of inuksuit were those that were meant to frighten caribou toward the waiting hunters. In south Baffin, they were referred to as *inuksuit tuktunnutiit*. They were often no higher than the hip, and when in use they exhibited a large clump of plant material on top with a stone to hold it in place. The long tendrils of plant material would blow about in the wind, creating the appearance of an eerie creature looming on the hilltop.

I learned of similar inuksuit in Nunavik (Arctic Quebec) that were referred to as *aulaqquit*, scarecrows or bogeymen. They tended to be a little more elaborate than their Baffin cousins. Some had the dried outstretched wings of seagulls dangling on sinew lines from their top. They would flutter in the wind and take on an appearance that threatened the caribou. Perhaps one of the most unique of these inuksuit was that with the capability to make sounds. These inuksuit often had bones such as caribou ribs and scapulas dangling from above, so that the slightest breeze would cause them to loudly click and clack in an otherwise silent landscape.

Perhaps the most fascinating aspect of inuksuit is how to read their meanings. For example, how do we know which type of inuksuk signifies a place where the ice is often dangerous at a certain time or where food is cached for winter? How would we know if what we thought was an inuksuk was in fact not an inuksuk at all but some other object, perhaps one of veneration, such as a *tunillarvik* or the dreadful *angaku'habvik* where shamans were initiated?

The simple answer is that each one of the inuksuk's unique shapes is its primary message. The faculty of visualization, of recording in one's mind every detail of the landscape and the objects upon it, was essential. Equally important was to memorize the location of places in relation to one another. Where there was a sameness to the vista, an inuksuk was a help to the traveller. It was important to memorize the shapes of the inuksuit that were known to one's elders, as well as their location and the reason they were put there. Without these three essential pieces of information, shape, location and purpose, the message was incomplete.

My mentor Simeonie Quppapik could illustrate from memory all the important inuksuit and other significant objects along the coast of southwest Baffin. He could relate them to specific places and describe their purpose. Had I possessed the faculty of acute observation natural to him and his generation, he would have performed *tauuunguatitsiniq*, meaning the act of conveying images onto another person's consciousness, upon me.

Inuksuit may appear as a single object on the landscape; in some instances two or more may appear in the same area while several are employed to form parallel lines called drift fences to divert caribou toward the shooting pits where hunters waited to kill them. There are, however, certain extraordinary places where one may encounter hundreds of these figures standing together. At least two such sites exist in Sikusiilaq, one known as Inuksugalait, located on the west coast of the peninsula, and a second known as Tukilik, far inland in the middle of the peninsula.

AN INUKSUK UNIVERSE

Some inuksuit, regardless of their intended purpose or age, look beautiful. One can see at a glance their careful arrangement of stones. Like pieces of a three-dimensional puzzle, they fit together with such precision as to be held in place by the force of gravity. They are not only a pleasure to behold but also are so well balanced and constructed as to have withstood the ravages of time and countless storms.

Often constructed on the crest of the highest hill so as to be seen from a great distance, these beautiful and enduring inuksuit, sometimes referred to as an *inuksuk upigijaugialik*, referring to an inuksuk that should be venerated, cause an amazing thing to happen. They create the conditions for the birth of a microcosm.

This is how it happens: standing on a hilltop for count-less years, the *inuksuk upigijaugialik* forms a windbreak, casts shadows, and attracts and holds the warmth of the sun on its south-facing side. Its shadow side tends to be moister than the surrounding area, often holding on to the remnants of winter's ice and snow longer than the land further away, which has dried under the prevailing wind. Thus the inuksuk creates a microclimate within a metre or so around itself. Though the temperature, wind conditions, and humidity in this microclimate differ ever so slightly from those of the surrounding area, a traveller can notice the differences.

Each bird leaves its signature upon the hilltop inuksuk. Many years worth of rich nutrients in bird droppings accumulate on its stones and work down to the warm surface. One of the first colonists to arrive in this new world is a tiny group of complex plants, some smaller than the head of a pin. They are a partnership of an alga and a fungus in a symbiotic relationship, with alga cells interwoven with filaments of the fungus to form a plant body. And so, over time, the inuksuk becomes draped in shades of black, dark green, and sometimes in the blazing orange of the lichen known as *Xanthoria*.

Nothing is wasted; even the remains of expired lichens add to the rich nutrients left by birds. And on one early summer's day on the sunny side of the inuksuk, an undigested seed carried there by an avian visitor sprouts and sends down its roots into a teaspoon-sized pocket of organic matter. The microcosm begins. Year after year, new colonists arrive, either carried on the wind or in the digestive tracts of birds. Pollen starts to be produced and an Arctic butterfly and a lumbering bumblebee discover this tiny oasis within the endless desert of rock. Under the protection of the inuksuk, carefully constructed by some traveller whose earthly journey came to an end long ago, a tiny universe comes into being and continues to unfold.

MORE REAL THAN YOU COULD IMAGINE

In the spring of 1979, a few days before leaving the Arctic, I went on my last solo trip. Carefully picking my way up the side of a worn down mountain, I reached its top, which provided a superb 360-degree view of the entire Cape Dorset area. A huge inuksuk had been erected here during a time now forgotten. Its very antiquity had transformed how it was regarded — then a landmark, now an object of veneration. All about its base and in between its carefully balanced stones could be seen countless *tunirrutiit*, little stones representing gifts of countless generations. I, too, placed a little stone within the inuksuk, hoping for some favour in return.

A vigorous cold wind prompted me to leave this place I would not see again for some time. Reluctant to depart and deciding to squeeze in a few more moments, I moved to the lee side of the inuksuk.

I now stood in the wind's shadow. All I could hear were the wind's sighs and whispers. I touched that part of the inuksuk facing the late afternoon sun and, to my astonishment, it felt warm. The sensation was what Simeonie Quppapik had described to me as *inuruqqajuq*, as if it were alive for a brief moment. Now sheltered from the wind, I sat down at the foot of the inuksuk and looked out toward the incredible beauty that surrounded me.

The noonday sun had slightly melted the entire mantle of snow on the land. Later, a cold wind swept up from the frozen sea and re-crystallized everything I was looking at into a vast, silent gleaming landscape. I was filled with a deep *unganatuq nuna*, an overwhelming attachment to the land. As the sun lowered, the appearance of the sky began to change. Thin wisps of cloud seemed to touch the tops of the hills in their path as they moved quickly toward the mountain.

I now lay down with my arms outstretched at the foot of the inuksuk, looking straight up into the sky. I could see only the top of the inuksuk. Ripple after ripple of low cloud passed rapidly overhead. I listened to the wind whispering through those still-warm, lichen-encrusted stones that sheltered me. I was enchanted by the sensation that the inuksuk and I were no longer earthbound. It was as if we had taken flight across a vast glistening landscape. I remembered an elder's words from years past — *Pillariktigulugu ... pillariugunniiqtillugu... asirurlugu... pillarirurlaqtikanniirlugu* — referring to an experience that seemed so unreal as to make it more real than you could ever imagine.

AN INTIMATE WILDERNESS

THE STONE HUNTER

Oshutsiak Publat was a quiet man, lightly built and often wrapped in deep thought. He was one of three brothers, all highly respected artists. Oshutsiak figured he was born around 1908, in the Qarmaarjuak (Amadjuak) region of southwest Baffin. As with everyone else of the same generation, Oshutsiak's birth was not recognized as a calendar date but as a personal event fixed in time that related to some other more important occurrence. For example, one might refer to the time of one's birth as the time of the great hunger or the time when the great ship from the South arrived.

Unlike his adopted brother Simeonie, Oshutsiak was never effusive in his greetings or farewells. Seeing me for the first time after a year, he would raise his eyebrows ever so slightly — a subtle sign of approval — make me a cup of tea, look straight into my eyes and, with a faint smile, wait for me to make the first move. He would watch me as a raven would watch some mildly interesting subject.

Oshutsiak talked to me at length about how inuksuit were used as hunters' aids:

> Some inuksuit are very old. They were made by the Tunniit long before we were on this land. I know of inuksuit that were made to fool the caribou. The inuksuit were made at places where caribou passed when they travelled together. They were placed in long lines on each side of the caribou trail. Our people would prepare themselves when the caribou were coming. The women and kids would hide on the ground between each inuksuk, and the hunters would hide behind a wall of stones in the middle, and at the end of the lines.

A very old inuksuk believed to have been constructed by the Tunniit at Itiliardjuk.

The caribou would come between the two lines of inuksuit. When many of them were between the lines, the women and kids who were at the beginning of the lines would jump up, yelling and waving things. This would frighten the caribou and they would start running toward the small wall of stones. They ran in a straight line because they saw people on each side of them. The inuksuit made it look as if there were many people. The caribou ran right up to the low rock wall and were killed by the hunters with bows and arrows.

Now I will tell you about some other inuksuit which have different names and are used for different things. When you go out on the land, I will tell you what to look for. If you see two or three stones one on top of the other beside a lake, they are tukipkota. *They are telling you that they mark a place where there are lots of fish.*

AN INTIMATE WILDERNESS

Sometimes when you come to an old camp beside a lake or at the mouth of a river, you see many little inuksuit. They tell you that this was a summer fishing camp and that many fish were taken at that place. They are called nappariat, and are about as high as your hips. The people used to string lines made from sealskin between these nappariat and hang fish on the lines to dry for the winter.

There are places which are marked by inuksuit as tall as a man. These are places which must be seen from a great distance and in winter, because they mean that an important thing, like food, has been left there. These inuksuit are called hakamuktak, and you can see them along the coast and inland where caribou are taken.

Sometimes you see two stones side-by-side with another stone on top. They look like a little doorway or window. These are called ikahimaluk, which means "attached to one another." Some of these are like windows which you look through to a distant place, so that you will know the right direction to take on the next part of your travels.

There are times when it is necessary for a hunter to set out on a trip over land without his wife and children. He will explain when it is safe to follow, and describe the landmarks to help his wife find her way. If the trip is a long one of several days, the hunter will make a tikotit, which refers to a "pointer." This is a tall rock leaning in the right direction, or a small rock on top of another which points in the direction of his camp. The tikotit was the helper that not only showed the way, but also was sometimes used to tell the family to change their direction because either there was danger ahead, or the hunter had decided to set up the camp in another location.

You asked if there were any strange inuksuit... Yes, there are some strange inuksuit in the nearby hills of old camps. They are very small and in the shapes of birds and animals. No, they have not been made by an inuga-ruvligak (dwarf). They were made by children. They are the children of a child's imagination.

The hauntingly beautiful site, Inuksugalait.

AN INTIMATE WILDERNESS

INUKSUGALAIT

Inuksugalait, or Inukso Point on Geological Survey of Canada maps, is a place of great significance in southwest Baffin. Designated a National Historic Site, it has origins that go back beyond recorded history. Here at least 100 inuksuit still stand within an area of approximately three hectares, making this site one of the most spectacular in the eastern Arctic.

No living person in the Cape Dorset area knows the age of Inuksugalait or the reason for its existence. Some believe that the "earliest humans" began erecting inuksuit there before making the journey across the open sea to Salliit Qikiqtanga (Southampton Island). It is also believed that the earliest ancestors of the elders in the Dorset area began building inuksuit at Inuksugalait either before setting out on a hazardous journey or having returned from one. I was told that this practice ended long before anyone now alive in Cape Dorset could remember. Every type of inuksuk (in a morphological sense) can be found at the site, except the human-like figure known as *inunnguaq*. Some inuksuit are beautiful to look at, where the mere arrangement of stones creates an aesthetic ambiance such as that found in a Japanese garden.

In whichever season I visited Inuksugalait, I couldn't help but be overcome by a sense spirituality and wonder. Visiting the site in early spring with my great friend Ohito Ashoona was a memorable experience. Ohito was part of a remarkable family. He was the grandson of the famous artist Pitseolak Ashoona who had provided me with much valuable information about intricate family relationships in the Cape Dorset area.

At the age of fourteen, Ohito's uncle Namonie had led his family some 160 kilometres across Sikusiilaq after their father died on the journey. Ohito's other uncle, Kiawak, and his father were master carvers whose works are collected by galleries and art collectors throughout the world. Ohito's own work ranks among the finest Inuit art today. Ohito was every bit as skilled in hunting and travelling in the vast spaces of Sikusiilaq as he once was the maze of streets in Toronto, where he lived for a short time.

On this day, Ohito, his 16 year old son, and I left Cape Dorset at 10 a.m. each hauling a sled with our snowmobiles. Ohito thought it would benefit his son to see "new territory." The young man was familiar with the landscape for the first few kilometres northwest of Cape Dorset, but after we stopped for our morning mug-up, everything looked new to him. From this point onward, Ohito carefully pointed out all significant features to his son.

"Significant features" did not just mean a prominent hill or bend in a frozen river. Ohito was pointing out the relationship of one hill to another and the shapes of certain valleys that were important to memorize. This valley might be in the shape of a kidney. That valley resembled a seal lying on the ice. So it went kilometre after kilometre, with Ohito's son noting and memorizing the shape of things and their relationships to one another. Even the shape and location of shadows were important to observe, for they could tell you not only how well you were maintaining your course but also how fast you were travelling. Every so often Ohito would stop, and I could see him gesturing to his son while explaining some very important detail I couldn't even recognize. Watching Ohito teach his son brought back fond memories of my own travels with elders. They explained the necessity of carefully observing such subtle elements as the colours of distant hills, the movement of clouds, the patterns of snowdrifts, the direction of waves, and even the play of ripples on a pond.

We arrived at Inuksugalait almost five hours later. Though it is only a distance of about 104 kilometres as the raven flies, ground travel is considerably more convoluted. In 1964, Charles Gimpel took about 28 hours by snow machine to and from Inuksugalait with stops along the way, whereas our actual travelling time to Inuksugalait and back to Cape Dorset, including mug-ups, not counting the time spent at Inuksugalait was a mere nine and a half hours. More powerful snow machines, excellent weather, ideal snow conditions, and the travelling skills of Ohito made for an incredible traverse.

Inuksugalait is known for its overcast days, howling winds, and profusion of polar bears during springtime. The bears give the greatest concern, for they are very hungry and ever-present at that time of the year. Once we had arrived, Ohito circled about until he found a place to his liking to set up camp. He set up the canvas tent on the side of the hill about a half-kilometer from where the inuksuit stood, lashing the tent ropes to each of our five-gallon gas cans. He said that using gas cans has an additional benefit because polar bears dislike the smell of gas. Ohito also pointed out that the location would provide a clear shot at either me or the polar bear — whoever seemed to be in the most trouble.

Having set up camp, we unhitched our sleds and pointed our snow machines back toward the trail. Leaving Ohito and the others behind to decide who would sleep where and who would cook supper, I headed warily for where the inuksuit stood at Inuksugalait. It is at twilight that the ice reveals the sheer power of the tides and currents that swirl about Inuksugalait. The powerful currents transformed the still-frozen sea into a vast field of icy spires about three metres high, making travel impossible except for polar bears. Where the landfast ice ended and the sea ice began, there stretched a line of fantastic icy shapes formed by the rise and fall of the tide. The impressive sight reminded me of the copperplate engravings in leather-bound books illustrating doomed sailing ships locked in the Arctic ice. Upon returning to our camp on the hill, I beheld a spectacle of indescribable beauty. The entire seascape of spires was illuminated by the setting sun. They appeared incandescent, their shapes and hues ever-changing as the sun descended to the surface of the frozen sea. I watched this incredible scene in silence. There was not a whisper of wind. I was witnessing *ijarovaujakpok*, the great shimmering. At times like these my old mentor Osuitok Ipeelie would refer to *nunaliriniq*, when we are at one with the land.

Visual aspects of weather conditions also seem to be amplified at Inuksugalait. I watched as the setting sun, for example, cast long plum-coloured shadows from each inuksuk across the land. When seen through a light mist, the site has a haunting quality, as if ghostlike figures move across the landscape. In early spring in the bright light, the place is absolutely dazzling. The inuksuit appear different because wind-driven snow has swirled about their feet and frozen in strange and wondrous shapes.

I've been led to believe that Inuksugalait was a place where people gathered to wait for favourable conditions before making their perilous journeys. They sought the favour of guiding spirits and constructed an inuksuk to show their respect. No doubt travellers constructed some inuksuit to pass the time while they waited for the winds to abate and the seas to calm.

The morning of our departure from Inuksugalait was windless with lightly falling snow. I went to the top of the hill to have one last look. On the day before our departure the entire landscape had been a vibrant, shimmering place with inuksuit illuminated by the rays of the setting sun. Now seen unlit and through the veil of falling snow, Inuksugalait appeared sombre. The inuksuit standing there looked like shadows. It was as if all were transformed into some distant and forbidding place.

Having travelled with the elders over the years, I had picked up some of their habits, one of these being to quietly thank the things that favoured me: the appearance of game, the conditions of the land, sea, snow, and especially, the weather. I stood on the hilltop, thanking Sila, the weather, for the gift of firm snow, brilliant sunlight, windless days, and *ijarovaujakpok*, when one sees the great shimmering. To my embarrassment, I noticed that Ohito had come up behind me and surely must have heard my conversation with Sila. Before I could utter some excuse, Ohito said, "I came here to do the same thing." I asked him who else he conversed with when out on the land. "Oh, with ravens, hills, clouds, all kinds of things," he said. We both said our thanks and headed back to our camp to pack up and return home.

Our departure from Inuksugalait, like our departure from Cape Dorset, began under a menacing sky and a shower of wet snow flurries. Having studied the texture of the snow in the vicinity, Ohito decided that we would take a different route back to Cape Dorset. He went on to explain that by the time we reached our

AN INTIMATE WILDERNESS

first mug-up, the sun would be out and the snow would begin to soften and make for tougher going than travelling along the coast. Trusting that his conversations with Sila were far more substantive than mine, I readily agreed to his decision.

Within an hour of our departure, the snow had stopped falling, the sky brightened and, as Ohito had predicted, the sun appeared. Within a short time we came upon fresh, widely spaced wolf tracks, all seeming to indicate vigorous pursuit. Yet we could find no caribou or hare tracks that would have indicated the wolves' quarry. Ohito followed their trail for a short distance, then returned to where we had stopped. "If my uncle Kiawak were here, he would pursue those tracks till he found the wolf, even if it took days." I learned that some hunters had an absolute hatred for wolves.

Ohito later went on to explain and demonstrate how he learned from Kov Tunnilie how to detect human footprints that were covered by a dusting of snow, as well as other vital signs a hunter must know. He described how he had felt searching for the footprints of his young cousin who got lost in a terrible storm and then later coming upon the young boy's frozen remains.

We had travelled on a few kilometres and came upon the fresh footprints of at least three separate bears. The varying degrees of sharpness to the prints' edges suggested that they had been made at different times, within days apart. Judging by the size of the prints in relation to the depth of their impression, Ohito concluded that at least one of the bears was starving, one was about a year old, and the other was a large bear headed directly toward the coast. Within a short time, we came upon inuksuit that reminded us that home was but a short distance away.

A kattak or entrance to a place where one must show respect,
Tukilik site central Foxe Peninsula (Sikusiilaq).

TUKILIK

While spending the next few days in Cape Dorset, I recounted my journey to Inuksugalait to some elders during our regular coffee break at the print shop. Paulassie Pootoogook, who happened to be there, mumbled something about a place far inland that had many more inuksuit than Inuksugalait. A few of the other elders nodded in agreement, though no one could remember the name of the site or its exact location. This took me by surprise. I'd never had the impression that Paulassie exaggerated things, yet I found this particular story almost beyond belief.

Later in the day, when Paulassie and I were alone, I brought up the subject again. I learned that the site had no name, was known only to a few elders, and seemed to be vaguely remembered as oriented between the Sugba and the north coast of the Foxe Peninsula. As Paulassie recounted, "It's somewhere in the area of the lake which is empty of fish and filled with ugly little creatures, known as *qupirqurqtuuq*. It is west of *Torngatalik*, the haunted hills."

Over the years, I learned to treasure these cryptic insights from Paulassie. He was one of the most important elders to teach me about life in traditional times, including travelling, living off the land, and having respect for the spirits. I still carry a vision of Paulassie hunched over my well-worn map of Sikusiilaq, one hand propping up his chin and the finger of the other pointing out places known only to a few elders and where no *qallunaq* had ever been.

Paulassie's description of a site rivaling Inuksugalait intrigued me. During the summer of 1995 we attempted to find the site while carrying out a reconnaissance of the general area but failed to locate it. Two years passed before our second attempt in July 1997, when I secured helicopter time with the support of the

Polar Continental Shelf Program. (For several years, I gratefully received logistical assistance from both Polar Shelf and the Geological Survey of Canada.) Upon the arrival of the helicopter in Cape Dorset, pilot Steve Horton and I plotted out the details of the western and eastern traverses. We made sophisticated calculations of fuel, weight, flying time, and distance by measuring with the span of an outstretched thumb and little finger placed on a map. The span between the forefinger and middle finger was about half the distance of the former. A knuckle was about one-sixth the distance of a span, and so it went. Thank heavens we had all our fingers and global positioning systems to back us up.

Paulassie explained to me and our fellow travelling companion, Mark Pitseolaq who often translated for Paulassie, that we were flying along the great pathway where the caribou travelled down from Nettilling Lake. During the fall, the caribou migrated westward to the interior of the Foxe Peninsula. So ancient were these trails that the very rock itself was etched by the hoofprints of countless caribou that had traversed this area, perhaps for centuries. To see the trails and the *nalliit*, the ancient caribou crossings, was wonderful. It was as if we were seeing the signature of life itself upon this vast Arctic prairie.

Paulassie asked the pilot to take us down. Upon landing, we got out and Paulassie scanned the horizon, looking for some sign that might tell us where we were. The most sophisticated navigational system was of no use at this time. He had to interpret a landscape he had seen only occasionally in his lifetime and translate into a summer landscape the vision that lay before him in winter. With some uncertainty, Paulassie decided that we should head south. The pilot reminded me that we had about twenty-five minutes of cruising time before returning.

Southward we went, the landscape looking as before, a vast prairie dotted with lakes and outcrops. Still nothing. My heart was sinking and the disappointment was evident on Paulassie's face. We saw a few inuksuit on some of the outcrops. One particular outcrop we flew over appeared to have glacial material scattered over it, but the lack of good light made it difficult to define the nature of the material. Our disappointment mounted as time was running out and our chit-chat faded into silence.

Time was up. The pilot said, "If we continue to head south we will be on our route home. Southwest will get us there more quickly. What do you want to do?" I asked if he could spare a few more minutes in the area before taking a direct flight path to Cape Dorset. I wanted to double back to the outcrops that appeared to be covered with scattered boulders. Paulassie was silent and disheartened. I didn't feel much better. The sky was lightening up a bit and we could observe faint shadows where small outcrops appeared. The pilot pointed out that the outcrops I wanted to revisit were lying just ahead of us. I asked that he take us down as low as possible and circle the outcrop to our left. There was a strange sense of unreality as we clattered above muskeg. Two caribou looked toward us and then bolted in opposite directions. Upon arriving at the outcrop in what seemed like only a few moments, I squeezed the talk button on my headset so hard it's a wonder it didn't break. "That's it!" I shouted. "Jesus Christ, that's it! We've found it!" Paulassie, then a Pentecostal lay minister, was beaming and pleased that I had expressed my gratitude so reverently.

We landed the chopper, got out, and just stared at inuksuit randomly situated in all directions. What a vision this site was. Each one of us seemed to want to discover some part of this place on his own, and so we walked off in different directions. I eventually met up with Paulassie, who was building a beautiful little inuksuk to celebrate our good fortune. It was to show the land we were thankful and would be in the company of those who hunted caribou with bows and arrows, long before the *qallunaat* appeared in this part of the Arctic.

I found a *kattaq*, an entrance, to a place of respect and asked Paulassie and Mark to join me in giving thanks for our good fortune. I passed through the *kattaq*, sat within a natural enclosure, and recited a prayer inspired by the moment. Paulassie and Mark joined me and began a beautiful chant in Inuktitut. I then set out to take photographs of the more prominent inuksuit and asked my companions to do a count of every feature on this outcrop. We counted 225 inuksuit — twice the number at Inuksugalait — one shelter, and one *tupqujak*, or doorway.

While I was photographing at the far end of the outcrop, the light had increased to make viewing favourable. To my astonishment, I could see the outlines of inuksuit on another outcrop a short distance to the southwest. I immediately walked across our outcrop in the opposite direction, where yet another outcrop lay. I crouched down so as to look at the profile of the third outcrop. They were there; from a distance they looked like pieces of scattered boulders, but when seen through binoculars... more inuksuit. (Later, as we were about to leave the site, I scanned the horizon to the east and saw what might be yet more inuksuit far in the distance.)

That day, I asked Paulassie if he now could remember the name of the place and to my surprise he could not. His father, the legendary Pootoogook who once traversed this area, had referred to the site only as the waiting place near Qupirqurqtuuq, meaning the lake where the water is empty of fish but filled with crawly things. I asked Paulassie and Mark if we could call it the *Tukilik*, defined as "a thing that has meaning," and they both agreed. The Tukilik site consisted of three large outcrops. The combined length of the outcrops, including the spaces separating them, is 2.3 kilometres. Using the Global Positioning System in the helicopter, we took measurements of the outcrops and the other features as we surveyed the entire site.

There are two important questions concerning the Tukilik site: Why is the site located so far inland? And why are there so many inuksuit concentrated on three small outcrops? The answers can be found by studying the particular area and knowing how people hunted caribou here before the arrival of white men. The three outcrops comprising the Tukilik site are situated in the middle of an ancient and still-travelled migration route from the Nettilling Lake region right across the central part of the Foxe Peninsula to its western region. Imagine this great path where caribou travelled westward in the fall. The females travelled about halfway, then remained behind to have their calves while the males continued westward.

About 145 kilometres west of the Tukilik site, still well within the caribou migration route, we observed a large pingo-like sandhill rising up from the plain. As we circled, I noticed that the downwind side of the hill was perforated with numerous holes.

On closer inspection from the helicopter, we noted from their size that these were likely wolf dens. Like their human counterparts, wolves would wait for the arrival of the caribou as they made their endless migrations from the Great Plain of the Koukdjuak. The males and some female caribou spent the winter in the west and then moved eastward in the spring back along the great path. The Tukilik site, being in the middle of the path, was in the region where the females were calving. Hunters knew that it was necessary to be at this place before the arrival of the migrating caribou.

If you drew a line southward from the Tukilik site, it would extend to the once-rich feeding grounds of walrus, beluga whales, and seals in the Sugba region and its outer islands, which acted as hunting platforms in winter. The hunting cycle began or ended at the floe edge. As the floe edge retreated, hunters began moving toward the land. On some islands, migrating ducks and geese lay eggs that the women and children would gather as the hunters moved ever landward, establishing their spring camps and, later, their summer and fall hunting and fishing camps along the coast. Whenever possible, humans and animals alike avoided travelling inland in summer due to the voracious hordes of mosquitoes. In the late fall, the mosquitoes were gone, the ground was firming up, and the caribou were ready to move into their wintering grounds in the western region of the Foxe Peninsula. Then the hunters, armed with lances, knives, bows, and arrows, moved into the area of the Tukilik site, took up their positions on the outcrops, and patiently waited for the approaching caribou. Paulassie explained that when you hunted caribou on foot armed with only lances, bows, and arrows, strict adherence to custom was observed for practical rather than "religious" reasons. It was imperative that the hunting area be "kept clean" and that any trace of the hunt be removed before one departed. As any good hunter knew, a wary caribou could detect even in a footprint the presence of the creature that had made it.

I believe that the absence of food caches, bones, and other refuse anywhere in the area attests to the fact that successive generations of hunters kept the site clean. When I asked Paulassie for his thoughts about the reason for the absence of food caches, he said the caribou that were killed were completely removed from the area. I believe that the guts and other refuse, such as human feces, were dumped into the nearby ponds and lakes.

This remarkable site not only held hundreds of inuksuit but also objects and places of a spiritual nature. I came upon a *tupqujak*, a "doorway" through which the *angakok*, or shaman, passed to a place where he propitiated the spirits. I assume this was to show respect to the abundance of spirits of the dead caribou believed still to inhabit the area.

At the foot of another outcrop were a series of hunting blinds arranged in a long row. I felt a strange sensation because everything was in perfect condition, giving the impression that the hunters had left but a few months ago. Sixteen blinds, or structures, one right next to the other, formed a continuous line or firing range along the entire length of the outcrop. Each circular structure was about one-and-a-half metres in diameter and constructed of loose stones piled to a height that would obscure a hunter lying on his side. This was the practice in southwest Baffin for those hunting caribou from a blind armed only with bow and arrows. The Tukilik site has by far the largest concentration of inuksuit now on record. I speculate that most were put there by hunters who waited for days or weeks for the arrival of caribou. They were largely confined to the outcrops, where they would be relatively dry above the muskeg and would not be spreading their scent over the established caribou tracks. On occasion, a young hunter bored with waiting would scour the edges of the outcrops looking for loose rocks to build his own inuksuk. And so the legion of silent figures grew each season.

Some were likely constructed as a form of thanks for a successful hunt or to leave a personal presence upon the land-scape, as Paulassie did when he constructed an inuksuk offering thanks to the site upon our arrival. The inuksuit were randomly scattered on the three outcrops, and there was nothing out of the ordinary in their construction. Interestingly, no *inunnguait*, human-like figures, were anywhere to be seen.

I asked the few remaining elders how I would describe the inuksuit that seemed to serve no purpose and were so far inland.

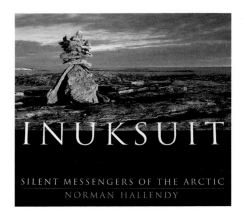
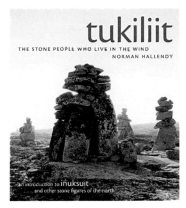

Their reply provided me with a new category of inuksuit called *inutsuliutuinnaqtuq*, referring to inuksuit that are created to shorten the time while one waits. The Tukilik site may also be described in Inuktitut as *tuttunik utaqqiurvik*, meaning the place where hunters would gather to wait for the arrival of the caribou.

A detailed account of inuksuit can be found in my previous books, *Inuksuit: Silent Messengers of the Arctic* and in *Tukiliit: The Stone People who Live in the Wind* published by Douglas and McIntyre.

LITTLE BEAR AND THE RAVENS

Anyone who has spent time in the Arctic is likely to have a few tales about polar bears, and I'm no exception.

Paulassie Pootoogook recounted to me the strange fate of his friend Niviaksiak, who died shortly before I arrived in Cape Dorset. As the story goes, Niviaksiak was obsessed with the terrible beauty of polar bears. He made exquisite soapstone carvings of them, pieces infused with so much power that eventually close friends warned him to be very careful of intruding into the spirit world of *Nanuk*, the polar bear.

In the spring, Niviaksiak went out hunting on the land with a few companions. They had spread out during the day, and as evening approached, Niviaksiak had not returned to camp. As the following day wore on, there was still no sign of him. The day after, Niviaksiak's companions set out to search for him and what they found was startling. "First they found his footprints," said Paulassie. "They followed them until they saw his body lying in the snow. There were no marks on him. When they turned him over, it was as if he just went to sleep. But from where he lay, the footprints of a huge polar bear had taken shape and eventually disappeared in the distance."

I've had a few close encounters myself with these beautiful and deadly creatures. One time, we were three families camping in the Sugba region beside a river where Arctic char had begun their run to the sea. We had a fresh supply of caribou that the women had cut into strips and placed on rocks for drying. We ate our fill of fish, many of which were also prepared for drying. These were hung on lines strung from small inuksuk-like figures called *nappariat*.

The mosquitoes were so voracious I was sure that they were sucking blood from one another. Fed up with this buzzing horde, the men picked up their rifles and headed out to sea under the pretext of going seal hunting, while the rest of us retreated to our tents. Sometime later in the day, little Irniq went out for a pee and then came bursting back into the tent crying, saying he had been chased by a big dog. We knew no dogs were anywhere near our camp, but to satisfy the child I stuck out my head from the tent only to see an Arctic fox making off with a large strip of caribou meat. Surely Irniq had been frightened by a fox.

A few hours later, Matta left the tent only to return screaming *Nanuk! Nanuk!* I rushed out, and there was a young, beautiful polar bear standing a stone's throw from of our tent. I called to my companions to get out of their tents, which they did with haste. To my chagrin, they formed a tight knot behind me. So I became the bait. *Nanuk* rose on his haunches, sniffing the air while turning his head from side to side.

"For Chrissake, don't stand behind me!" I shouted. "Spread out!" The tight knot of women and children spread out and the sight of them frightened the bear. From this young bear's behaviour, I assume that he had never encountered a human creature. He dropped to the ground and quickly headed off to the nearby hills. Our encounter that day was relayed throughout the entire southwest Baffin Island via sideband radio. I had just heard part of the conversation in which my name was mentioned when someone in a camp further along the coast said, "He wouldn't have tasted very good anyway."

Though polar bears frequently prowl the southwest coast of Baffin, they are most prevalent in spring. Later in the season, they visit the multitude of small islands strung out along the entire southwest Baffin coast. Some of these islands have been the nesting places of eider ducks as long as anyone can remember. In early summer, entire families eagerly gather eggs and eiderdown. The eggs are very nourishing, and the down is used locally and sold abroad, commanding a price as high as $150 per 0.028 kilogram on the German market.

One time I met an ornithologist, Bill Barrow, who offered an interesting perspective on polar bear activity and eider ducks in the region. Bill had been working among the islands scattered about the treacherous shoals in the Sugba and Markham Bay areas. His job was to survey the state of nesting eiders in that region. It meant days of travelling among the outer islands, often in wind and rain, and sleeping night after night in a water-drenched tent. Bill was kind enough to go over with me his maps indicating the existence of ancient camps, tent rings, inuksuit, graves, caches, and other formations unfamiliar to him. Of particular interest was a site where a black soapstone was quarried, which in years past was used in the making of *kudliit*, seal oil lamps.

I learned from Bill that the peak breeding time of the eiders in the area is from mid- to late July. It's a fact well known to polar bears that, like Bill, frequent the islands at peak production. Polar bears do phenomenal damage, devastating colony after colony of nesting birds. When they come upon an island of nesting eiders, they wipe out one hundred percent of them. Bill recounted the time when two bears had wiped out four thousand eider nests on Southampton Island in just one week. The only saving grace in the area we frequented is the existence of about two to three hundred eider colonies.

The polar bears in the Sikusiilaq region usually come in from the east and work their way westward to the Foxe Basin. Cape Dorset is a handy place for them to pick up snacks along the way. When the bears come into town, whoever is operating the FM radio station announces that bears are roaming and warns that children should be kept in the house until hunters have driven the bears away. More often than not, warning shots will convince a bear to lumber off to the dump to compete with the ravens for scraps of food. If the same bear returns to town, it is once again driven off with a few shots. If that bear persists, though, it is killed for everyone's safety.

The Sikusiilarmiut, the people of southwest Baffin, have a long history entwined with *Nanuk*. The meaning, relationship to humans, and spiritual significance of the polar bear appeared throughout the accounts of hunters and legends in times past. Some of the most beautiful and significant carvings by Cape Dorset artists depict polar bears transforming into humans and other animals. Some represent the spirit helpers of the *angaquiit*, or shamans.

It was Iyola Kingwatiuk who said: "We respect the seal, we love the caribou, but it is the bear we revere."

What I found most beguiling about the polar bear came to my attention one overcast day in April. I was startled by what I saw lying on the ice. For an instant, I thought it was the headless body of a child poking up out of the snow. Upon closer examination, I realized that it was the headless and skinned body of a young polar bear. The following day, I went out onto the ice to see the little bear again and beheld a strange sight. A flock of ravens had gathered in a circle around the bear. As I approached, the ravens flew off to the nearby hills and returned again on the following day.

The raven, known in Inuktitut as *tulugaq*, has many names, some spoken with reverence, others in scorn. However you regard this bird, the raven is one of the smartest and toughest creatures in the Arctic. *Tulugaq* has an astonishing repertoire of sounds, ranging from a deep-throated "gronk" to the almost mystical timbre of a crystal bell. The ravens play in the sky, harass dogs, steal meat, and cleverly topple garbage cans to get at the delicacies hidden inside.

Each day, I returned early to observe them. First I noticed that upon landing at the site, they appeared to remind one another of their pecking order before the feast began. After the dominant ravens had checked things out and had their fill, the other birds moved in.

The ravens were far less aggressive than gulls when feeding. They appeared quite tolerant of youngsters darting in between the adults' flashing black beaks to snatch a scrap of food. Within a matter of a day or two, the birds had worked out a pattern that remained constant throughout all their visits to the site. The entire flock of about twenty birds would arrive around 6 a.m. Some would land near the bear while others would fly about, diving, tumbling, and performing a wide variety of aerial acrobatics. Some birds would strut around visiting one another while others communicated through gronks, gargles, and croaks. Only after a period of considerable interaction would they would walk over to where their breakfast lay and begin to feed.

By now, the birds that had been fooling around in the sky would descend in a roll or some other aerial flourish on their way to land on the tips of snowbanks. Each bird appeared to have its own style of landing. Some would give a little twist before they landed while others would fan their wings and momentarily hang in the air before their feet touched the ground. Whatever the particular manoeuvre, it was a graceful expression of each one's individuality. I was able to recognize several individuals not by how they looked but rather by their antics.

Each day after the birds had completed their feeding, they would take off in various directions. Some would head for the dump and others would check out house porches for food left lying outside while others would fly to where the dogs had been chained out on the sea ice. The dogs never seemed to learn an old raven trick. One bird would tease the dog until it lunged out to the full length of the chain while the other would dart in and steal the poor dog's last scraps of food, a ruse that never failed.

After the fifth day, the remains of the little bear had been picked perfectly clean. I now assumed that the ravens would have no reason to return, thus bringing an end to my morning ceilidh. To my surprise, they still arrived each morning. They continued to visit one another, some of the younger birds playing inside the rib cage of the bear. This socializing took place every morning for many days and then, one morning, they were gone. *Tulugaq* had vanished.

Try as you might, it's difficult not to anthropomorphize the behaviour of ravens. Their gestures, antics, behaviour, and downright cleverness have earned them a revered place in the minds and hearts of Native North Americans. Anyone who has observed ravens will tell you that their behaviour often approaches the unbelievable. Inuit elders will tell you that *Tulugaq* is revered for its wisdom and seemingly supernatural abilities. I've heard of hunters calling out *"Tulugaq-tulugaq-turaarit-tuttuit-mitsaanut,"* imploring the ravens to show the hunters the whereabouts of the caribou.

I travel through places of vast horizons.

WHERE NORTHERN LIGHTS ARE BORN

When first arriving in the Arctic, you experience a sense of overwhelming vastness. You may see a horizon that extends 360 degrees, with no single vanishing point. It is as if you are staring into infinity without having to raise your eyes to the heavens. You lose your sense of scale and distance. A distant hill may be much further than you thought. A seemingly high cliff is not so difficult to climb when you finally approach it. In the crisp, clear Arctic air, light and its attendant moving shadows appear to ornament a solemn landscape. Pale hills become illuminated, sombre ice-fields begin to glimmer, and open water seems carpeted with stars. You stop for a moment and ask yourself, *Is what I'm seeing wondrous merely because I have made it more appealing than it really is? Can the sun really dance and shimmer?*

If you have spent time on the prairies, in the desert, or at sea, you will undoubtedly have seen phenomena that seem to occur only in such vast open spaces. The Arctic is also a place of strange and wondrous sights. There are, of course, scientific explanations for all these natural phenomena, yet how they affect our senses is what matters, not just why they happen. Someone from NASA once told me that the astronauts who had experienced the Arctic described it as akin to travelling through outer space, for both journeys invoke a sense of the spiritual deep within the traveller.

The iconic phenomenon associated with the Arctic is the aurora borealis — the northern lights. They have fascinated humans since earliest times. They illuminated the imagination and wonder of Chinese astrologers, Sami reindeer herders, Viking navigators, Greek and Roman philosophers, and North American Native peoples, including the people of the circumpolar world. Northern lights are entwined with northern folklore as day is with night.

In the land where one lived at the very edge of life, this ghostly phenomenon was called *aksarneq*, which refers to the sky dwellers playing a celestial game of kickball with the skull of a walrus. Some believed it to be the other way around that the walrus and other slain creatures were playing with the skulls of humans.

The common thread that runs through practically all Arctic legends of *aksarneq* is the belief in spirits. Those mysterious luminous vapours could be the souls of animals or humans. They could be messages from the dead or spirit messengers of departed relatives seeking solace in their living kin. It was believed that every strand of light represented a human soul and thus one beheld an eerie parade of sky dwellers.

Rummaging through the dog-eared pages of one of my notebooks, I came upon a little tale about *aksarneq*. I was once told that there is a place on southwest Baffin Island, past Itiliard-juk, where the ghost children dwell. They are the spirits of the stillborn, including children who died while still in their mother's *amauti* and those who were lost and died alone on the land. A very long time ago, a hunter who had been lost for many days and was near death wandered one dark winter night into this ancient place. He was met with whispers, pleas, and soft cries. He had neither food nor fear, he had nothing except a short time to live and a small white stone called *qaummaqquti*, meaning "light." His mother had given him the stone to protect him from harmful spirits.

Knowing he had little time left to live, he searched for a place to die. He found a crevice in a nearby cliff and, before lying down to die, took the *qaummaqquti* and placed it atop the nearby ridge. All of a sudden, out of the darkness, came a long cry — *aiii-aiii aiii-aiii* — and the *qaummaqquti* gathered up the lost souls of all the children and focused them into the dark sky. For the first time and there ever after, the sky gave the appearance of an approaching dawn, and for each little soul there was a strand of light in the darkness. And so, this is how *aksarneq*, the northern lights in Sikusiilaq, came to be.

I would learn later that the *qaummaqquti* was once placed on the graves of loved ones, especially children, to focus their life force upward.

VISIONS

You can be exposed to strange occurrences when travelling on land or sea. They may be as simple as *uujurumiaq*, when the earth appears to tremble because of heat rising from the stones, or as profound as *tautuqaqarviuqattaqtuq*, when one may have visions.

During one of my visits to Arviat, Luke Suluk, a friend introduced me to a gentle old man who was a respected elder known for his skills in reading the landscape. I asked the elder to talk to me about the most unusual place or event that he had experienced during his lifetime of travel. He asked if I had ever seen *tautoquaq*. I replied that I had no idea what he meant. He proceeded to talk about "lightning in the ice."

I'm not afraid to admit that I have been scared of things in my life. One thing that aroused great fear was when I found myself overtaken by the tautoquaq. *It happened one winter when I camped by a small lake. I was on my way to get some caribou. I was alone because my partner was sick and dogs were too yappy to take when hunting caribou.*

Sometime during the night, I heard a loud crack that startled me. As I rushed out to see what it was, another and yet another crack broke the silence. To my horror, a great streak of light flashed through the ice on the lake, making a terrible crashing sound. Soon there was light flashing through the ice in every direction, followed by sounds that crackled and hissed everywhere. I climbed to the top of a small hill nearby, leaving my belongings behind, and watched this frightful thing until it finally spluttered and went out. I am not the only one who has seen such things. The thought of it still frightens me.

He would not be the last to tell me about the mysterious *tautoquaq*. Joanassie Salamonie of Cape Dorset recounted an experience while hunting in early January.

You know my father's camp at Ikirasaq? Well we were travelling to Ikirasaq one winter, which is a place where some people are afraid to go. Some older people claim that if you fall asleep there, ghosts will strangle the life out of you. I have no reason to be afraid of going to Ikirasaq — I spent my boyhood there and it still beckons me. There are several small lakes on the way which makes for nice level crossings in winter; the whole area is familiar to us. Yet one evening, we were confronted by something we had never seen before.

We saw a glow on the horizon which seemed to flutter, coming from the direction of one of the small lakes. We stopped to talk this thing over and decided to approach the glowing thing with caution and readiness to flee if necessary. We came closer. To our surprise, the glowing came out of the ice around one part of the lake. It was a cold blue-green light that lit the things around it. It was one the of the most beautiful things I have ever seen, though I'm reluctant to talk about it. Some people might think I have just imagined it. I have never seen it again, though I know others who have seen such things.

LUNAR ATTRACTION

During one of my solo sorties in southwest Baffin, I had a strange experience. I was travelling up a pleasant valley when my snow machine momentarily went out of control. Just under a light covering of snow lay a vast flat sheet of blue-green ice that had caused me to go into a spin. Even above the roar of the snow machine, I could hear, or more likely feel, a deep hollow sound as I crossed over the sheet of ice. I carried on and thought no more of it until the following day.

Travelling through the same valley on the next day, I discovered that the sheet of ice had not only grown larger but also had assumed a distinctly convex shape. It now looked like a huge lens. By the third day, a large hump about one metre high had appeared in the middle of the ice sheet. When returning on the fourth day, I was startled to see that the hump had grown into a huge pingo-like structure that was now about three metres high. All the more fascinating was the fact that there were no cracks. It was as if the hump had become a blue-green glassy dome. The ice appeared to be in a very plastic condition.

Upon my return to Cape Dorset, I described the experience to my old mentor Osuitok Ipeelie and asked him what had happened. Osuitok was not only a master carver and historian, he also was a walking encyclopedia. He had a vast knowledge of his world.

After listening to my account, Osuitok described an occurrence known as *iqniqanitusiutut*, which refers to the pull of the moon not only on the tides but also on springs deep in the Earth. It applies as well to people and to the behaviour of animals. This phase of the moon can usher in a dangerous time, known as *iqniqani-tut*, when the tides are their highest and the currents strongest. This condition is at its peak in spring just after the full moon, and occurs during a *syzygy*, a Russian term referring to when the sun, moon, and Earth lie in a straight line. At such times the upwelling of water in freshwater lakes can occur, creating dangerously thin spots where the ice otherwise can be more than one metre thick.

GHOSTLY CARIBOU
AND PHANTOM DOGS

There are times when you experience a moment out on the land which, though brief, can be divine. For me, such a moment occurred one early spring while I was travelling with my companion by dogsled on the ice south of Iqaluit (Frobisher Bay).

The day started out soft and grey, the kind of day when sounds are muted and the land and the sky blend together. With no wind, the snow fell lazily in large flakes, creating a screen through which we could see only the faint outlines of distant hills. Having endured the wrath of violent spring storms, the land seemingly had fallen into a gentle sleep.

We decided it was time to give the dogs a rest and have some tea before we headed back home. Sitting on the sled and feeling the touch of snowflakes on my face, I had an overwhelming sense of peace. Then, as if in a dream, I beheld the shadows of caribou materializing in the distance. Slowly, one by one, they began to ascend into the sky. Having reached some invisible summit, these ghostly caribou suddenly vanished into thin air.

For a moment, I wondered if we were experiencing one of the many tales of magical occurrences I had been told about. Were these the *ijirait*, the caribou spirits, that Oshutsiak Pudlat often spoke of? Illusion or not, the sight was beguiling.

By the time we were ready to leave, the mystery of the ghostly caribou had been revealed. In front of us a hill, invisible just a short time before, began to emerge from the whiteness. Approaching the hill, we saw them — the fresh tracks of caribou leading to the summit and disappearing over the other side.

On the way home, listening to the sound of sled runners on the ice, I relived the day. Making a sled journey in good weather can be a wonderful experience. You sit a few centimetres above the ice on a comfortable pile of caribou skins and, except for the sound of the sled's runners gliding over the ice, experience a serene quietness. You gaze at the moving panorama of a white landscape and, though you've seen it countless times, marvel at its eternal beauty. You have time to think of experiences that shaped your life or thoughts and embed themselves in fond memories, such as the illusion of the caribou that vanished into the sky.

I recounted this experience to my dear friend Joanassie Salamonie, who told me of the *qimmuksiujait*, the phantom dog teams that can sometimes be seen racing across the ice. "They are like ghosts pulling strange-shaped sleds as they seem to fly in the air. Sometimes they appear to dissolve and then reappear again until they vanish into a hole in the sky. They are real, a real *puikkatuq*, a real mirage!"

Reality assumes a fullness when it is enriched by comprehension of being, and illusion. Many things that vanished into "thin air" were not illusions. There were the ancient snow traps to capture caribou, the inuksuit made of hard-packed snow placed by dangerous spring currents, the great ceremonial snow houses, as well as the countless igloos constructed by generations of hunters. There were human effigies, some used for target practice, others, such as the deadly *apumik inunguaqutilik*, created to destroy human souls. There were snow blinds put up for hunting seals, and even the cutting edge of a bone knife that was licked to take on a sharp icy edge. But the greatest vanishing act of all belongs to the icy landscape that covers both land and sea, which can vanish and reappear in the space of about one hundred days.

TIME OF THE MAGIC LIGHT

During a trip to Kiawak Ashoona's camp in July 1997, my travelling companions and I were treated to yet another episode of light and shadow. The effects were particularly noticeable due to the rapidly changing weather that spring. In the course of a single day, it was not unusual to experience at least four different conditions.

We began our journey when the light was perfectly flat, making it almost impossible to distinguish dangerous cracks, crevasses, or serious drop-offs when travelling over new snow. In combination with the flat light, we encountered mist or haze, slowing our progress as we tried to assess where we were. Under such conditions, maps are of little or no use. During the trip, it was not unusual for sudden storms to overtake us. The phenomenon of a bright whiteout in contrast to the flat light experienced earlier would stop us in our tracks until the landscape became visible again. Within a very short time, any trace of bad weather could vanish as brilliant sunshine illuminated the land.

At times it was so bright that ordinary snow goggles had to be replaced with dark glacier glasses. Removing our glasses, even for the short time it took to change film or tend to some minor repair, would affect our vision if repeated throughout the day. In these conditions, shadows were welcome. They helped us see clearly any hazards along the way and indicated sheltered places or entrances to passes. Shadows gave depth to the landscape and gave us a better sense of direction and the passage of time.

On clear evenings we observed what cinematographers refer to as "the time of the magic light." As the sun descended to about the width of my hand, a golden glow illuminated the entire landscape. Shadows took on plum-coloured hues; the normally forbidding pressure ridges of sea ice glowed like crystal spires. This time of magic light lasts only a few minutes and is gone, replaced by a sense of coldness. On rare windless nights, moon-light flooded across the landscape.

Travelling through the valleys, across the plateaus, and then up the sides of mountains was a profound experience, sparking a sense of unreality. A scene of haunting beauty replaced the stark, rugged landscape seen just a few hours before in the cold light of day. It was as if all that surrounded us had taken on the colour of the moon.

On another evening, around 11 p.m., the sea near Itiliardjuk was relatively calm. We had just hacked off a nice piece of ice from a large floe to make fresh water for tea as the sun set behind the hills. We were enjoying ourselves looking for seals and talking about old times. At times like these, the sense of freedom and joy is indescribable. A good boat, the sound and smell of the sea, a welcome companion, and an enchanting evening do wondrous things for the human spirit. The light all about us was continuously changing, from blue to a soft violet-grey. Clouds hanging in the air became incandescent, set glowing by a sun that had dropped below the line of the dark and distant hills.

As the sun set, a startling sight appeared. A fiery and then-glowing column of light formed and reached skyward, touching and illuminating the bottoms of clouds. Its sharp, clear edges gave the impression of a great beam of light bursting from the Earth to ignite the stars. At that moment, my companion, Davidee Saila, shouted, "Look! Look!"

"What is it?," I shouted, startled. "Where?"

He pointed behind us to a huge full moon that appeared to rise out of the sea. The atmosphere was magnifying the image of the moon, creating an illusion that the moon was intent on overtaking us. It was huge and luminescent, like a great paper lantern floating heavenward. As it rose, it illumined a pathway from the horizon to the very edge of our boat. All the while, the pillar of light from the departed sun grew deeper in hue as it touched the clouds in an ever-darkening sky.

On one side of us, the sea was bathed in golden moon-light, while on the other, pale green-blue and orange-yellow hues of light fell upon the sea from the undersides of clouds. We drifted in this radiance as if floating on light.

A FEARFUL TWILIGHT

Davidee Saila is the adopted son of Pauta and Pitaloosie Saila. He is twenty years my junior, which causes me to regard him as a young man. His mother, Pitaloosie, and I were such close friends that she regarded me as her southern brother, which was fortunate because she would often order Davidee to be my travelling companion whether he was up to the task or not.

Davidee has a lot of spirit. Several years ago, I was travelling with two companions by snowmobile. We were several kilometres inland from the coast on a northward journey when we spotted a lone figure on the horizon travelling at high speed. He was zigging and zagging, climbing almost-vertical slopes and plunging down their sides in daredevil fashion. This lone hunter burning up the slopes turned out to be Davidee. He often travelled alone and over considerable distances, hunting for food to help support the family.

I thoroughly enjoyed travelling with Davidee; he was highly competent and had a great sense of humour as long as I didn't feed him a chocolate bar. Sweets turned him into a madcap comedian, causing the both of us to become momentarily hysterical. It was Davidee who often accompanied me to places where I documented inuksuit and who patiently waited for me for hours without taking off to hunt seals or some other equally sensible activity.

On a trip with Davidee, I had a frightening experience I had only heard of in vague terms. Some refer to it as the "kayak sickness," a condition in which you become so disoriented you do not know up from down or your own position in relation to the surface of the sea. I'd heard the experience could be so frightening that even experienced kayakers were seriously affected.

Though this condition could arise on a glass-calm sea when the horizon was clear, a similar and most frightening experience occurred to us under somewhat different conditions.

It happened near the end of a wonderful sunlit day. From our canoe, we eagerly anticipated the appearance of an afterglow on the horizon. But on this evening, something was happening of which we were not aware. A vapour more delicate than mist seemed to be slowly coming toward us. The violet afterglow was still visible through this vapour, yet the surface of the sea seemed to disappear beneath this delicate shroud. Our state of euphoria gave way to one of unease. The stillness, silence, and sense of everything around us dissolving into nothingness created a feeling of apprehension. Suddenly, our canoe was thrust up from the sea, as if by unseen hands, and then dropped.

We were frightened. All we could see was the sea welling up and rolling toward us from some invisible place. The swells threatened to roll us over. As we turned to meet them at our stern, for a moment I thought we would surely be drowned. Presuming that the swells had their origin somewhere far out in the Hudson Strait, we rode them to where we hoped the south shore of Baffin lay. And just as suddenly, we passed through this phantasm and could see a thin black line on the horizon. Land was ahead. The swells continued to raise and lower us in a threatening manner. Just before the sun rose, our perilous ride came to an end; the tide turned, and we approached the shore of south Baffin.

Upon reaching home the following day, we recounted our harrowing experience to Pauta. He said he'd had a similar experience on rare occasions but gave us little comfort in describing how dangerous such great swells can be. "It is when the ocean swallows you," he said.

Indeed some poor souls were swallowed by the sea, as related to me by Ikkuma Parr. The southwest coast of Baffin and the entire north coast of Nunavik, or Arctic Quebec, are subject to very high tides. They average from five and a half to seven metres and may exceed ten and a half metres at the flood tide. In places, when the tide goes out, the ice remains suspended like huge vaults above the sea floor. Into this frightening and gloomy region, women descend through a hole in the ice to the ocean floor to gather little clams.

"Our spring camp was in the direction of the fish lakes." Ikkuma told me. "There are many clams in that area. Nothing is more delicious than the taste of fresh boiled clams after a long winter, and so sometimes we went below the ice to gather them. I remember such tales from Nunavik. There were places so far below the ice that they could only be reached by using a homemade ladder. It was strange walking on the bottom of the ocean. It was scary at times when you heard unfamiliar sounds coming from dark places in the distance. You could hear your own breathing. I know a lady who disappeared forever down there. You felt different in that place, drawing breath from another world. It is a world inhabited by many *tuurngait* (spirits)."

The mysterious *Sukaq* or Sundog.

AN INTIMATE WILDERNESS

SIGNS FROM HEAVEN

While travelling with Pauta Saila and his family, between Qaumainnasuq (where the land is bright, where there are sounds of life) and Iqianaqtuq (where the land is in shadows and silence), we were enveloped by a vast *puikkatuq* (mirage). Spellbound, we watched ghostly islands rise from the sea. Some attached themselves to one another. Others grew into grotesque shapes, hovered over the sea for a moment, and then vaporized. The distant shoreline trembled at the feet of hills that became mountains whose peaks detached themselves and drifted off into space. We too drifted among the clouds reflected in a calm sea. How would we appear to someone standing on the shore? I wondered. *Inailangaartuq*, a wanderer or changing spirit, I thought.

The *puikkatuq* disappeared as quickly as it had overtaken us. In a matter of moments, reverting to our familiar perceptions of land, sea, and sky, the more ethereal images left only an imprint on our memory.

One may experience a number of other phenomena in the North. Arctic haze appears red-brown when the viewer is facing the sun but grey-blue from the opposite direction. Ice blinks are often seen at sea during the spring when there is a field of ice and low-flying clouds. As you turn your gaze toward the horizon, you observe the bright underbelly of the clouds, a visual experience caused by the light reflected upward from the field of ice in the distance. Ground drift occurs when snow is being blown very low across the surface of the earth. When backlit by the sun, the blowing snow appears as water flowing around and just above the rocks. A sundog, or mock sun, can be seen in the South as well as the North. A luminous halo appears to surround the sun.

Two small suns to either side of the actual sun will often appear on the halo in an atmospheric phenomenon that was once believed to be a sign from heaven.

The Inuit also used another phenomenon to give direction in early spring, known as *tunguniq*. To the inexperienced traveller, *tunguniq* appears as a forbidding deep black patch in the sky. To the experienced traveller traversing inland, it indicates the direction of open water at sea. It is the opposite of the ice blink; here the darkness of open water is reflected skyward.

One of the most enchanting sights, known as "diamond dust," occurs when the air appears to be filled with minute glittering ice crystals. You become enveloped in a million pinpoints of light that create a dreamlike world around you.

ESSENTIAL WOMAN

Some of my fondest memories are of times spent with women elders, many of whom talked openly about all manner of things: love, life, times past, and the future for them and their children. Usually, we experienced an ease and comfort in our times together — and plenty of silly talk. I recall once sitting on a stoop when an elder placed her hand on my thigh and giggled to her girlfriend, "If I was fifty years younger, there'd be nothing left of him." Or the time when we were all together in an old hut, bathed by the light of a seal oil lamp flicking shadows on walls insulated with old newspaper. Oqsuralik was pretending to pluck lice from my hair while her three girlfriends were conducting a mysterious chant. I soon realized that it was my fifty-fifth birthday, and they were singing "Happy Birthday" to me in Inuktitut.

At cocktail parties in the South, I was often asked, "Do the Inuit really rub noses and share their wives with you?" My stock reply was, "I've never had the pleasure of either." If I'm in the right mood at a party, I may invite a female guest to help me demonstrate how some Inuit show affection to the opposite sex. The man and woman come together and ever so gently place their heads on the other's bare neck and shoulder. They wait for a moment, then slowly and delicately inhale each other's scent. I assure you it is an experience never to be forgotten.

Though at times the desire to make love to a woman was almost overwhelming and regarded as natural, with great restraint I chose, sometimes regretfully, not to do so. Much later in life I asked a few women elders if they had ever regarded my behaviour in such matters as aloof or insulting; they assured me they had never felt that way.

In the summer of 2005, I took my wife Diana and partner for the last twenty-six years, to the Arctic for her first visit.

She found herself warmly welcomed by the elders and, I later learned, inspired a collective sigh of relief from the numerous male companions I had travelled with in previous years. As Davidee Saila put it "When Mom told me to take you out on the land, I was always worried." I heard that the mystery of my sexual orientation had become a topic of local chatter on the sideband radio for an entire day.

In time, the old adage of beauty being only skin deep became abundantly clear. I would learn that the beauty of a woman was once measured not by her superficial appearance but by her knowledge, status, and level of skill. I remember the time when, at our usual morning mug-up, I went on at length to some of the male elders about the beauty of "K's" two daughters. My *qallunaq* perception of feminine beauty was dismissed as trivial. The most desired woman, as described by Osuitok Ipeelie, was one who attained status and who was respected as an *arnammarik*, a great woman — one who is inspired to do all things in an exceptional manner.

I also received multiple lessons in the nature of "women's work," Arctic style. Mary Pudlat made me some beautiful drawings illustrating what women had taken out on the land on long journeys in traditional times. She was obviously respectful of tradition and the role women played in sustaining family life. "Don't think we just sit around in the tent when our man is out hunting," said Mary. "He just shoots the animal, skins it, and brings it home. We have to prepare the meat. We take the skin, scrape it clean, then stretch it. In the meantime, we remove the sinew from the back of the caribou and dry it. When the caribou hide is ready, we mark out the pattern of whatever we must make and carefully cut the pieces out. Then we take the sinew we saved and strip it into threads for sewing together whatever we are making. If we are making boots, we have to do all what I have told you and more. We have to chew the skin for the bottom of the boots until it is good for sewing.

"All my husband had to do," Mary added with a chuckle, "was throw me the skin."

I recall a particular comment by my old friend Qugjuq (the swan) when we were sitting on the outer edge of an ancient tent ring eating bannock and dried caribou meat. "There are times when our women get together and speak in such a way that we men can't understand them," he said. "It's like they have their own special language. We call it *arnait uniqautigusingit arnaqsiu-tinik*, and not only that, there are places out there we call *arnain-narnut qaujimajaujuq*, places known only to women. We don't know what goes on there. If you see a woman walking off on her own, don't follow her or you will get a good scolding."

I had the opportunity to follow Qugjuq's advice during a long and hazardous journey along the west coast of the Foxe Peninsula. The Saila family and I were beset by a gathering storm. The sea became so violent that standing waves began to appear. Having never seen such fury before, I was both fascinated and frightened. The waves appeared as huge white feathers rising up from the sea, warning of the grave danger created by violent winds and a surging outgoing tide. Just below the surface lay hidden sharp shoals the likes of which destroyed many ships that sailed these waters.

So frightening was this scene that the children hid beneath the canvas that covered our provisions, so as not to see the huge waves rising and falling all about us. Pauta, with skill honed by years of experience, guided our canoe to a small cove at Tikiraaqjuk, the Great Finger. Upon our landing, I'm certain that each one of us in our own way offered thanks to whoever was listening.

Pitaloosie and the girls immediately headed off toward a nest of large rocks. Recalling Qugjuq's admonition, I walked off in the opposite direction. That evening when we were snug in our sleeping bags, I asked Pitaloosie about places known to women, in particular about a place on the way to Kangisurituq (Andrew Gordon Bay), where women were said to leave things (gifts) to the land. She confirmed that such a place existed and revealed its location by name, but added that this was no longer done. On the second day at Tikiraaqjuk, before taking down camp, Pitaloosie took me to a place that held much meaning for her, the type of place that many mothers and daughters throughout Sikusiilaq held close to their hearts. It was a small sheltered alcove among the rocks — a puzzling scene at first glance. We had come upon a collection of small stones of various shapes and colours placed upon little shelves of flat rock. Among the pebbles were fragments of little bones so old that bright orange lichen found nourishment in them. To me, the place had a mysterious quality, but for Pitaloosie, it was no mystery: Here was a special *ungatinnguit*, a playground for girls and the spot where Pitaloosie's mother had played and her imagination still lingered. Far out on the land, places where children had played and left traces of their imagination upon the landscape were rarely disturbed.

The women's role was not only to stay in camp, mend clothes, and mind kids. Often, they stood side by side with the men spearing fish and later netting them when the char ran in the icy rivers. Women often assisted in the caribou hunt by standing between the lines of inuksuit, guiding the caribou to the shooting pits. A friend from Labrador informed me of an Inuit woman who regularly went out hunting alone on the land for many days. She was regarded as one of the most skilled hunters in the entire region.

I had met such a woman many years ago at Qaqqaq Ashoona's camp on my way to Itiliardjuk. Majuriaq was Qaqqaq's wife; her beautiful name referred to "a gentle rising slope." Majuriaq's eyes spoke of a life that was anything but gentle. A year after I had visited Majuriaq and Qaqqaq, Qaqqaq died. But because of treacherous ice conditions, several days elapsed before the men of the family could go to the camp and bring Majuriaq and her dead husband back to Dorset.

The following summer, on my return to Cape Dorset, I asked Majuriaq if we could visit, have a bite to eat, and talk. This is what Majuriaq shared with me that day.

I've lived most of my life in an outpost camp. From the beginning, I learned how to live on the land. I was always watching others, learning all things necessary to survive. I not only learned things women must know, I learned about the behaviour of animals, how to read their tracks, and all the things required to be a good hunter.

I learned from my elders that one should wake up very early to go hunting, for this is the time when animals are the most active. In spring and fall they are migrating and therefore are more abundant than at any other time of the year.

AN INTIMATE WILDERNESS

Knowing how to hunt and survive on the land made me feel independent deep inside, even though I behaved as a wife. My husband, Qaqqaq, was often carving, so we took turns hunting. It was during these times that I went out on the land alone. Sometimes I would be trapping, sometimes I would be hunting or fishing. Sometimes I would be walking for miles inland, and other times I would be hunting at the floe edge. I even learned how to get Qaqqaq's boat going, and I would go out to sea by myself.

There were times when I knew that I was not capable of swiftly killing an animal or having the strength to handle it even if I did kill it. At times such as these, I would walk away and leave the animal alone. I always made sure that I was well prepared, just in case I couldn't get back to our camp for several days. Whether you are out on the land or the sea, alone or with someone else, it's important to be cautious. I was always prepared for the worst. I even kept things and food for emergencies, not only for us but for unfortunate people who wandered into our camp. Sometimes they came in on foot from far away. All the things I've learned I try my best to give to my grandchildren.

Since my husband died, I've had to live in the community but my heart is out on the land. I know that some day I will go back to the land and be whole again.

Majuriaq turned toward the open window and watched a pair of ravens flying low over the hills. She turned to me and said softly, "Thank you for listening to me."

Majuriaq revealed to me the real meaning of a beautiful woman.

NEEDLE, THIMBLE, AND ULU

During the summer of 1960, I began photographing people and collecting stories and accounts in a systematic way. One afternoon, Ikkuma Parr asked a small group of women to her house to talk to me about their experiences. As usual I provided the food, which consisted of a brick of old cheddar cheese, garlic-laden dried sausages, and Red Rose Tea. Ikkuma began:

> I grew up in a very small camp. We didn't travel to other camps and so the things I have to tell you have been learned from only a few women and from the things I found out by myself. Remember that the things that happened to me happened in my life and in our camp, so do not think that it was the same with all women.
>
> It was important in our camp for each person to behave well. People who misbehaved, including children, were severely punished. I remember the time when a little boy had stolen some meat from another family. He was taken into the tent, tied up by his parents, and not released until he was painfully hungry. You may think this was cruel, but it was so important for everyone to know that they could not do as they pleased.
>
> The two worst things that could happen to a woman in the camp was for other people to say that she was a gossip or that she was a woman that could be had by any man. Gossips cannot be trusted, and loose women not only are resented but also can be the cause of serious trouble between men.
>
> I think that many young women like me had their marriages arranged by their parents. Whether or not you

loved the man didn't matter. Sometimes the parents of little children would agree that the two kids would marry when they were old enough, and other times a man known to the family would convince the parents that they should allow their daughter to be his wife. Such a thing happened to me.

A man who was old enough to be my father came to our camp to speak to my parents. They told me to leave the tent and stay in his boat until I was given permission to return. I was in the boat all day and all night, and I knew what was happening. My parents told him that he could have me as his wife, and I was sick with anger and sadness, but could say or do nothing.

There were many times when he would go out on the land or to the floe edge to hunt, and in my heart I wished that he would never come back alive, such was my feeling for that man.

You see, a husband can do no wrong. He can be very hard on his wife and she has nothing to say. She must continue to serve him. If he complains to her parents that she is lazy or not good to him, they are angry with her and will even beat her.

The most important thing for a woman to know was how to make clothing. Life depended on two things: food and clothing. The man got the food and the woman made the clothes to keep him alive to get that food. A woman's reputation was determined by how well she handled a needle.

I know of one instance of a man who could not keep his wife. Another hunter came into our camp with his young sister, and when he saw my uncle's wife, he said that he wanted her. He was a powerful man who had much influence throughout the camps along the coast and so his wish could not be denied. He gave his young sister in trade for my uncle's wife. Both women were not happy and could say nothing about the wish of that one man. I was told that, in later years, he felt sorry for having demanded the other woman and was kind to our family until he died.

AN INTIMATE WILDERNESS

I told you that the status of a woman was determined by how well she did things, especially in the making of clothing. She also had a different kind of status as she grew up. The word that was used to describe her before she had her first period was niviaqsiaq. *After her first period she was* uvikkaq. *If she went through life without having slept with a man, she was* ooigasuk. *It was important for a woman to have her first child when she was young because her hip bones could spread and delivering her baby would be easier.*

I was told that pregnant girls must get to their feet as soon as they opened their eyes in the morning or they would have a hard labour. We were told never to braid things or make a loop with any cord or thread for fear that the baby would be strangled in the womb. We had to be careful when eating seal meat because the seal has a very small kneecap that can easily be swallowed, and if you swallowed it your child would be born with a small, unpleasant face. We also believed that cleaning a bone when eating, so that there wasn't one speck of meat on it, would ensure the birth of a sweet child.

At this point, I asked Ikkuma to describe the virtues of her favourite daughter to me, as though to entice me to take her as a wife.

The room was filled with other women who looked on with amused anticipation. Ikkuma began by telling me how good her daughter was, how clean she kept her hair and, above all, how well she could make things. I replied that this was not sufficient to take her as a wife because I didn't know all the things that the girl could not do. "Never mind what she can't do," the mother said. "I will show her or do (the things) myself. It will be a good match." Then the mother looked at me with a smile spreading over her face and asked, "What kind of boat do you have?" I replied that I didn't have even a small canoe, and she shot back, "Then who needs you for a son-in-law?" The room was filled with gales of laughter.

She continued:

There were two medicines I knew that were used. One was pujualuk, *which is the powder inside a small, round mushroom. It was very good in stopping bleeding. The other was* qingmingivak *(the hairy mantle of Arctic willow), which was put on the baby's belly button so that it would heal quickly. Sometimes a mother had no milk in her breast, and then she had to feed her baby on soups made from blood and meat until it was old enough to eat food that she first chewed. The mother fed the baby from her own mouth. When the baby was older, it could be given a piece of meat to suck and chew. In order to prevent the baby from swallowing the meat whole and choking on it, we stuck a piece of wood or bone through the end of it. It worked like those nipples you buy in the store to keep kids quiet.*

A good medicine to stop the "runs" in kids was to give them a mixture of udjuk *(square- flipper seal) fat and rabbit droppings. We had no soap in the early days, and in the spring we used the yolk from duck eggs to really clean the skin.*

At this point Ikkuma's friend picked up the conversation.

I remember the first time that I was a midwife. I was trembling with fear because I had never seen it done before. I also remember the feeling of joy when it was over. We say angusiaq *(I brought forth the boy) or* arngnaliaq *(I brought forth the girl) when we have made a good delivery.*

That little boy who was in Ikkuma's house when you came in, was delivered by me. He came by to give me the first duck eggs he found for bringing him into the world. I love him for that.

Women not only prepared the way for life but looked after the dying and the dead. We made the dead person clean. We closed their mouths and their eyes. We dressed them in clean underwear. We were the last to touch them.

You asked me what is a beautiful woman. I think that the sign of beauty is in the eyes. We did no special things to our hair and faces. I have heard that in other places women had themselves tattooed, but it was not the custom where we lived. I know of two women who were tattooed a long time ago by whalers who hunted in this area. But this was an unusual thing.

You were told by another lady that a gossip or a loose woman was resented by other women. A selfish woman was not just resented — she was detested by everyone. Selfishness was the worst kind of behaviour in any camp.

It is true in many ways that the life of a woman was hard. She was the first to rise and the last to sleep. Her husband was always right — she could be punished by her parents for not pleasing her husband. She could do nothing if he slept with another woman. All of this did not mean that she was without feelings. It hurt to know that your man was in bed with someone else, and even if he was a demanding old man, you felt jealous of that other person.

I remember being so hurt one time that I was determined to smash my husband's rifle in half, then go over to his girlfriend's tent during the night and slash it to ribbons. My friend remembers the time that her husband decided to take a young woman along on a hunting trip with them. My friend was so angry that she attempted to turn over the canoe and didn't care if she drowned along with the younger woman.

I remember the time that my husband crawled into bed and wanted to get on top of me. I told the old fool, politely, to go and undo his pants in his girlfriend's tent. I guess I was a pretty independent woman. Once when I was young, a man from another camp kept chasing me. I heaved stones at him, and after a while he gave up. When men get the idea in their heads, they can become pests. Once a pest got me onto his sleeping platform, but finally gave up when he knew I wouldn't take off my parka, pants, and boots. We used to dress very well!

Though sometimes a man forced a woman to lie with him, this was a most unusual occurrence. Forcing a woman (rape) was not known to happen in our camp.

People who camped together behaved very well. It was necessary to do so. Young girls who were growing up were forbidden to talk or ask questions about what it was like to lay with a man. We didn't even talk among ourselves about the kind of man that we would like to have as a husband when we grew up.

I can add a few things to the conversation that you had last night when you were listening to my friend talking about pregnancy. The pregnant woman could eat only the lower parts of an animal. She could not eat the meat from the head of a caribou nor its fat or marrow. She was to eat only cooked meat; she could never eat raw meat or fish while she was pregnant. In the old days she had to eat separately from other people and she ate her cooked food from a separate pot.

It was common for an angilijaiguti *(midwife) to help the mother deliver a child, and even some men knew how to do this. I remember the time when I assisted a friend who was in great pain and discovered that the baby was dead inside her. I had no choice but to take out the baby in pieces, to save the mother's life. Sometimes the baby was in the wrong position with its head high up in the belly, and then the* angilijaiguti *had to very carefully try to turn the baby around by making movements on the mother's belly. You asked if we ever took a baby out by cutting the mother's belly; the answer is "No, we never did such a thing." You must remember that a mother's life came first. If things went badly, our first concern was the life of the mother — another baby could be born but not another mother.*

You told me that you spoke with a woman who said that there were no tattooed women in her camp. I knew of a woman who was tattooed all over her body. Being tattooed was painful, especially when done on the face. Tattooing was done by mixing soot with grease, and rubbing it on thread. The thread was then attached to a small needle and the needle was pushed through the upper part of the skin. When it, along with the thread, was

AN INTIMATE WILDERNESS

pulled out, the soot remained in the skin; and that's how tattoos were made. One girl who was about to be tattooed protested and was threatened with being put into the pot below the kudlik *(stone oil lamp). That frightened her even more, and so she gave in and was made beautiful. Women with pale skins were especially good-looking when their faces were tattooed. I know that some women were tattooed long before the whalers came into our area — it was a very old custom. I have seen a few men who had a tattoo across the bridge of their nose. This was not a mark of beauty, but a sign to let everyone know that he had killed a fearsome person.*

We decided to take a break and have some tea. I took out my tobacco and began to roll a cigarette. "Oh," Ikkuma said, "I haven't seen those cigarette papers for a long time." I gave her the packet of Vogue Cigarette Papers with the picture of the lady on its cover.

Just as the hunter is associated with the harpoon, the woman is associated with the needle, thimble, and ulu. These three things were her most precious tools, for with them she made everything for the family members to wear. Their clothing was highly specialized, superbly designed, and modified for the seasons. Animal skins and sinew were used to fashion garments that allowed the family to survive in a climate where death by exposure was an ever-present possibility.

We were always making and repairing clothing. Our needle case, thimble, and ulu were the things of the greatest importance. Yes, we had other women's things in the camp and, though not as important, they were necessary. Some of these women's things were a skinning board, a big ulu for skinning, a sharpening stone, a stone scraper, cooking pots, cups, drying racks for clothing, thread made from caribou sinew, and, most importantly, the kudlik. *We burned seal oil in the* kudlik. *The flame was tended with a* takhut *(tamper made from wood or stone) and the wick for the lamp was made from a very fine moss mixed with the fuzzy part of the Arctic willow.*

Another important thing was our teeth. We had to chew skins before we made them into things, and when some things were made — like kamiks *(skin boots) — we continued to chew them every night until they wore out and we had to make another pair. See my teeth,* she exclaimed. *They are only half worn down. My mother's teeth were almost flat to her gums.*

You said that when you were in the western Arctic they made underwear from rabbit skins. Well, we didn't make underwear where we lived. We were naked inside our parkas. We made clothes for babies from rabbit fur with the hair facing inward, which was very soft and warm. The making of clothing was a lifelong thing and, even so, a woman took pride in what she made.

Earlier this evening, you asked if some women slept with other women. I never knew of such a thing; besides, they've got nothing to "do it" with anyway, she said accompanied by giggles in the background.

I don't know how other people behaved in other parts of the Arctic, but let me tell you that we had to behave well where we lived. Men did not freely exchange wives. Swapping wives never happened in our camp.

Life was often hard, and there were times of loneliness and sadness, but there was also love. How can I tell you about love? Perhaps I will try to talk to you as if you were my own child and so you will understand the simple things I have to say. Try to love those around you equally; it's better than hiding it. If you love a certain woman more than you love me, I cannot love you less. Talk to this woman about your love for her, but do it with the feeling and in that simple manner as when you try to share an idea with a child. She may be afraid of you. Remember that she has lived her life so far in her parents' tent. Make your intentions and feelings known to them. If they like you, you will be allowed to come again and again. It takes time for a girl who has never slept with a man to overcome her fear of leaving her family to begin a new and uncertain life with a stranger. Your presence with her family will help overcome her fear, and the time will come when her parents tell her that she should leave their tent and begin living with you. Even though you have a good wife, you may be tempted by the appearance of another woman. Try not to sleep with another woman; your pleasure will be your wife's pain. If you do it once, tell her then, even though it is painful; forgiveness lies in her love for you. If you are often in another woman's bed, then keep it to yourself, even if it is no longer a secret.

It was getting late, and the women were preparing to return home. But Ikkuma had one final thing to say:

I will always remember my mother. She was a woman who served every member of the family. There were times when she was hurt and disappointed and times when she was happy. For all the years she gave of herself, she received very few rewards and made no complaint. You may think that this is being submissive. It is not, it is the expression of strength. Her strength is known to all of us and, now, to you.

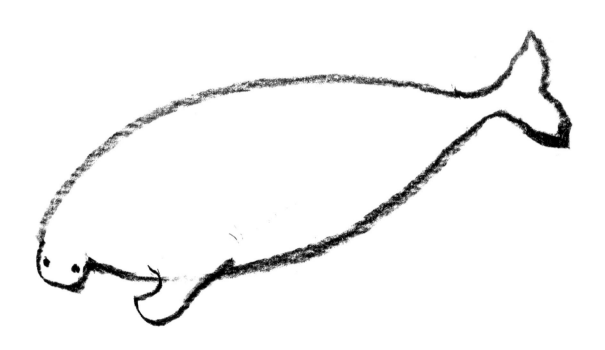

Osuitok Ipeelie's drawing of an Aivioyarq.

WITCHES AND MERMAIDS

Osuitok Ipeelie remained one of the most important people in my life. He befriended me the first time I set foot in Cape Dorset (Kinngait) and has been a lifelong influence. Osuitok was born near Cape Dorset in 1923 and lived in various camps along the southwest coast of Baffin. One of the finest carvers in Canada, Osuitok seems to have absorbed the mystical entities into his work, which shows humans, animals, and terrifying spirits transforming from one into the other. His masterful creations depict practically every aspect of traditional life and beliefs, and are still sought out by institutions and serious collectors throughout the world.

The first of my many conversations with Osuitok about life, tradition, and spiritual belief took place in his tiny house in Cape Dorset. We began with easy banter. "Surely you don't believe in stories of shaman, spirits and magical powers," Osuitok said with a smile. I replied that I was not sure whether I believed in them or not, but I did know that stories of such things persisted in the villages I visited. He looked into my eyes and said, "You say that you have been told that there is a woman shaman living here. I don't know of any such person. Perhaps the only one who told you such a thing is the only one who knows if it is really true."

I asked him how he knew the difference between what he believed to be true and what he knew to be true.

Illustration of a Stellar's sea cow.
(GOOGLE IMAGES)

That's easy, I will explain the difference. A long time ago some whalers were shipwrecked and were found by hunters from a camp a long way from here. They were afraid of these white men yet wanted the things that they had. The hunters' desires became more powerful than their fears, and they killed the whalers and took their things back to the village. I have been told this story by different people at different times in different places and I believe it to be true.

Now I will tell you a second story. My grandmother once told me that there was an evil old witch who lived in a cave near Igaqjuaq. This witch would gather beautiful bright stones from a special place in the hills and arrange them into a trail leading to the entrance of her cave. In those days people lived on the other side of the island, and some of their children found the trail of beautiful stones and disappeared forever. It was said that the evil old woman killed them and ate them. Every one of us believed this story. When I was much older, I went with my friends to the other side of the island. Do you know the place, I mean?

I told him that I knew it well, but that I had never heard of caves, witches, or brightly coloured stones being there.

He continued, *We searched around and found the cave and found the place where the stones came from. They were the colour of blood (garnets). But the most frightening thing of all is that even though she is no longer there, you can see the shadow of her footprints in the stone at the entrance of the cave. This I know to be true.*

"Do you know of anyone who has seen Sanna (Sedna), the sea goddess?" I asked.

Yes, I know of people who say they have seen her, but I have never seen her. Twice in my life, many years ago, I saw Aivioyarq. She is a sea creature so rare that few hunters have ever seen her. I saw her during a long trip to Nuvudjuak. She was beautiful. She had the shape and

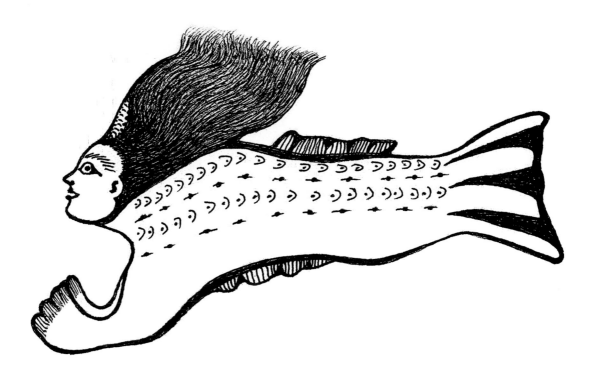

Pitaloosie Saila's drawing of the sea goddess Sedna or Sanna.

size of a beluga whale. Her skin was dark like that of a
walrus; but unlike walrus skin, it was smooth. She had
flippers like a seal, but her tail was shaped like the tail
of a beluga. She had a head that was like the head of
a young walrus without tusks. We knew that we must
not harm her and that it was a gift just to see such a
wonderful creature of the sea.

Osuitok then took a pencil and drew *Aivioyarq* on a scrap
of paper. *Here, a little present to remind you of our afternoon*
together.

A short time later I met two young biologists, one of whom
had done considerable studies of Arctic marine animal life. I
recounted the story of *Aivioyarq* and showed them the drawing.
The young man looked at the drawing and then at me, slowly
shaking his head. "It can't be," he said. "That's a Stellar's sea
cow (hydrodamalis gigas). It's supposed to have become extinct
around the turn of the century."

The midnight sun at Lancaster Sound.

AN INTIMATE WILDERNESS

WHERE THE SUN DANCES
AND THE EARTH SHIMMERS

Spring in the southwest Baffin region is a beautiful time. Simeonie Quppapik described it as the *immatuuti*, when the very first water is released from the snow that covers the land. You can still travel on the sea ice in spring although vast glistening sheets of water lie on its surface. My friend Kananginak Pootoogook pointed out that these pools of water, known as *imamatatinnirk*, have been created by the heat of sun and are not to be confused with the pools of water called *qalluq*, which are created when a dark object, such as a piece of seaweed lying on the ice, soaks up the heat of the sun, thus causing a pool to form.

Though the sun grows stronger each day, remnants of snow are still evident on the land. At sea, ice algae now colonize the bottoms of the ice pans. The algae form vast green pastures of phytoplankton upon which krill graze and, in return, fill the bellies of bowhead whales. High upon the surface of the Baffin glaciers lie remnants of the great ice sheet that once stretched as far south as the Ohio River. Sunbeams carve into the surface of the ice little pools of fresh water about the size of cupped hands. Embedded in each indentation are small plant-like organisms without roots, stems, or leaves.

Upon the vast rocky landscape are other countless small impressions on the surface of the lichen-encrusted rocks. Some are no larger than a teacup. The black lichen on their rims attracts the heat of the sun, which begins to melt the ice trapped within the indentations. Tiny pools of water begin to form, each bearing its own reflection of the sun. You can discern traces of minute plant life lying in wait at the bottom of each Lilliputian pool.

These are the days when you behold *ujumirapuq* — when the sun dances, the earth shimmers and the very air feels incandescent.

Now that water is on the sea ice, the sky is reflected beneath you. It is as if heaven has finally been brought down to Earth and you fly across the tops of clouds as the runners of your sled shatter their reflections beneath you. Once drab hills that looked like shadows laid upon faded shadows begin to show a faint blush.

Stop for a moment and listen carefully. You can hear the distant sound of streams and the faint calls of birds returning from as far away as Antarctica. Eider ducks are returning to their favoured locations out on the islands. Overhead, Canada and Snow geese, followed by swans, can be heard as they fly further north to the Great Plain of the Koukdjuak.

Everywhere, the myriad freshwater ponds are awakening from their deep sleep. The mantle of ice that covered them begins to soak up the sun's energy, triggering a transformation as old as the beginning of time. As the ice melts, vertical fingers of ice take shape, forming into countless crystal prisms each reflecting sunbeams. You lie down on the tundra and rest your chin on the back of your hands, gazing at the dance of a thousand lights. A slight breeze arises, and the icy crystals now touching each other create a sound reminiscent of the one created by those little glass wind chimes that came all the way from China. You are as fascinated as when you were a child and still believed in magic.

The floe edge of ice is quickly disappearing and soon you will be travelling on open water to a distant camp. You feel a renewed sense of energy and urgency to repair the boats, mend the nets, check the equipment, gather supplies, and prepare to journey to *inigijuminaqtuq*, the place you favour above all others. There is an unexplainable sense of freedom when you are out on the land. *Inigijuminaqtuq* is your place, wherever it may be, where you feel truly at home and very much alive.

DREAMS, DREAMING, DREAMERS

As I spent more time with the elders, I developed an interest in dreams. I wondered if dreams were shaped by tales of the past, legends, and belief in spirits, and was curious about a possible relationship between dreams and the remarkable drawings produced in Cape Dorset. I was told to talk to Mannumi Davidee, but for some reason Mannumi became vague on the subject, which often signals that a person does not want to discuss a given topic.

A few days later, Leetia Parr, my interpreter, and I sought out Osuitok Ipeelie. We arrived at his house to find it filled with his children, his children's children, and his neighbour's children. A Coleman stove hissed with boiling water for tea. It seemed strange to enter into a private conversation as we were surrounded by laughter, pleas for biscuits, and gentle reprimands.

"I want to know about dreams and dreamers," I said when we had settled in. Osuitok sighed, looked at a religious picture hanging on the wall, and then quietly said, *I will tell you what I know, nothing more.*

All things that breathe have dreams. I do not know what dogs and ravens dream, but they do dream. Dreaming is a state of mind we call seenuktumjuk. *It is a time when we see things that come from a place beyond our normal vision. There are many kinds of dreams, and I will tell you about some of them.* Irkahliuk *is when you dream of things which you know to be real. They are not special dreams and are close to, but not the same as, what you call daydreams. A daydream that allows you to see something that is about to happen or has happened is more impressive because it is certain. That very moment in the daydream when you see what is happening is called* issohrho.

There is another kind of dreaming called nireuzaktuk. *These are dreams of things seen that have yet to happen. Most people have little dreams like those, and some people have the power to dream often about things which are sure to happen in the future.*

I asked him what he thought was the difference between a shaman's state of dreaming and our own, but he claimed not to know. I came back to that question in a different manner from time to time, and the answer was always the same.

He asked me if I had ever dreamed of someone coming back after a long absence and they had later reappeared *(tikkitu-siaktuk)*, or if I had ever dreamed of horrible demons and terrible creatures *(ohhumanniaktuk)*. I said of course, and he laughed, So why do you ask me what a shaman dreams?

He continued: *There is another kind of dream, and though I have forgotten its name, it is important because it has come from time to time to all of us. It is the dream of a special person who appears in your mind when you are troubled. You know that this is the only person who can help you.*

There are two more kinds of dreams which are opposites to one another. The fearful dream is called hunujak. *It is the dream of death, and it will surely come to the person the dreamer dreams of, and to the dreamer in the end.*

At this point, he turned to the two children sitting next to us on the battered old sofa and good-naturedly told them to leave. He lowered his voice and raised his eyebrows, and asked, *Do you know the word* ahnajowtuk?"

No, I replied.

It means you, that boy who was seduced by a beautiful woman in your dreams a long time ago! This was met with great laughter from everyone in the room.

Pointing to one of the girls, he said, *Ahnrgusjrizuk, she has probably had the same kind of dream. It comes to all of us as we leave our childhood.*

I asked him if the woman or man who comes in our dreams and makes love to us has a name. *Achoo?* he said. *I don't know.* Was anyone in the settlement especially known for the ability to have important dreams? Again, he replied, *Achoo?* The thread was broken, the bannock was cooked, the tea was made, and it was time to play with the kids.

The first meeting of Osuitok Ipeelie, his daughter Pishukti and wife Nipisha in 1958.

The last time we were together early summer 2005.

AN INTIMATE WILDERNESS

FIVE STATES OF MIND

My conversation with Osuitok Ipeelie continued. He asked me if I knew a certain man, and if I knew that the man had been possessed at one time during his life. I replied that I had been told that he had gone mad for a time. "It is true," he said. "Madness comes in different ways, and the most frightening thing is knowing that it is moving toward you. People don't talk about such things because they want to appear to be strong.

"There is a state of mind that is dreamlike — either you go one way or the other. One way is good and the other is terrible. To escape from a terrible situation in that dreamlike state is called *oqumagiisiavak*. It happens in different ways, like a woman who is in great pain during childbirth and thinks she will go crazy with the pain. Yet she remembers slipping away in a dream more real than when she was awake, and the pain goes, and the fear of going crazy is melted away by a dream."

Osuitok, Leetia, and I were tired. It was late, and we could hear the rain on the roof. It was time for the last cup of tea. We sat silent for a while and then Osuitok said, "You seem disappointed. Haven't I told you enough?"

I replied that he had told me more about dreams, dreamers, and dreaming than anyone else, but that perhaps we had missed something along the way. I said casually, "Perhaps there is a state of mind that goes beyond dreaming, which is so difficult to express that we seldom talk about it. Perhaps all these questions that I have been asking you are really childish."

His eyes lit up and he sat on the edge of the sofa. Leaning toward me, he lowered his voice as if to begin unfolding a secret.

Yes, there is a state of mind beyond dreaming. It is called quiinuinaqtuk. *It is like a window through which one can see into things as never before. It's as if you have moved out of the tiny space you occupy in this world and can see the world whole and can see past its shadows. There are five shades in this state of mind, each one different, each one lighting the fire of powerful thought.*

There is qiinuituk. *This is when you are alone, the only living thing far away from earthly things and filled with peace. This sense of peace fills every corner of your mind. It is more satisfying than any joy you have experienced in your conscious life because it runs deeper than happiness. It can mend broken thoughts and feelings, and having experienced it gives you the knowledge that it can come again when you feel there is nowhere to go.*

There is angnatsiaq. *Because you and I are men, I will describe it to you as a man. This is the state of mind when you think deeply of a woman. No, it is not thinking about making love to her or her earthly charms. It is thinking about her as a beautiful and totally necessary part of your life. Her smell, touch, voice, movement, and presence are as important to you as breathing. She is ageless. The both of you ensure each other's survival, and at the bottom of your hearts you know that you will travel together forever. She is that one missing part of you that has made you a whole person. Every sunrise begins in her eyes.*

Then there is angutiisiaq. *How can I describe this to you? There are certain people who are known by all others as special people because they do everything well. They make the best things. They are the best hunters because they know the behaviour of animals, weather, seasons, tides, and other things better than anyone else. It is not that they strive to be better than their neighbours. It is that they have a state of mind that does not allow them to do things in an ordinary way. They are compelled to do the simplest things as perfectly as can be done by a human being. Sometimes when you come across an ancient campsite you may find a cooking pot or harpoon tip that is the most beautiful thing you have ever seen. Yes, even an old cooking pot can be a special thing if made by a special person. The important thing to remember is that this state of mind doesn't mean that you can do just one thing — it is a way of living.*

Now I come to issumatujuk. *This is a state of mind that allows you to think deeply of many things. Our minds move from thought to thought, hardly stopping to turn one over to see what the underside looks like. "Achoo?" we say, because it is easier to leave behind the things that are hard to understand.*

There are riddles, puzzles, and secrets everywhere. Some things which appear to be simple are complicated things in disguise, and it is so the other way too. To think deeply of things is not daydreaming. It is moving through shadows and never staying in one place forever.

The last state of mind is called siilatujuk. *I find this the hardest to describe because it happens to me. It is that state of mind that allows me to see a large world which is my very own place. Here, I am not subject to unnatural forces. Here, I can create things which are beautiful and can give me great pleasure. It is a very strange place because you know that it can never be, yet when you leave it and come back to the world we know, you discover that you have created a beautiful thing which you have brought back with you. I am a carver, so I bring forth carvings, but there are songs, stories, and magical things that have been brought back by others from their own worlds.*

I thought of what he was saying and recalled an incident many years ago, when I asked a well-known artist the definition of art. She replied simply, "The ability to take that which is real and make it unreal in such a way as to make it more real than ever before."

I heard Osuitok say, *Remember the five shades. The words themselves* — qiinuituk, angnatsiaq, angutiisiaq, issumatujuk, *and* siilatujuk — *are seldom spoken and have a beauty as spoken words which is as powerful as their meaning.*

As I was walking Leetia home, she said, "I have lived here all my life and I never knew that such words existed. Those words are in my mind forever."

Composite spirit figures drawn for the book by Pitaloosie Saila.

THE SPIRIT HELPERS

Forty years ago, to encounter Inuit elders whose entire lives were lived on the land was not unusual. A lifetime of travelling in search of food not only required acute hunting skills but also a profound understanding of the sky, sea, tundra, and ice in order to stay alive. The hunters' language was complex, an articulation of accurate observations, omens, and, where appropriate, incantations. If hunters were out at sea, the *angakok* would be implored to utter *uqausiit saimaqsaigutiit silamik*, the ancient and magical words to soothe and calm storms. *"Aklairadlarnaekl Aklairadlarnaek!"* he or she would shout toward the sky, calling upon spirits such as Ikkuk to bring fair weather.

There was a time when the Inuit believed in the existence of *tuurngait* or spirits. Some spirits were believed to be evil, others benign or even helpful to humans. *Tuurngait* inhabited all things and all places. They were not gods or deities. They exacted no sacrifice but possessed powers far greater than those of humans, and so humans had reason to fear them. Both evil and good *tuurngait* were the spirit helpers of shamans, who called upon the *tuurngait* to perform all manner of tasks.

My mentor Osuitok told me that ten shamans had lived throughout the Sikusiilaq area in the 1930s and '40s. Of the ten, eight were men and two were women. Of the eight men, two were regarded as dangerous by virtue of having magically killed a human. "A" possessed the spirit of a vicious dog that would devour his victim from the inside. He derived his power from the process of having himself eaten alive and then reconstituted, thus he was regarded as the most powerful of all the shamans in the area. "Ak" possessed two spirit helpers. One dwelled in a nourishing seaweed that tastes like dulse. The other was the spirit of a young caribou.

Aq, a female shaman, that was able to transform her helping spirit into a vicious dog with enormous teeth. "I" possessed the spirit of a small ermine yet was one of the most powerful spirit helpers of any shaman in Sikusiilaq. "P"'s spirit helper was believed to be the instrument of curses.

Some of the most helpful *tuurngait* were those who not only made the animals available to humans but also served as the providers of light. Some *tuurngait* lived in light itself, others contained light within their being, while still others provided it. Nanniruaq was a *tuurngal* who provided light. He roamed the land and, dressed like the hunters of long ago, wore a long cloak that hung down to his knees. Inside his cloak Nanniruaq carried a fire that would burst into a shower of bright light and consume him, leaving only a pile of bones and ashes where he stood. But then, Nanniruaq would come together and be whole again. He would continue his journey, carrying the fire in his cloak and thus be consumed and reborn over and over again.

One of the rarest forms of light seen in the Arctic is a *kataujaq* or, in southwest Baffin, a *sugaq*, a rainbow. As it appears only on the horizon, the *kataujaq* can never be approached, except symbolically through the intervention of an *angakok*. In constructing a low portal of stone, bone, or driftwood, the *angakok* replicated the rainbow's ethereal shape. This portal was a magical instrument. The suffering and gravely ill would lie under it, listening to the *angakok*'s incantation — *piusiq aulaniusuuq taqairsuititsinirmut tarnimik* — which was the ritual act of appeasing the spirit who infected the sufferer.

Those who were fortunate enough to be relieved of the afflicting spirit or spirits were known as *aaniaqtuq*, ones whom the *angakok* had healed.

PLACES OF POWER,
OBJECTS OF VENERATION

Munamee Sarko was reputed to be one of the greatest travellers since Atsiaq who is said to have travelled throughout Qikiqtaaluk (Baffin Island). Munamee claimed that he travelled alone for many years and during all seasons throughout southwest Baffin Island. I loved the old guy; he was tough, shrewd, and enigmatic. I never knew when he was pulling my leg or testing me.

I decided that I would seek his advice and that of other elders as to where I might find special places such as *saqqijaarviugia lik*, places where one must be respectful. My intention was eventually to map the unusual sites I had heard mentioned in various accounts over the years. I explained to Munamee that I was interested in places that were dangerous or important ceremonial centres or that were believed to be haunted, or where one encountered spirits and strange creatures or a murder or execution had taken place.

Before I could finish listing all the places I had in mind, Munamee interrupted. "Have you got cigarettes?"

I replied that I had none.

"Too bad," he said. After a moment, he added, "In all my travels, I have never come to places which frightened me. I have never been overtaken by ghosts, *tuurngait*, or *ijirait* (caribou spirits behaving like humans). I don't know where such places are, and I don't know why you think such places exist."

Katauga, Pauta Saila's daughter, was with me at the time. She smiled and whispered, "He knows. I know he knows."

Munamee brought our brief visit to an end with a puzzling remark. "Go and ask others about such places, and if you find nothing, then come back to me."

A few years later, I saw Munamee working on what turned out to be his final carving before he died. He was covered head to toe in white dust. In Inuktitut, I shouted above the racket of his electric grinder, "Greetings, white man!"

"Have you got cigarettes?" he asked with a smile. Then he asked if I had found what I was looking for. I replied that Oshut-siak, Osuitok, Pauta, and Simeonie had revealed many places that were to be respected and in some cases avoided. "Good," was the last word I heard from Munamee. Some time later, it occurred to me that Munamee had never denied the existence of the many mysterious places I would eventually learn about.

Listening to the Inuit elders led me to understand that the Arctic landscape had two characteristics, the physical and the metaphysical, both inseparable. Some places upon the landscape were benign, whereas others were powerful and dangerous. The places that earned the highest respect were those where the possibility of losing one's life was greatest: locations known for their fierce storms, vicious tides, dangerous ice, or a host of other hazards. Associated with such places are the *tammanaqtuq*, places having a topography so deceptive that even seasoned travellers have been known to lose their way and perish. Some places were avoided owing to their association with terrible events, such as murder, pestilence, or starvation. These places included *inuktorviit*, places where humans were known to have been devoured.

Among the most revered places were those where life was renewed, such as the fish spawning beds, calving grounds, nesting sites, and, most important, the *nalliitt* — the caribou crossings, where custom and tradition were exercised not simply for religious purposes but as part of preparing the site for the arrival of the life-sustaining caribou.

The expression *aglirnaqtuq* refers to places where strict customs were observed. These ranged from the most dreadful, the *angakkuksarvik*, where shamans were initiated, to places of celebration, games, and festivals.

On Kinngait Island the strikingly beautiful site, commonly called Igaqjuaq consists of a small cove providing shelter from the violent storms that can sweep across Hudson Strait. A beautiful Arctic meadow gently rises from a sandy beach.

The area is carpeted with a profusion of Arctic grasses and wild-flowers, and the meadow is crowned with a small freshwater pond that is attached to two other ponds leading to the interior of Kinngait Island. But Igaqjuaq does not mean an overturned kettle; it refers to a great fireplace. The profusion of Arctic grasses and wildflowers grow there because they are nourished by the remains of countless feasts.

I had heard of a special place for celebrations, where people came to feast and gorge themselves on walrus, polar bear, caribou — virtually all the food that could be had during the brief period between late summer and early winter. The Inuit came from camps all along the coast. It was a joyous occasion when families would meet, when young boys and girls would satisfy their curiosities.

But my inquiries about the existence of such a site were fruitless. Even the elders who guided me through the arcane subjects of shamanism, curses, incantations, spells, and charms conveniently sidestepped my inquiries with the simple reply *"Achoo?"* Who knows? Some three years after my attempts to find this mysterious site, Itulu Itidlouie referred to "places from which one returns to earth refreshed." He went on to disclose that the site was not only where feasting took place but also where *tivajuut*, the celebration of life, was held. "Its name is Qujaligiaqtubic."

Now I had the archaic name of a great place and the name of the ancient ritual once practiced there. I begged Itulu to show me the Qujaligiaqtubic on my map, but he asked why. I explained to Itulu that learning about such things is my *tukisiuti*, my pathway to understanding.

"I don't need to point out where Qujaligiaqtubic is," he said. "You've been there many times. The name we use when talking with outsiders is Igaqjuaq!"

As Pauta Saila and Paulassie Pootoogook later explained, the *angakok* was at the centre of the *tivajuut*. It was he who walked among the people, touching a man and a woman on the shoulder with an *ushuk* (baculum, or walrus penis bone), thus pairing them off for sensual pleasures. The *tivajuut* was a festival, as well as a celebration of carnal pleasure. It was the anodyne for periods of hardship, isolation, and, in some cases, hostility.

The *tivajuut* was not unique to Sikusiilaq. My friend Natar Ungalaaq, the actor in the movie *Atanarjuat: The Fast Runner*, described a similar celebration that took place in Igloolik in days past, and a woman I met who was originally from Sachs Harbour in the western Arctic also confirmed the existence of such a celebration in her region.

When I visit the old camps along the coast, I'm touched by a sense of melancholy. All the camps are deserted, and all the camp bosses, including the few I knew, are no longer alive. The ceremonial places are abandoned. It is as if all the stories of life once lived on the land, with all their pleasures and perils, have been turned to stone.

Yet amid the stones are signs of life. I remember the summer afternoon when Elissapie a charming young lady spoke of *takussunaittuq*, places of great beauty. "There are places where wild flowers grow in abundance," she said, "where there are little hollows and where it is warm. These are the places where people have made love and that's why these places are so beautiful."

The most powerful feeling about the land was given to me through the words of a young woman who once came very close to ending her life.

After being ashamed, after feeling hopelessness
I need to get to go out on the land.
When I am there, I talk to the earth and it hears me.
I know this because it shows me all its flowers and
I hear the songs of birds and the sound of storms.
And when I go to sleep on the land, it is with a feeling of
anxiousness to see the next day.

IN THE FIELD, ON THE LAND

There is a world of difference between being "in the field" and "on the land." I navigated those worlds in different ways, using different mindsets.

When I was doing fieldwork, I examined and recorded the conditions, places, and objects that interested me in a disciplined manner, shaped by how I was taught to perceive the world. I used a variety of instruments to measure and record material objects, noted weather, flora and fauna, and employed scientifically acceptable techniques and methodology.

The following excerpt from my field notes, relating to a visit to the Nurrata site, reflects one way of capturing knowledge of a site:

> ...The site is quite exposed to the prevailing NW winds, leading one to speculate that there was a diversity of food and other resources prominent enough to trade off against ideal settlement criteria. As its name suggests, it is a gently sloping plain dipping toward the sea. The predominant feature of the Nurrata site was a field of grass, probably Cochlearia officials, about one square hectare in size. The site is approx. 311 m in length and 316 m in width, containing over 190 features. The features include graves, stone shelters, tent rings, and refuse pits. The most numerous of the features were the caches. A particularly interesting feature was an alignment 9.1 m in length of walrus jaws arranged in a herringbone pattern leading toward the sea...

When I was out on the land, the experience was sensuous, hence the expression *unganatuq nuna*, a spiritual connection to the land. I became acutely aware of the sound and touch of the wind, the feel of warmth and the bite of the cold, the glare of the sun and the silence of darkness, the movement of shadows and the stillness of stone, the magic of nothingness and the sense of infinity. My sense of scale was as elastic as my sense of time and distance. I towered like a giant where plant life reached no higher than my shins, yet felt like an insignificant microbe as I looked out on the vastness of the tundra.

Inevitably, the insights that came to me while out on the land differed from the information gathered during a field trip. Consider a solo trip I made back to Igaqjuaq to revisit the ceremonial site known as Qujaligiaqtubic.

The most striking feature at the site is a huge granite hill at the edge of the sea. Rising about thirty-five metres, it has very steep sides, making climbing to its top quite dangerous. At the top is a small, ordinary looking stone that is a *tunnilarvik*, an object to which one presents a gift in the hope of seeking a favour.

Below the hill, which once was littered with the skulls of polar bear, seal, and walrus, are at least five graves, one having been made with great care. This particular grave was constructed in the form of a domed vault, so that no stone touched the interred body. A single upright stone sat atop the dome. The grave looked like a miniature of the huge dome-shaped hill with a *tunnilarvik* upon its summit.

Here, at this grave next to the place where life was celebrated during the festival of the mid-winter moon, I beheld what was, at first, a curiosity. This curiosity would become a mystery, then an insight. The insight would later become what the Inuit elders refer to as *tukisilitainnaqtuq*, seeing or understanding a thing for the very first time.

The curiosity began with a single line of fresh caribou tracks made in the crisp white snow. The tracks indicated that the caribou had descended the side of the steep hill to my right in a perfectly straight line. The caribou had stopped when it was approximately sixteen metres below the hilltop and directly opposite the grave. It was then drawn to the grave for some unknown reason.

I followed its footsteps to the side of the grave and discovered that it had gone to that spot to feed on the now-dry but still-nourishing grass that grew there sheltered from the biting winds. These very winds had sculpted a shelter out of the snow that helped to protect the grasses. Once more, I beheld the fantastic shapes of the *uqquiqqsiniit*, the footprints of blizzards.

Having eaten its sparse meal, the lone caribou returned once more in a straight line to the path it had been on in the first place. It continued its journey in a straight line across the valley floor to the sharply rising hills. It ascended the steep slope without wavering from some imaginary path. I sat on my snow machine, convinced that there was a lesson here. All I had to do was to fit the pieces together.

My concentration was broken by a flurry of snow buntings that swooped down to where the caribou had nibbled the sparse grass. One bird alighted atop the upright stone on the grave. He pooped, as had all the other birds that alighted there throughout the years.

I visualized the companions of a revered hunter now dead as they carefully constructed a vaulted grave. No stone touched the hunter's body; to place a stone by the body would likely cause the dome to collapse when the body disintegrated. Because the hunter was laid upon bedrock and not preserved in permafrost, all except his bones returned to the earth and nourished it, as did the remains of his feasts. Over time, the earth around his grave became enriched, causing moss to grow, which in turn captured precious water. The grave itself captured the heat of the sun in summer and provided shelter against the winds of winter. Snow buntings, Arctic terns, gulls, and ravens visited this place, which began as a grave but over time became a microenvironment.

The birds not only provided nitrogen-rich nutrients in their droppings but also seeds from distant meadows. In this vast Arctic desert now flourished a tiny oasis. Seeds became plants, flowers, and grasses, which in turn provided nourishment to a variety of insects, birds, lemmings, and voles. A solitary caribou came by this way. It picked up the delicate scent of grass and so visited this oasis of life that began when a hunter died here so many years ago.

And so the *inua*, the life force, continued.

Three charms given me. One to save my life (left), another to protect me against unseen things (centre) and the third (right) to ensure I don't loose any essential piece of equipment.

A CHARMED LIFE

I fished around in my pocket, searching for a lighter. Finally, I dumped the contents on the table, hoping to find the lighter in the assortment of junk that somehow finds its way into every pocket I have.

The elder from Kugluktuk (formerly Coppermine) asked, "Why do you carry that walrus tooth in your pocket?" I told him that I had found it among some bones on a beach and that, as silly as it might seem, I carried it with me as a good-luck charm. He asked to hold it, and I gave it to him. "Do you really believe in such things?" he asked.

"*Achoo?* I guess I do, if I carry such things in my pocket." We both laughed. I asked him if he had a good-luck charm, but he didn't answer.

Then he said, *You know, in the old days we were very superstitious and we had many charms. We believed in Sattqwa (Sakka?) (spiritual power), and we had many different kinds of charms which were made from many different things. A human cannot simply make a charm. A real charm possesses power. You can try to make charms and hope that they will protect you, but they never can protect you unless they have power. A shaman can invite certain spirits to enter into objects, and when they do, a charm is made. Spirits can enter into objects without being invited and that object becomes charmed. There are evil charms, and there are good charms. Old charms have more power than new ones, and charms which have passed from hand to hand are the most powerful ones to have.*

There are different kinds of charms, and each kind gives you a different kind of power. There are charms which attract good luck — ahtehtat. There are super charms, those which are very powerful and can allow you to do things that no ordinary human can do — attetawk. There are other charms; those are ones which protect you from harm. They drive off danger and so are most important — sweenakmin piktakitit. Then there are charms which allow you to look into the future — tunektat. There is a special bag that is made to hold the different charms. I have seen one made from the skins taken from the heads of two wolverines. This bag which holds magical things is called anuhrawak.

There is one more thing that I will tell you before we turn out the lamp. It is a thing that happened to me when I was a very young boy. My uncle was an old man. He respected the shaman who lived in our camp but never lived in fear of the shaman's powers. He had the power to protect himself not with a charm but with a song. I know what you're thinking, but just listen. My mother told me that he had the power of song; I think she called it atudluk.

I asked my uncle one day if he had the power of a song, because I had never heard of such a thing. I suppose being a child protected me from his anger. He didn't speak to me all day, and I knew I had offended him and was afraid. The next day was windy, and the men could not go out to sea. My uncle came to our tent and told me to come out. He told me to follow him, and we walked over the hills without speaking. We came to a shallow river and he stopped. He turned around, looked straight at me, and said, "Listen to me very carefully. You will stand behind me. You will look at only the big rock in the middle of the river. You must never look at my face, no matter what happens, until I tell you. If you don't obey me, a terrible thing will possess you." I was a young boy and very frightened.

He turned away from me, so that only his back showed. He began to sing a slow song, using words I had never heard. Slowly, his voice began to change, becoming lower and lower. What started out as a song began to transform into sounds coming out from the centre of something that was not a human being.

I was so terrified I thought I would die. I wanted to scream at him, to tell him to stop this thing, but fear froze me solid. The only thing that was still living in my whole body was fear itself. I can't remember how long these sounds went on. I can remember that they began to change and slowly became like the sounds and words that I heard at the beginning.

He stopped singing and slowly turned around to face me. He looked very, very old. He looked like a person who had suffered a terrible pain. He reached out and took my hand and held it very tight. He said, "Look at the rock that was in the middle of the river." It was no longer there.

The terms the elder used were totally unfamiliar to me, so I was only able to record them phonetically.

Top left: The strange figure of a shaman with his drum held captive in a stone.

Top right: Inuksuk anirniqtalik, an inuksuk believed to contain a spirit.

Bottom: The spirit imbedded on the cliff face at Ijirallik.

AN INTIMATE WILDERNESS

SPIRITS IN THE STONE

The elder from Kugluktuk also spoke to me about spirits that inhabit stones.

You asked me if there were inuksuit that had magical powers. I have never heard of such a thing, nor do I know anyone who knows such a thing. There are many things that happened a long time ago. There are many things that have been forgotten — even the words to describe them have been forgotten. These things are not just lost, they will never be found again.

Though I don't know if inuksuit ever had magical powers, I will tell you a few things. I was born in an igloo and lived in small camps most of my life. Our families travelled from camp to camp during the seasons. The camp boss and the shaman were the two most important people in our camp — everyone was very respectful of the shaman. Our shaman was an old man when I was a young boy. He had many spirit helpers and could call on them when he needed their power to help him see and do special things. He could call the spirits of the dog, caribou, lemming, wolf, and many other creatures to help him. But even with all his powers, even though he could do things that were magical, he knew that he would soon join the , the dead people. He knew that he would die when we would set up our spring camp. He told his son that he had a vision of dying, and he spent much more time with him describing all the spirit helpers and each one's special powers. His son was never a shaman, but he knew that there was a reason for his father carefully explaining many things before his death.

The old shaman died at our spring camp, just as he had seen in his vision. None of the old people go back to that place any more, not because they are fearful, but because it would be disrespectful. If you were to go to that spring camp you would see strange inuksuit. Those inuksuit are different from any others. The last thing that the son did to show respect for his father was to build an inuksuk for each spirit that helped his father. Each inuksuk is in the likeness of a spirit, and the hill behind the spring camp is where they live.

Now, I will tell you another thing, because you asked if shamans ever used inuksuit to do magical things. First, you should know that inuksuk is not the same as . Many people call a thing "inuksuk" when they see stones put one on top of the other. Inuksuk is a thing made by a man to help him in various ways. From a distance, inuksuit can even look like a man, but that is not why they were made.

is different. means "in the likeness of a human." looks like a person. There are not many real to be seen. I have heard that your children make their own in the wintertime. You call it snowman! There is a special kind of — I have forgotten its name — but it too was made of snow. This was a fearsome snowman because it was made by a shaman. It was made to capture the spirit of the person that the shaman wished to harm. Secret words were spoken to it until it possessed the person's spirit. Then the shaman would take either a knife or a harpoon and kill the snowman. I have been told that the person, even if he was far away, would surely die.

THE STRENGTH OF SPIRITS

All living things have spirits, one Cape Dorset elder told me some time ago. Even plants have spirits.

Do not be fooled into thinking that the spirit of a polar bear is greater than the spirit of a lemming because the polar bear in life is stronger. The strength of a spirit is measured by what it can do and not where it resides.

There are good spirits as there are evil spirits, and there are spirits which are neither good nor bad. It is these neither good nor bad spirits which cause those things to happen for which there is never any answer. They are above men and above all other spirits. Together, they are the condition in which everything will happen, happens, and has happened. When, because of the condition, a woman dies while having a child and the child dies or lives, there is nothing more to say than, "It cannot be helped."

I have told you that all living things have spirits. All living things are also houses for spirits. Spirits can come and go, like you and I when we choose to enter and to leave places. Spirits also may choose to live in real houses, in air, the sea, and even in small stones.

Spirits are respected in different ways. The greatest respect is given to those which are feared the most, and that is why they are the most powerful. That is why when we see a thing which we never knew about we are respectful, because the spirit which lives within it is also unknown and could be evil. Even things that at first look harmless can be the house of a terrible spirit.

It is not the man, animal, or thing which is terrible, but the spirit which lives within it.

A shaman has a special spirit that comes to him and gives him strength. The spirit will make it possible for the shaman to see and do things that other people cannot do. You asked me, "When does an ordinary person become a shaman?" A person becomes a shaman when a spirit enters and allows that person to do things which other people cannot do, as I have told you. Even a child can become a shaman if the spirit wishes it to happen.

The power of the shaman is the power of the spirit. A powerful shaman can become invisible, can visit distant places without moving, and can see through things to their centre. A powerful shaman can see forward and backward at the same time, and can speak with the dead. A powerful shaman can kill living things with his thoughts.

There was a shaman here who was a friend of Qiatsuq. He wondered if he had the power to kill a man with his thoughts. The spirit that came to him was not an evil one, and through it he killed a caribou. When the caribou was opened, its insides were found to be smashed as if something had crushed its bowels with a rock. There are people who can still remember the event. This shaman knew he had a great power, because it's harder to kill a caribou with a thought than it is to kill a man.

INURLUK

I was in Rankin Inlet (Kangiq&iniq) at a Northwest Territories housing meeting when I met three elders from Cambridge Bay (Iqaluktuuttiaq). I found them sitting comfortably on the hotel corridor floor and joined them by saying, *"Qannuitpit, uvunga apirsuqti kinngalt miavunga"*: How are you? I'm the inquisitive one from Cape Dorset. During that evening, one of the men offered the following story about a dark spirit.

What I am about to tell you happened a long time ago. There lived in a small camp a young girl who was very beautiful. Her face, voice, behaviour, and the way she could make clothing made her very desirable.

Young men often visited this camp, bringing food to the girl's father, hoping that some day he would say, "Take my daughter, you are a good provider. She will make you a good wife." But the father was not able to part with his daughter. He loved her, and she looked after the old man as if he were her child.

As I have told you, she was able to do many things well. Her father once gave her a special stone which is called inurluk. *This stone is most valuable because you can make fire with it. You make a small bed of dried moss and take the fire stone in your hand and hit it against a rock next to the moss. Bright sparks jump up and fall into the moss; there is smoke and then the moss catches fire. The fire that jumps out of the stone lights our* kudlik, *which gives us heat and light during the darkest time of the year. The old man's daughter could make the fire stone give out sparks better than anyone else and could start a fire faster than any man using a* pitikserak *(bow drill).*

She must have been fifteen years old when a stranger came to their camp. He had the best qajaq (kayak) they had ever seen. His harpoon and all the other things that were in his qajaq were made in such a way that you knew he was a special person.

He spoke softly, but he could be heard clearly. He moved quietly, but you could feel great strength in his every movement. He did not speak like the people in the camp, and they asked him where his home was. He gave the name of a place that no one knew, and said that it was a very long way from their camp. This stranger stayed with the people for many weeks, and everyone was happy because he was a good hunter. He could find food when others failed.

One night the old man said to his daughter, "The stranger is a man who will always provide us with food, for he is a great hunter. You must become his wife; he will look after us when I can no longer hunt." The beautiful young girl had strange feelings about the visitor. She knew that the stranger had often watched her, especially when she made fire. But her father told her that every young girl who has never slept with a man (every ooigasuk) has the same feelings.

The summer was passing. The weather was becoming dangerous at sea, and the stranger told the people in the camp that he would have to leave before the days became dark. He came to the tent of the old man and said that he must go. He asked the old man if he could take his daughter as his wife and promised to return with her when the geese came back to the land. He gave the old man much seal, caribou, and dried fish, so that he would not be hungry through the winter.

And so the beautiful young girl was promised to the stranger. You must realize that in those days, it was the parents who made the final decision. Before anyone was awake in the camp, the stranger took the girl to his qajaq, saying that they must leave now because he could smell a change in the weather, and they must get past the dangerous narrows further down the coast.

The girl said, "But I can't leave without saying goodbye to my family," and was about to cry, when the stranger told her that he had made this arrangement with her father.

"Come," he said, "Get into the qajaq. *Hurry, the tide is going out." He grabbed her hand, and as he pulled her toward him, she screamed. She had looked into the centre of his eyes — they were not black; they were filled with fire.*

She screamed once more, "You are Inurluk," *and with all her strength, pulled away from him. He shouted a warning, but she fell onto the rocks by the shore and died.*

Even though this happened a very long time ago, the beautiful young girl is still there where she fell. I am not sure whether Inurluk *felt a great anger or a deep love, but one thing is known, and that is, he changed her into an* inunnguaq. *That* inunnguaq *will stand forever by the sea looking toward the sunrise.*

The wonderful old man, Ottochie, who with Etidlouie, looked after
Lord Tweedsmuir when he was in Cape Dorset (Kinngait) in 1938-9.

AN INTIMATE WILDERNESS

HAUNTED BY HUNGER

I first met Ottochie (Ottokie) in 1966. He was an elder, inwardly focused, who bore the marks of a hard life lived on the land. At the time I was surprised that he was willing to talk openly with me, although later I realized that his openness must have been due to a mutual friend. He and I both knew Chesley Russel or, as he was known, "Red Face." Chesley's red face was the product of wind, sun, and long travels on the land when he was tending the Hudson's Bay Company Post in Cape Dorset. When I revealed to Ottochie that Red Face and I were friends, Ottochie began to trust me.

I was anxious to talk with Ottochie because he had experienced a great deal. He was considered a skilled hunter, the kind of man to whom you would entrust your life knowing he knew how to survive under the most severe conditions. He had helped Lord Tweedsmuir, (Sir John Buchan) who spent a short time in Cape Dorset and later became the Governor General of Canada from 1935 to 1940.

The old man sat quietly in a chair for quite some time before finally saying, "So little has happened in my life and so many things have gone from my memory. I fear there is nothing much to say."

I asked him about Lord Tweedsmuir and our mutual acquaintance, but he could recall little. Then, with no prompting, the old man said, *I can remember the first time that I saw a ship. It was the ship called Arctic. I saw the ship when I was still a boy. It had a mast on it that was so tall I was sure that the ship would tip over when the first wave came against it. I was frightened, knowing that I would have to go on that ship because some of our*

*people would leave Ivujivik (a place in Arctic Quebec)
and go to Baffin Island. There was much hunger in Ivujivik when I was young. We did not go into the ship but
set up our tent on top. Yes, we stayed in our tent on top
of that ship that took us to Baffin Island.*

I asked him if he had known Alariaq, the shaman. *Oh
yes, there are many people who knew Alariaq; he was a
powerful shaman. I was with other people who heard a
spirit devouring Alariaq. You could hear animal sounds;
you could hear the tearing of flesh and the crunching of
bones coming from Alariaq's body.*

*I knew another shaman, but I have forgotten his name.
This shaman came into a big tent after we had gathered
there at his command. He put several things into the
hood of his parka and walked out with them. He said he
was going out to chase a spirit, but some of us thought
that he was making an excuse to leave with some of our
possessions. He stepped out of the tent, closed the tent
flap, and told us to wait. We could hear his footsteps and
those of another as well. He soon returned to the tent,
demanded a knife, and then quickly left the tent again.
This time he was gone for a long time. When he came
back, he was very strange. His knife was covered with
blood, and there was blood all over his hands and blood
frozen to his arms. He was possessed with spirits, and it
took a long time for them to leave him. He became quiet
and said, "All of you go! leave this tent now."*

*One of the hunters picked up the knife and smelled it.
"It smells like the blood of an* udjuk *(square-flipper seal)."
Everyone was surprised because no* udjuk *had been taken
in that area for a long time. The shaman looked at my
father and said, "Go. Tomorrow there will be an* udjuk *in
the bay and you will kill it."And my father did see an* udjuk
and killed it, and we had food for our hungry bellies.

I asked other questions, but the old man seemed
tired. I had the feeling that for him to remember things
was an effort and that only politeness kept him in his chair.

I was both disappointed and frustrated because I knew that beneath the overburden of time lay a wealth of stories and experiences. I asked him one final question, "Is there anything in your life that can never be forgotten?"

> He replied, *Oh yes, hunger, starvation, and dying. The one thing I do not have to be reminded of is starvation. Dying of hunger,* pirliliqtuq, *still haunts me and it will until I die. You will never know what it's like to be starving. There were times when there were no caribou, no seals, and no other food. People did starve in some of the camps. I remember my father telling of a time when he and some other hunters came across an old igloo and found the dead starved bodies of a family inside. There were pieces of meat missing from some of the bodies. He was never sure if they had been eaten by foxes or by the last person to die.*
>
> *Starving is something I have known more than once. I can still remember the burning pain in my stomach. You become so weak that there is no outward sign of suffering. You know that you are dying and you are helpless even to try and find food. Finally, you say to yourself, "It's too bad, but nothing can be done; it's too late." And you accept the coming of death. All you can do is wait, and you know that death is about to swallow you.*

Armand Tagoona, an Anglican deacon, gave me the word for such a terrible fate, describing it as *tungujariaqaligtunga*, facing death quietly.

> *The first time I felt the burning pain of starvation was when I was a child. My father, mother, grandfather, grandmother, and two aunts were together in a small camp in winter. We had run out of food, and the weather was so bad that no one could go anywhere to find food. Though the grown-ups had nothing to eat, my mother kept me alive by feeding me small pieces of an old, sticky sealskin. We had eaten our dogs a long time ago, and all that was left were bits of sealskin. My father became so weak that he could not get up even when the storm had passed.*

It was my grandparents who left the igloo. I don't know how they had the strength, but my grandfather took his gun, and we were sure that we would never see them again. The next day, my father dragged himself to the entrance of the igloo, hoping to see a sign of his father and mother, and could not believe what he saw.

A small herd of caribou were passing only a short distance from the igloo, and he called to my mother to bring the gun. She could not believe that there were caribou out there, but she managed to bring my father his gun and, with his last bit of strength, he shot a caribou. My mother's feeling of joy turned to one of fear because she thought my father had died when he shot the caribou, but it was not so. He had passed out from weakness, even though there was food to save our lives just a short distance away.

My mother managed to get us something to eat, and that same day, three more caribou could be seen in the distance. My father got his gun and crawled along the snow to try and kill another one. Then he saw them. He couldn't believe his eyes. His mother and father were returning — they were alive.

Later, my grandfather told us what had happened. He and his wife had found a sheltered place and lay huddled together to try and keep warm. They don't know how long they had been there when a single bull caribou came very close to where they lay. My old grandfather shot the caribou, and he and my grandmother cut pieces of it and put them into their parkas to carry back to us. They did not stay but turned around and came back to save us from dying. We survived.

Oh yes, I remember starvation. I can remember being in camps with other families when the only food left to eat was so rotten that you could cut it by pinching it with your fingers.

You asked me if it was true that, during the period of great hardship, the oldest people would leave the camp to die, so that the younger ones might have a better chance to live.

It is not true, at least not in my experience. From the youngest to the oldest, we shared everything. We shared food and we shared suffering. If you were my son, I would say to you, "Always behave yourself; understand kindness, and never be a threat to others. The greatest hurt that you can ever throw at me is not obeying these things I asked of you. The greatest gift that you can give to me, is food for our family."

MIRKUT AND THE SHAMAN

At the end of a housing conference I attended in Pond Inlet (Mittimatalik), I took a walk down the dirt road with Iyuka, the conference interpreter. We came upon an old man with a beautiful face and engaging smile. I asked Iyuka to introduce us and to ask the man if we could visit him and listen to him tell some stories. Without hesitation, *Atattasiaq* (I called him "Grand-father" out of respect) agreed.

For some strange reason, the first thing I asked Atattasiaq was what he thought about death. He replied that he didn't give it much thought. He then asked me about my thoughts on the subject. A beautiful conversation ensued about what was once for me a doleful subject. I asked Atattasiaq about stories that remained vivid in his memory, and he shared the following two tales.

> *Sometimes we hear stories that are the children of some-one's imagination, and sometimes we hear stories that are real and very hard to understand. I will tell you two such stories told to me by my father. He had not heard of these stories. He saw the events with his own eyes. They only became stories when other people began to talk about them.*
>
> *There was an old man who once lived here called Mirkut. He had no children, no wife, and no skills that can make one a special person. No one paid much attention to Mirkut, who lived in a little tent across the bay within sight of the village. He did a little seal hunting in and around the bay, but he was too old to go on long trips or out to sea. Some-how he managed to get just enough food to keep living.*

Each time the hunters left the village, they would pass by his camp. Each time they saw signs of life, and some would wonder if old Mirkut would live forever.

One night, when some of the hunters were unloading their boats down by the shore, flames could be seen burning from Mirkut's camp. We knew that there was nothing we could do to save the old man and that he must have been burned in that horrible fire.

The next day, some of the older men paddled across the bay to put stones over Mirkut's burnt body, so that the foxes could not eat his remains. As they came around the point of land, they were surprised and frightened, because the camp was still there. They called out, "Mirkut! Mirkut!" but the old man was nowhere to be seen.

The men cautiously landed and walked with a feeling of fear to his [Mirkut's] camp, calling out his name. Nothing in the camp had been touched by the fire. They looked everywhere around the camp, and there was no sign of a fire anywhere. The most frightening thing of all was when they went into his tent and saw the impression of his body, as if he were still lying in his bed. Only then did they smell the smell that lives in an old firepit. Mirkut had vanished forever.

Now I will tell you my second story. This too was witnessed by my father and not only the Inuit know of it, but there was a qallunaq who was a part of the strange thing that happened.

As you know, there are good and there are evil shamans. There was an old woman, whose name I have forgotten, who was an evil shaman. She was so feared by everyone that no one would dare to cross her path. We were told by the young minister who came to our village that there were no such things as real shaman and that what we thought were "magical" powers were nothing more than our own fears of things we didn't understand, yet the book from which he read was full of magic.

No matter what he said, we continued to fear the old woman and secretly wished her dead. That same winter, when the four stars called Kutujuo (collarbone) were in their nighttime position, the shaman died. None of us wanted to go into her house, but we knew that we couldn't leave her body there and that we would have to bury her behind the village. We asked the minister if he would go to the house and see if the old woman was truly dead.

He said that he would go and pray for her soul, and that if she had died last night he would help us bury her. We followed him to the house, and he went in alone. He stayed in there for a long time, and when he came out, he looked terrible. He spoke to some of the old men, and after much urging, together they went into the house and brought out the old woman wrapped in her bedcovers and buried her behind the village.

That qallunaq is gone from our village, but what happened will remain for many lifetimes. He had entered a house so cold that the tea was frozen in the mug, and his breath came out in clouds. He looked at the body of the old woman lying dead in her bed. There was frost on her face, but when he touched her body, it felt like fire. The minister never wanted to talk about what happened, ever again.

Osutsiak Pudlat's drawing of Ijirait made into a print.
(courtesy, West Baffin Eskimo Cooperative)

AN INTIMATE WILDERNESS

LOVE, LIFE, DEATH, AND IMMORTALITY

The *ijiraq* (singular) is a being that looks like a caribou but really is a spirit in animal form. Stories about these creatures vary from region to region; some stories describe the ijiraq as a benign creature, others as a creature to be feared.

A common belief is that *ijirait* (plural) not only have the power to change from a caribou- to a human-like shape but also to become two-dimensional: They can be seen only front on and disappear when turned sideways. A few hunters claim to have met an *ijiraq* on their long journeys inland and say they were not frightened. Though Simeonie Quppapik had never met an *ijiraq*, he said that some hunters had slept with a female one. I myself have often visited the area where the *ijirait* are known to live but have never come face to face with one of these fantastic creatures. My questions to various elders about *ijirait* prompted Lucassie Arragutainaq, who was from Sanikiluaq (Belcher Islands), to recount a fascinating story of love, spirits, death, cannibalism, rebirth, and immortality.

Many years ago in Sanikiluaq, there lived a pleasant woman who had no husband. One day when she was out on the land picking berries, she encountered an ijiraq *who had taken the shape of a man. The woman had no idea that he was in fact an* ijiraq. *She often met him when she left the camp. Over time they became attached to each other. But the* ijiraq *longed to leave the island and return to the mainland where there were caribou. The woman agreed to go with him; she said goodbye to her family and, with a few dogs, departed for the mainland.*

On the mainland with its herds of caribou, the woman's husband confessed to being an ijiraq. *Being an ijiraq, he would live forever while she, being human, would age, sicken, and die. But there was a way to change this terrible fate, the ijiraq said. He would slay the woman and eat her flesh until all that remained were her bones. These he would carefully lay out and, soon after, her flesh would begin to grow back.*

And so it came to pass. The woman was consumed and, in time, became whole again, appearing as young as the day she and the ijiraq had first met. It is said that her dogs eventually returned to Sanikiluaq and were recognized as hers. The elders on the island knew that the dogs had returned from the mainland because they had the smell of caribou on their fur.

And so, from time to time, the woman from Sanikiluaq and her husband, the ijiraq, carried out this ritual, and she remained forever young and in love.

FOR THE LOVE OF JESUS

Many years ago, while gathering information from Inuit elders, I came across references to how the arrival of Christianity affected them. At the time, I paid little attention to these accounts. My bias toward documenting only what I considered to be traditional beliefs was, in retrospect, short-sighted. I missed the rare opportunity to hear described what, in essence, was a critical interface between two concepts of religious belief — animism and Christianity.

Long after realizing I had lost this opportunity, I sought out the highly respected Armand Tagoona. Armand was the first ordained Anglican deacon in the eastern Arctic, renowned for his depth of knowledge about Christian and traditional beliefs. He was born and raised in Repulse Bay (Naujaat). I first met him in Rankin Inlet, where I was asking the local elders for information about inuksuit in their area. I had heard that Armand was a truly charismatic person, so I attended his service in the little Anglican church where he preached. In my entire life, no other speaker has so impressed me. He had the grace to speak in English from time to time for the benefit of the few *qallunaat* in the congregation. At the end of prayers, he asked translator Deborah Evaluarjuk (linguist) and me to come forward and, in front of the congregation, presented each of us with a small silver heart in memory of the visit.

Armand invited us to his modest little house, where we spent an enchanting day with him. We talked about several things. I was curious to know how his traditional beliefs had been affected once he became a minister of the Christian faith. He began by giving me a brief account of a journey he had taken after his ordination.

My partner and I had been travelling by dogsled for some time. Each night, if I wasn't too tired, I'd read a little bit from my Bible and each night my partner would mumble something about my new faith. And so it went. Approaching Harvaqtuuq (the Kazan River), we paid more attention to our surroundings, for this was a place of great importance to generations of Inuit. There was cause to be very respectful where so many people had lived and died. There were many revered objects and places in that area. Coming upon a huge inuksuk with a great round boulder perched on top, my partner stopped his sled and refused to go any further. To do so, he explained, would attract great misfortune if we did not show it our respect. He went on to tell me the story of how this inuksuk, which is really called kibvakattaq inuksuk, was placed there a long time ago by a powerful man just before his death. It was said that travellers thereafter must attempt to move the great stone on top of the inuksuk or suffer terrible things on their journey. Observing such a traditional custom is called tiriguhungniq.

So there I was, an Anglican minister, standing before an inuksuk believed to have the power to harm the disrespectful. As you know, only the foolish take chances on long journeys and, besides, anyone who worked so hard to make such a big inuksuk should be complemented for his efforts! To the great relief of my partner, I performed the old ritual of trying to move the stone resting on the top of the kibvakattaq inuksuk. Eventually we arrived at the family camp, tired, happy, and well, as was to be expected. You can never be too careful!

ALIGUQ'S WARNING

The first person who revealed to me the existence of a spiritual landscape was a gentle man originally from Arctic Bay (Ikpiar-juk), whom I referred to as Angak, or Uncle. Angak's mother was an *angakok*, a shaman. What I learned from him, he had learned from his mother and his uncle, also an *angakok*. His mother was known for her healing powers. His uncle was known for his ability to perform frightening acts, including the laying of curses, conjuring ghosts, and instilling fear in people, including the *qallunaat*.

From this remarkable man, I would learn about the behaviour of shadows, the differences among amulets, the purpose of incantations, the method of dispelling malefic spirits, and more. I believe his candour was a response to the nature of my curiosity. I sought his knowledge about traditional spiritual matters better to understand my own. Though my grandparents were devout Orthodox Christians from eastern Europe, they were intensely superstitious and quite familiar with amulets, incantations, and ways of dispelling malefic spirits. It was as natural for them to hang garlic in the doorway of the house as to kiss the holy icons in places where spirits dwelled.

I revealed to Angak that during my infancy, I had become gravely ill. My grandmother, who was regarded as a healer, in-structed my mother to bathe me in the first urine I passed in the morning. I was to be bathed with a piece of garment she wore next to her body. My mother was then told to throw the cloth used to wipe my body onto a pathway, with the intent that some unfortunate passerby would carry off my affliction. This personal account apparently delighted Angak, and he proceeded to tell me of a similar traditional Inuit practice where he lived, which was known as *qoqsiuarira*. As the evening wore on, he began to talk about spiritual subjects as casually as one might discuss the kinds of provisions necessary to undertake a long journey.

"When you are alone at night on the land," he said, "take this precaution. Tie two slender objects together to make an X. They can be bone, wood, anything. Then place the X on the threshold of your tent. The X will protect you even while in your deepest sleep. We knew of such things long before your men (missionaries) came with their Xs and stood them on their end."

Angak caused me to think about the spiritual features of the landscape and the sensuous communion with the land. Yet it was Pauloosie Tulugaq, (the Raven), who caused me to reflect on my own perceptions of spirituality, which lay shrouded in my consciousness. Tulugaq as I preferred to address him, was a huge man who had difficulty in walking. His skill as a mechanic had enabled him to modify his old snow machine into a land buggy that he used to travel about the community. That snowmobile on wheels puttering down the street in July was quite a sight. On occasion, he would make a beautiful ulu, a crescent shaped woman's knife that he would give as a gift to some fortunate woman. I knew that Tulugaq had lived in Arviat (Eskimo Point) at one time, and a friend who had lived there for a number of years suggested I try to talk with Tulugaq about spiritual matters.

I remember one day pausing at the door of Tulugaq's dwelling. I thought, "Is it possible that he has the power some people believe he has? If I open that door, what might happen? Should I just walk away?" I decided to push on, opening the door. I called out my Inuktitut name, Apirsuqti. Tulugaq beckoned to me to enter. He sat in the gloom clad only in a pair of shorts; a half-eaten walrus flipper lay before him on a piece of cardboard.

"Why have you come to see me?" Tulugaq asked. I replied that I heard he had been initiated as an *angakok* when he lived in Arviat many years before. Tulugaq exploded with rage. "Who dared to tell you such a thing?" he said with a fury that made me tremble. I was shocked by the violent outburst. "Tell me, who dared tell you such a thing? Was it him?" He pointed to my companion.

I felt pinned to the wall yet obligated not to reveal who had told me of Tulugaq's powers. I apologized for being so ignorant. I asked his forgiveness and prepared to leave his home at once.

"Stay!" he commanded. My companion sat on the floor next to the door while I sat on the floor facing the Raven. We were afraid of him, and Tulugaq knew it.

We southerners have one term for fear while the Inuit of southwest Baffin define different forms of fear. *Iqsizuq* is the general term. *Illira* describes an awesome sense of fear, such as one experiences when a terrible storm is brewing at sea. *Kappia* is the fear experienced upon sudden violence, as when facing death. *Sivuuraginiqpaara* means "my greatest fear." *Tatamittuq* refers to a fear so powerful that one is paralyzed by it. Then there is *kijigijaak*, which is not fear but a person who is feared and to be avoided. This person causes you to remain silent. Tulugaq fit that description.

"Why have you come to see me?" Tulugaq asked once more. I replied that I was sorry I had angered him and that I should leave. He leaned forward and drew out a long sharp knife. Without taking his eyes off me, he sliced a piece of fat from the walrus's flipper. He placed the knife within my reach, its tip pointing toward my companion. I sliced off a very small piece of rancid fat and swallowed it. I desperately groped for something to say, anything that would reduce the tension hanging in the air. Remembering a strange experience I had faced the previous year, I asked if he would help me understand what had taken place. I recounted what had happened on the island of Mallik, which means "a breaking wave."

Some three hundred years ago, several families lived in permanent dwellings on Mallik, an island connected to Cape Dorset by a small esker that can be traversed at low tide. They were Thule culture Inuit and, though ancestors of the Inuit living today, were regarded by them as a different people called Tunniit. All that survived of the Tunniit on Mallik were the remains of several dwellings. These appeared to be little more than round excavations in the earth, roughly five metres across and with stone walls about one metre high. The floor was paved with flat stones, and at the back of the dwelling was a raised sleeping platform about the height of a chair, also built of flat stones. The frame forming the roof would have been constructed of whale ribs, covered with caribou skins with a layer of turf laid on the whale bone frames.

A strange mask of soapstone carved by Pauloosie Tulugaq.

The whale bones were long gone. They had been carved into various figures for sale in southern markets.

A rich carpet of plants grew about the dwellings, nourished by the refuse of many years past. The dwellings formed a semicircle at the edge of a small pond. The shallow bottom of this pond was littered with all manner of bones and bits of broken implements. The effect of sunlight falling through the water to the floor of the pond was mesmerizing. The ancient bones of walrus, seal, whale, and caribou appeared to move and change their shape with each breeze that rippled the surface of the water. Now and then the dark shape of an Arctic Triops would appear and then vanish into the shadows. These little water dwellers in the shape of a tiny horseshoe crab are considered to be living fossils. A steep hill about twenty metres in height rose behind this camp, providing shelter as well as reflecting the heat of the sun toward the settlement. Even now, one could discern two pathways leading to the camp from opposite sides of the island.

Tulugaq patiently sat as I recounted my first visit to Mallik. I began by telling Tulugaq that, for some reason I couldn't explain, I had felt an urge to go to Mallik on my own. I remember starting out on a day that promised to be clear and mild. The tide had gone out, exposing the esker that formed a narrow bridge connecting

AN INTIMATE WILDERNESS

Cape Dorset to Mallik. It took me about an hour to get to Mallik, and in that short space of time the weather had changed. The sky had darkened and a cold wind began blowing across the island. I remember how, looking at the hollows in the earth where people once had lived, I felt a sense of unexplained sadness.

I started shivering and decided to find a place where I could be protected from the wind. About halfway up the cliff, I came upon a niche into which I could neatly fit my body and escape the wind. I could see the effect of the wind on the surface of the pond but no longer feel its bite. The shadowless landscape revealed only faint outlines of the camp. I stared without looking at anything until a daydream overcame me.

In this dream, I saw the camp come alive with women and children. There was a large platform made of flat stones upon which meat lay and another platform upon which lay bundles of skins tied together with lines. What looked like harpoons and other objects were heaped alongside the bundles. I heard the laughter of children; and upon turning in the direction of that sound, I saw them. They were chasing something, pushing and bunting one another.

Pauloosie Tulugaq.

They all seemed to be very young and dressed in tunics of caribou skin with the hair removed. Their trousers were also made of caribou skin. Their clothing was covered in patches and looked very worn. I saw three middle-aged women and an old woman dressed in the same manner as the children. One woman tended a fire made of twigs and Arctic heather, which gave off much smoke. The other woman was returning from the pond carrying water in two skin buckets. The third woman, with her head bowed, sat beside the old woman and appeared to be listening intently.

I was startled by a sudden outburst of yelling and shouting in the distance, to which those in the camp quickly joined in. Four hunters dragging seals came into view. They were not dressed like the hunters I've seen wearing traditional clothing for hunting at sea.

They wore long sealskin jackets with high collars that reached to the tops of the backs of their heads. One hunter's jacket was open and I could see that his sealskin boots extended up to his thighs. No decoration of any kind appeared on anyone's clothing. Upon reaching the camp, the hunter in the lead looked up to where I was sitting. Pointing directly at me, he turned his head toward the old woman and said angrily, "Who is that strange white human looking at us?"

The old woman replied, "Pay no attention, my son, it is only a ghost!"

At that moment everything seemed to dissolve like a *pulkkatuq*, a mirage at sea. I was once more conscious of how everything was before my *sinnatuuti*, my dream.

Tulugaq said nothing for a while. He just sat there staring at me. I felt it necessary to continue telling Tulugaq about the strange experience on Mallik that had taken place the following year.

We had a short period of bad weather the following summer. So one dreary day, I decided once more to visit Mallik. With a small pack on my back, I crossed to Mallik on the esker. The day was cold and grey, much like the day I had visited Mallik the year before. I saw the remains of the camp; I neither noticed nor felt any apprehension. I was convinced that what had happened on that strange day a year ago was merely a vivid dream. I found the little niche in the cliff face without difficulty and, as I had before, inserted myself into it and settled in. I looked about the landscape in a very slow and deliberate manner, attempting to absorb the details of everything in sight. This small Arctic meadow bearing the signature of human habitation was silent. An abundance of *nunariat*, plant life, was reclaiming the site. Then, it happened again.

At first, everything I had seen on the previous trip appeared to be gone. There were no dwellings or people. Then out of the corner of my eye, I caught a slight sign of movement coming from a small heap of skins at the side of one of the dwellings. The old woman I had seen before emerged, gaunt, covered in tattered skins, and sobbing. I called out to her: "*Anannatsiak*, Grandmother, what has happened?"

She uncovered her face and, looking squarely at me, cried out, "I am alone and I will be alone forever. If ever you come back to this place, you will not be able to see me again. But I warn you! You must never sleep where you are sitting, because if you do, you will die before your time!" The old woman then faded away.

Tulugaq stared at me. After what seemed like a long time, he spoke very deliberately. "You have been visited by Aliguq," he said. "Listen to what she has told you. She knows."

Tulugaq died shortly after our encounter. I still remember the cries of anguish during his funeral. The summer after the episode with Tulugaq, Osuitok Ipeelie unexpectedly began to talk to me about the *angakok* Aliguq. He told me about her powers to heal and the love that many had for her. "She was a source of light," he said, and shared the following account.

Many years ago, one of our men who went hunting during winter alone. He did not return to where his family was camped in the time expected. There had been no storms to delay his return, so his family were sickened by the thought of him being lost. Though people searched for him and some shamans tried to find were he might be, all failed. It wasn't until early spring that the family finally went to Aliguq and pleaded with her to call upon her helping spirits to reveal where Qilikti could be found.

Aliguq summoned everyone to her place. She took a small stick, dipped it into the oil in the kudlik (stone oil lamp), and set it afire. She then held the flames to her throat, slowly moving the fire from side to side, and called upon her helping spirits. When the two spirits, seaweed and caribou, came to her bidding, she uttered sanngijualuit uqausiit, *powerful words we could not understand.*

When she opened her eyes, she spoke to all of us and told us that Qilikti could be found at Itiliardjuk Point near Tariungazuq, by the shore. He would be dead. They were to bring his body back to her.

It was early morning when they found him where Aliguq said he would be found. They brought his body to the igloo where Aliguq and the dead man's family were.

But before the body arrived, Aliguq warned everyone not to look directly at the body and not to make the slightest move when it was brought into the igloo. She warned them again when the body was brought in to do as she commanded or he would disappear and we would lose him forever. Standing beside the body of Qilikti, she sang a strange magical song.

Osuitok began singing:

*Here I am Harmless and considered to be nothing
I have powerful helpers
Here I am Harmless and considered to be nothing
Now come back to life!*

Osuitok continued: *When she finished uttering those words, she spat upon him and she spat upon his clothes, helping bring back the dead man's inua, his life force. At that moment, Aliguq told everyone that they could look upon Qilikti. There he was, sitting before them with a faint smile upon his face.*

Osuitok abruptly stopped talking about the incident and moved on to other things.

BRIDGING WORLDS

Over the years, I was told of the existence of ghosts, witches, and demons. I came across accounts of spiritual possession and shamanic powers, and what we southerners would regard as arcane entities. The subject matter was not new. It had been well documented during the Fifth Thule Expedition to Arctic North America from 1921 to 1924, led by the legendary ethnographer Knud Rasmussen.

Hearing about such things seventy-five years later, from those who still believed in them, was interesting. I recall an early Sunday morning when my dear friend Joanassie Salamonie and I sat together overlooking the sea. It was a dreamlike time. We watched gulls gliding above a glass calm sea. The scent of the land drifted on air that carried the faint sounds of distant ravens.

Breaking the silence, Joanassie turned to me and said, "It's strange how being out on the land can make you feel young at any time of your life. Though I've seen many different places and things, I only wish that I could see the spirits, the ghosts, and all the other things I know are out there. Have you ever seen a ghost?"

With some hesitation, I replied that I believed I had, but I was not certain. My ghost was no more verifiable than the belief that I had a soul.

Many years ago, my companion Luke Suluk and I met a remarkable old woman who had lived on Arviatjuaq, an island once known as Sentry Island, which lies close to Arviat once known as Eskimo Point on the west side of Hudson Bay. The woman had become a devout Christian, yet she talked at length about traditional beliefs. She surprised me by divulging intimate information about *apirqsait* and shamanic powers. I became absorbed just hearing her utter words once spoken to attract animals, move stones, calm storms, and raise the dead.

In the very room where these names were pronounced hung a lithograph of Jesus. Close at hand was a small black Bible embossed with a golden cross. Observing me staring at the tattered book, she proceeded to tell me how it had saved her husband's life.

At first he was just sick and I was not too worried. As each day passed, he became weaker and I became frightened. He told me that a sickness had been cast over him, so that he could be hunted by some evil thing. Then during the night between the fourth and fifth day, he cried out, "Help me, help me — they're coming — the tupilait, *evil* tuurngait, *hunger for my entrails! They're about to tear me apart. Oh woman, help me, I'm about to die!"*

I knew he was telling the truth, and the tupilait *were about to devour him. I grabbed my Bible, which I could see my husband trying to reach. I pressed it hard against his chest. I cursed the* tupilait *in their own language, which caused them to come together. They transformed themselves into an* angakok *who was covered from head to foot in strange charms. The* angakok *looked at us hatefully, then turned away, became mist, and was gone. My dear husband was left alive, though you may have noticed he's lost his power to speak. Our faith drove away the* tupilait. *Our fear is that they're waiting to come back.*

With utmost care and with the assistance of Luke, I asked the woman to help me understand how it was possible to displace the belief in the spiritual powers of the shamans with the adoration of Christ. She replied simply, "The *angakkuit* deceived us. Following them never changed our lives. We just continued to be fearful. Faith in Jesus was a promise of a better life. It was our release from fear but not from our past."

She went on to explain that belief in Jesus in no way diminished her respect for tradition, reverence for the land, and the words it continued to whisper to her.

"And what does the earth whisper?" I asked.

Many things. If you go to a place only a few days from here, there is an uppiguhungniq *(a place deserving of much respect) where there is a crack in the earth. If you listen carefully, you will hear the sound "Ahimaa" repeated over and over again. It is the land asking you, "Are you really what you appear to be?"*

Several years later, as I was walking on a cold winter night in downtown Ottawa, I shared the account of the old lady in Arviat with a young woman from Iqaluit. That prompted her to tell me about an experience involving her mother that beautifully bridged traditional beliefs and the belief in Jesus, miracles, angels, heaven, and hell.

As the young woman recounted, her mother felt it was time to follow Jesus and yet, in a way, the idea saddened her. One night her mother had a dream in which she learned what she must do. The following day, she summoned all the women in the camp and told them about her dream. They understood its meaning. Working together, the women selected the finest sealskins and made the most beautiful *amauti*, woman's parka. They took the gift to a place overlooking the sea and spoke to Sedna, who lived at the bottom of the sea and was said to possess the power to provide or withhold the sea creatures that sustained humans. She could be generous but dangerous at the same time. The women called out to Sedna and told her about their sadness. They begged her to accept the gift that they had made, believing that they would never see her again, and threw the beautiful *amauti* into the sea.

Top left: Fertlity effigy carved from Stellar's sea cow bone, Alaska.

Bottom left: Hunting effigy carved from ivory and whale bone, Kugaaruk (Pelly Bay).

Right: Inunnguaq carved from drift wood, Thule culture, Dorset area.

INCANTATIONS, CURSES, AND THE POWER OF WORDS

Chance meetings in different places, either with strangers or old acquaintances, often yielded unexpected insight into a different realm of belief. Knowing where the very fine line existed between trespassing on another person's beliefs and seeking advice so as better to understand your own beliefs was important. Invariably, people would inquire, "Why do you keep asking us about the *angakkuit*, spirits, and old beliefs?" I could reply only that when I was out on the land, the solitude awakened in me a deep, unexplainable feeling — the sense that moving around out there were things I couldn't see, touch, or rationalize. Even if I tried to dismiss this feeling as merely a figment of my imagination, the mystery remained: Why did I sense such things? My attempt to convey this feeling to the elders was accepted, though regarded as strange coming from a *qallunaq*, a white man who was *qiniinaqtuq*, ever searching.

Learning about the *tuurngait* and the *angakkuit* occurred over several years of conversations with elders from Kivalliq, the Keewatin (central Arctic) and Kinngait regions. Among my most important teachers were Osuitok Ipeelie, Oshutsiak Pudlat, Simeonie Quppapik, Pauta Saila, Mannumi Davidee, Munamee Sarko, Namonai Ashoona and Kiawak Ashoona, Ikkuma Parr and Kov Parr.

These elders revealed much about beliefs in traditional times. Munamee Sarko described living at a time when spirits dwelled everywhere and in all things. "That time we remember as *ungajuq* (ever travelling). We killed every living thing that we and our dogs could eat. It was the *taimaigiakaman*, the great necessity." Munamee spoke of human lives sustained by the death of animals whose spirits still hovered where they were killed. Failure to appease these spirits could lead to the disappearance of their kind in time of need. In times of stress, the *angakok*, with his *tuurngait* helpers, would be called upon to appease the offended spirits. The *angakok* had *sanngijualuit uqausiit* (magical words) that he had acquired during his initiation to become a real shaman, a real shadow-maker. Real shamans — *angakkuruqsazausimaazuq* — differed from those who called themselves shamans the *angakkuruqsaqtausimangitut*. The latter had never been initiated and were not powerful. As Osutchiak said, they could not call upon important *tuurngait*, such as *pamiuliktaaq*, who could provide humans with seals, whales, and walrus by crushing their souls.

Real shamans started out as *anakkurusazuq* (learners). They would have to learn *uqausiit angankkurnur atuqtausuut* —words spoken only by shamans. Osuitok explained that long ago people believed that powerful words contained the very essence of the thing they described, and so they had to be treated with utmost care and never wasted. Some words offered protection from different forms of danger, others cured illnesses by driving out the cause.

Sanngijualuit uqausiit, what we would call "magical words," would be strung together to form incantations. Incantations were numerous; some were used to heal while others, such as *illihiirut*, were curses. I learned of incantations to attract animals, calm storms, protect oneself against evil spirits, and even give thanks for a safe journey or successful hunt. But never was I given a single word that was a curse or even a part of a curse. The existence of such things was never denied, simply avoided. In retrospect, I still wonder if those words dangerous to use are explicit performative utterances, that is, when spoken, they are the very instruments that cause things to happen.

When I asked Osuitok where the most powerful words had originated, he revealed a bit of information that still echoes in my mind.

AN INTIMATE WILDERNESS

"The most powerful words," he said, "were gathered from the Tunniit angakkuit, the shamans of the Tunniit, the people who we know were here before us and prepared the land for our arrival."

One of the first hunters to take me out on the land was believed to have fallen victim to a curse. He was a quiet and gentle person who had angered someone. I don't know whether or not the offended was an angakok, as non-shamans could also lay curses. The poor man first lost his hunting equipment in an accident that almost took his life. Shortly after the accident, a person dear to him suddenly died. I was told that when he went out with others to hunt, no seals or caribou would appear and the hunters would return empty handed. Finally, he received a visit from the phantom Nuliarsaq, a beautiful woman who first appears in the dreams of boys when they are just discovering their sexuality. Nuliarsaq seduces them and then vanishes, leaving traces of her seduction in their sleeping bag. At first, Nuliarsaq's return to my friend's dreams freed him from his deepening depression. She pleasured him greatly. He began to long for sleep so as to be enchanted by dreams of Nuliarsaq. Sometimes, she would not come to him and he would awaken depressed. As time went on, Nuliarsaq's appearances became fewer and fewer and then stopped altogether. I was told that the gentle person whom I had known years before had entered a period of madness and now was regarded as "a little strange." I did go out with him once more to Itiliardjuk. He spoke very little and seemed distracted by something I could neither sense nor detect.

It was Simeonie Quppapik who revealed the existence of certain words spoken by the *angakkuit*. The day I returned from a trip with Paulassie Pootoogook to an *angakkusurvik*, a place where a shaman once practiced, I decided to drop in and have tea and bannock with old Simeonie. Simeonie was well aware I had been inquiring about the things that the *angakkuit* did, the words they used, and the spells they cast, and he suggested that

I turn my attention to something useful. He was also aware of my fascination with *tulugait*, ravens. "I will give you the gift of a useful utterance," he said. "When you go hunting caribou and see a raven overhead, speak to it. Shout *Tulugaq tulugaq turaarit tuttuit mitsaanut* (Raven, raven, show me where the caribou are!). The raven, hearing you, will tumble downward and then fly up and away in the direction of the caribou." I was touched by Simeonie's gift. The following summer while having tea and bannock with him, I mentioned that I had followed his instructions when I had been out on the land with Itulu Itidlouie later that summer. I had struggled through the incantation but nothing happened; the *tulugaq* just kept on going. Simeonie merely shrugged and said, "You never spoke Inuktitut very well, and even the *tulugait* knew that there were no caribou near here last summer."

ETERNITY

I met Issuhungituk in 1958 during my first visit to Cape Dorset. Issuhungituk, whose name means Eternity, was born in 1939 in the camp at Igallalik, some sixty-five kilometres east of Cape Dorset. She was a thin and somewhat fragile woman. She had a slight cough and a melancholy look about her. Issuhungituk had suffered much during her relatively short life. Her health was never very good and was further weakened by a series of miscarriages. Though my interest in shamanism was well known, dear Issuhungituk continually chided me, suggesting that I give up that dark pursuit and embrace Jesus. A lithographic likeness of Jesus hung prominently over my head whenever I sat on her sofa having my cup of tea and piece of warm bannock.

Though her health limited what she could do, Issuhungituk was a good soapstone carver and she sewed beautifully. When I brought my underwear to her for mending, I was always a bit embarrassed; I used to wonder what she thought seeing the deplorable state of my long johns. Her teeth were worn down, attesting to years of softening the skins from the caribou and seals her husband Paulassie Pootoogook brought home from the hunt. Her thin fingers were always busy. Everything about her was gentle, and for this she was widely esteemed.

When I think of Issuhungituk, I see a gentle, caring wisp of a woman. I think of how it felt when we embraced — a wonderful feeling of love, that ecstatic moment of release of one's self to the other. Yet, considering how close we were, I knew very little about her. We spent hours together at the kitchen table talking about all manner of things. Apparently she was too unassuming to insert herself into any conversation. When I asked about her childhood, her maiden years, or, for that matter, any vignette from her life, she seem embarrassed by the attention.

It's interesting how certain things stand out in one's memory of a person. Often they are simple things that define what that person really meant to you. And as in a remembered dream, the meaning is often symbolic. Such an incident is at the centre of my memory of Issuhungituk. One sunny afternoon shortly after I had arrived in Cape Dorset, her daughter, Malaya, tracked me down, asking if I would come to visit. Realizing that this was as much an admonition as an invitation, I told her that I would visit on the afternoon of the next day.

As I entered her kitchen the following day, Issuhungituk feigned surprise. Yet everything in the little house was tidy. The plastic tablecloth was gleaming. Not a single dish lay in the sink. "Oh," she said, "If I knew you were coming I would have made some fresh bannock." Issuhungituk then went to the back of the little oil heater and carefully brought out a little metal bowl. "I made some *misiraq* for you," she said. *Misiraq* is seal oil that has been allowed to ferment and is considered a great delicacy, often tasting like a cross between castor and cod liver oil. But Issuhungituk could make *misiraq* that tasted like a delicious melted blue cheese. Little Malaya brought something wrapped in a scrap of newspaper. Issuhungituk unwrapped it, revealing a bright green Granny Smith apple. She carefully sliced the apple into eight pieces and joined me on the sofa. While dipping slices of Granny Smith into the *misiraq*, we licked our lips and fingers in a state of euphoria.

I will never forget the moment, while Jesus watched us, when Eternity said, "I love you."

QIATSUQ AND THE IMAGINED WINDOW

The summer before she died, Issuhungituk talked to me about her father, Qiatsuq. Qiatsuq's family tree had its roots in Nunavik, Arctic Quebec. The *Nunavikmiut*, the people of a great land occupied by animals, were known to Baffin Islanders as the *Akianimiut*, the people of the other side. I was told that Qiatsuq was born in a camp between Ivujivik and Salluit, which was a very long winter journey to Kuujjuaq (Fort Chimo, Arctic Quebec), where the family lived.

Around 1890, while still a child, Qiatsuq and his immediate family left their camp and began the perilous journey to the distant shores of Qikiqtaaluk (Baffin Island). They set sail in an *umiak* with a frame made of driftwood or whalebone lashed together and over which square-flipper sealskins were stretched. The boat was equipped with a small square sail and oars. Unlike the kayak, the *umiak* was a large boat, up to nine metres long, that could hold as many as twenty people with all their gear and several dogs. The *umiak* was regarded as a "woman's boat," since the women did much of the work in building it, preparing the skins, and finally rowing it filled to the gunwales with tents, food, hunting gear, kids, and anxious dogs.

Qiatsuq and his family reached Tujjaat (Nottingham Island), some fifty-six kilometres into Hudson Strait, where they were beset by roving ice and set up a temporary camp on a large ice floe. When the ice moved out from the island, good fortune prevailed. The supply ship *Arctic* picked them up and took them the rest of the way to Cape Dorset.

Qiatsuq's great uncle Inukjuarajuk was a commanding *angakok* (shaman) from whom sprang the powerful Pootoogook clan, for many years the dominant family in southwest Baffin Island. Qiatsuq's formative years were no different from those of any other young boy learning how to hunt, survive on the land, and provide for his family. I was told that the thing he feared most was the wind out at sea. This fear compelled him to learn the signs that foretold the approach of bad weather in all seasons. He made detailed observations of the shapes of clouds, the colour of the sky, the tint of the horizon, and the hue of distant hills. Qiatsuq became so good at forecasting weather that many hunters consulted him before they undertook long journeys out to sea. He was also said to be a singer of songs and a teller of stories, and the possessor of a fine skill in carving. When he was carving one of his exquisite bears, he reportedly could be heard singing softly to the creature emerging from the stone.

Qiatsuq lived all his life on the land except for the few remaining years when he came to Cape Dorset, where he now lies buried. He spent his last five to six years documenting everything of importance to him in an astonishing series of more than six hundred drawings. These are the visual record of what went on in his mind, the mind of an *angakok*; like his great uncle Inukjuarajuk, Qiatsuq was a shaman.

I came upon the Qiatsuq drawings in the archives of the West Baffin Eskimo Co-operative in Cape Dorset in the early 1960s. I was searching for ethnographic material amid the several thousand drawings in the collection; people such as Simeonie Quppapik, Oshutsiak Pudlat, Kananginak Pootoogook and Qiatsuq, and others made drawings depicting scenes, objects, legends, and memorable events relating to traditional times.

Qiatsuq chronicled various aspects of life on the land. There is a beautiful rendering of women covering a kayak with new skins. There are numerous scenes of hunting caribou and seals, walruses and whales. He depicts the tranquility of a winter camp; you can imagine him snug in caribou skins in his snow house while outside his *komatik* (sled) is perched on snow blocks high above the hungry dogs. Qiatsuq illustrates a young hunter travelling with his wife on the land. One can see clear signs of affection between the couple, suggesting the fond memory of Paksau, Qiatsuq's wife of his early years, whom a friend later killed in a hunting accident. We see how moulting geese were herded into stone pens, how inuksuit were built, and how sleds were prepared for long journeys.

Occasionally I would come across drawings that were puzzling, such as three sheets with a number of birds on each one. At first glance the birds appeared to be merely repetitions of one another, but upon closer examination each bird revealed slight variations, such as the position of the head, wings, or feet. I then discovered with great delight that if you quickly scanned the birds on each line from left to right, working your way to the bottom of the page, you had the illusion that you were looking at single frames of only one bird in motion.

One drawing that stands out in my memory is a scene with several men rolling oil drums up the beach to the Hudson's Bay Company warehouse. The men at the beach were large and the rolling drums small, whereas the men arriving at the warehouse were diminutive and the drums they struggled with huge. The illustration was brilliant. It depicted how the longer you labour, the harder the job; by the time you had rolled that drum all the way up the beach, it was a monster.

But there is another side to Qiatsuq's chronicles. As light is to shadow and shadow to darkness, Qiatsuq illustrated a world in which demons dwelled among strange beasts that could transform themselves into humans. He depicted scenes of violence and killings, evil creatures with sharp teeth embedded in their victims; scenes of terrible beasts and *tuurngait* (spirits) tearing and devouring one another. Most likely such frightening and evil images originated in an incident from Qiatsuq's early childhood.

What was it that intrigued me when I studied Qiatsuq's drawings? Two things stand out: the many gentle, even humorous, themes, and the violent and terrible depictions. With Issuhungituk's help, I began to understand the source of these visions. I asked Issuhungituk about the most beautiful thing and the most frightening thing that had entered into Qiatsuq's life.

She said that the most beautiful thing Qiatsuq had experienced was having a place where game inhabited the land, sea, and sky; where hunger was infrequent; and where a man had time to think about what moved the forces around him. The most frightening thing was a terrible event that occurred during his childhood.

Greater than the fear of dying is the dread of being eaten. A man driven to hunger because he is a poor hunter is not only hungry, but also ashamed before other men who can find food. Such a man came to the camp where Qiatsuq lived when he was a child. There was very little food in the camp, and the stranger began to kill people for what scant resources they had. The survivors found out that this man was eating the bodies of those he had killed, and so Qiatsuq's family fled along with the others. Fleeing from the man-eater did not save them from death; some were later to die of starvation. I asked Qiatsuq's daughter why they didn't kill the man-eater and was told, "Because they were afraid of killing him."

Some time after the killings, the man-eater returned to being a normal man, and a family from another camp began to care for him. As winter approached, he again became strange. The family who cared for him was afraid that he would once more turn into a man-eater, and so they killed him.

Over his lifetime, Qiatsuq had had his powers as an *angakok* tested on many occasions. I learned from Mannumi Davidee that *angakkuit* at times were threatened by other *angakkuit*. The threat might come from an *angakok* in the same region or from one a great distance away. The instrument of harm or even death contained the *illihiirut* (the curse). The physical object in which the curse was placed could be as innocuous as a carving of a small knife or polar bear, a peculiar stone, a tooth, or perhaps some strange little creature. These articles might be wrapped in a piece of sealskin in the guise of a gift.

I was told that Qiatsuq had received such a curse from an *angakok* who lived in Salliq (Coral Harbour, Southampton Island). But Qiatsuq had his way of dealing with dangerous shamans. Osuitok told me that Qiatsuq had shaped an *apumik inunguaqutilik* — a human-like figure made of snow — into which he placed a powerful *illihiirut*. Qiatsuq then "killed" it, and so dealt with the *angakok* who had tried to destroy him.

It was not unusual for two shamans living in the same region to test each other's strength or power. These challenges ranged from minor displays to acts that could involve the death of an opponent. Osuitok told me of one incident well known to various elders in Cape Dorset. "You asked me who was the most powerful *angakok* of all the *angakkuit* in Sikusiilaq," he said one day. "The most powerful one was Alariaq. He was respected by all the others. A long time ago, when Alariaq was alive and Qiatsuq was still gaining his strength, they had a kind of test. They were both out on the land with other hunters waiting for the caribou that had come down from the great plain in the north and were seen north of the Sugba. Some say that Qiatsuq claimed he had enchanted the caribou to come their way. Alariaq said nothing. As they and the other hunters waited for the caribou to approach, Alariaq pointed to the bull caribou and said to Qiatsuq, '*Taika!* (Look!).' The caribou fell to the ground as if struck dead by lightning. The hunters nearby only saw a caribou that had fallen and rushed up to it to make sure it was dead. They then prepared to skin and cut it up, but first they had to slit open the belly. The moment the belly was slit open, a dark and evil-smelling mush poured out, and they fled in fear."

Although an *angakok*, whether male or female, was very involved in day-to-day camp activity, the real power resided in the camp boss. There were two kinds of camp bosses: The *angajuqqaaq* was respected for his toughness, experience, and commanding bearing; the *issumataq* was respected for his intelligence, judgment, and planning skills. I knew of one instance where three *angakkuit* had resided in the same camp and at the same time, with the approval of the camp boss. Qiatsuq was one of the three.

Though he had lived in several camps generally east of Cape Dorset, Qiatsuq settled in a wonderful place called Igallalik. Igallalik simply means "window." Curious about the name, I asked Lukta, Qiatsuq's son, for more information. Lukta explained that when the summer sun moved across the sky, a shadow appeared on the face of the cliff behind the camp. When the shadow darkened, a window appeared as if cut into the face of the cliff and then faded, seemingly disappearing into the rock face. In that sense, Igallalik was referred to an imagined window.

Issuhungituk described Igallalik as her father Qiatsuq's *inninariva*, a place so beloved that one would not wish to live anywhere else. I was transfixed by the description. With all the courtesy I could muster, I beseeched Lukta to take me to there.

The scant remains of the once thriving camp at Igallalik.

And so early one morning, we headed east along the coast. Though Lukta was Qiatsuq's favourite child, he apparently had not inherited his father's spiritual powers. Lukta was a fine artist, a good provider, and a very gentle person who spoke little. He was the perfect travel companion. After a lengthy full-day journey across long stretches of open water, we turned north toward the distant shore of the mainland. We finally landed at the end of a rocky point.

To my disappointment, Lukta announced that we had landed at Igallalik. All I could see was shattered rock, small patches of tundra, and a sullen sky taking shape. We set up our tent, unpacked the canoe, and spread out our sleeping bags. I'm sure Lukta could see the disappointment on my face, but he said nothing. When all was done, he pointed to a distant hill and said, "Go that way." I did as he said.

It was twilight by the time I could see the outlines of old tent frames. Looking at the skeletons of places in which people had once lived and dreamed, and where some had faced dying with quiet resignation, was eerie. Bits of pots, lamps, and bones were strewn all about. Dense clumps of Arctic wildflowers grew in patches where refuse from meals eaten long ago still provided nourishment. The sound of a bird bursting out of the Arctic willows shattered the total silence. The sun lay just below the horizon, the imagined window had vanished, and a chill wind began to flap the remnants of tattered canvas hanging from the frames of the long-abandoned dwellings.

As I was about to return to our own camp, I happened to look down upon a patch of moss. There she was, a little *inunnguaq*, a doll made of rags with her face pointing toward the sky — a touching yet disturbing sight that inspired a myriad of questions. I wondered to whom she had once belonged and why she had been abandoned. I wondered who had created her: Qiatsuq for his daughter Issuhungituk? If Qiatsuq had made the doll, did he sing to her as I'm told he did when he carved in stone?

Upon returning to camp, I told Lukta about the doll, hoping he would shed light on what life had been like at Igallalik, but he chose not to speak about it. In retrospect, I realized that we had camped some distance from the old camp and that Lukta had never come to visit the site.

I have visited the imagined window several times since. On a bright summer day, it is a beautiful place to see. But when twilight descends, the dark, skeletal shapes of dwellings and the debris of daily life seem to evoke a sense of apprehension.

I remember recounting my impression of Igallalik to Osuitok. In particular I described finding the little *inunnguaq* lying embedded in the moss. "Did you touch it?" he asked. I replied that I had not. Osuitok then surprised me by revealing the existence of a very special *inunnguaq*, known as *aanguarluk*, that only an *angakok* could create. The *angakok* made the *aanguarluk* for people who could not have children and were desperate for a solution. If the *angakok* was an *angakkuruqsazausimaazuq* — a shaman who had been initiated — then he had the power to make an *aanguarluk*. The *aanguarluk* I had found looked like a child and contained the spirit of a child.

"Was it like a make believe child?" I asked Osuitok.

"No!" he replied emphatically.

He went on to underline the fact that the little *aanguarluk* was regarded as real. It was given a name and sometimes had a secret name to protect it from being invaded by a harmful *tuurngat*. It was loved and looked after like any other child.

I asked Osuitok if the *inunnguaq* I saw at Igallalik could have been an *aanguarluk*. He just shrugged and replied *"Achoo?"* Who knows? "Make sure you don't touch things like that," he admonished me, "especially if they are near a grave."

Much later that same summer, Joanassie Salamonie asked "When you visited Igallalik and slept there, did you see or hear the ghost children?" I was speechless. I was on the verge of asking if he was kidding but held my tongue. I remembered an unpleasant incident in the past when I had doubted another person's credibility. I asked Joanassie to tell me about the ghost children, and he related the following story.

Some people believe that ghost children inhabit the hills behind Igallalik. "They are the spirits of the stillborn and children who died while still being carried in their mother's *amauti* and those who were lost or drowned." This account is practically identical to the story "Where the Northern Lights are Born" told to me by Paulassie Pootoogook.

I remember the conversation with Simeonie Quppapik when I asked him about myth and reality he explained to me that there are things said to have happened that may or may not have happened. It doesn't matter, as long as they are believed. The expression he used was *sulinngikkaluaqtut ukpirijaujut,* the reality of myth.

TUQU: DEATH

Early in our lives, we regard the subject of death simply as an event that happens to others, especially old people. As we grow old and lose our sense of immortality, the subject of death begins to shift from an abstraction to a morbid reality. To those of us who are superstitious, the reality of death is a subject best not thought about. No matter how we attempt to rationalize our immortality, the spectre of death is frightening. There are, of course, exceptions to the fear of dying, as Osuitok Ipeelie explained, "When suffering is all there is, *tuqu* is welcomed and *inuusiq* or *inua* (life force) is set free from our bodies to go elsewhere."

Several years ago, on a quiet afternoon, I watched a flightless flock of snow geese wandering about the settlement of Arviat. The geese appeared to be in moult and, though vulnerable, were unharmed. Had they been in moult out on the land, they would have been herded into stone pens like sheep and later killed for food, as was the custom for generations. Being in town, they were in a safe haven. In some instances, their antics were amusing as they waddled about picking up bits of food while oblivious to people and four-wheelers that skirted around them. I happened to see a young snow goose amid the flock that had a broken wing. I watched her feeding and moving about seemingly unaware of her condition. I was saddened by the thought that in about a week or two, the entire flock would take to the sky and she would be left behind to die before the first snow fell. Perhaps the curse we bear is not death but the knowledge that it exists.

The deaths of strangers, friends, children, teenagers, or elders, whether natural, accidental, or violent, have been part of my experience in the Arctic. It seemed natural to talk about dying, death, and grieving with the elders, not just because they were nearing the inevitable, but so was I. These conversations have been casual and speculative, usually beginning with "I wonder if…" or "I wonder why…."

One of the several conversations on the subject occurred when I met a woman Majuriaq, whose name meant "a gentle rising slope." Now residing in Cape Dorset, she was born in 1926 in a remote camp on the shores of Nunavik, Arctic Quebec.

She began, *Some people were terrified of the dead. I was more afraid of the dead than of death itself. If there was a dead person nearby, I was afraid to kill the flame of my kudlik (oil lamp). Being in the dark gloom of the qarmaq (sod house) was sometimes frightening. Now that I'm an old lady, I am frightened by death only because it would prevent me from looking after my grandchildren who I love dearly. My greatest sorrow is the death of my brother. He was my light. He was my guide all during all the growing-up years of my life. Later I was once more visited by a great sorrow when my husband died. And then I was overcome by a great pain in my heart when my grandchild was murdered.*

When we lived on the land, most deaths came because of old age. Very few people died of accidents. We hardly had suicides then. We looked after our old people as we expected to be looked after when we became old. When they were close to death, we tried to fill their every wish even if it was difficult. They might want to have a new warm bedcover or piece of whale meat, and we did our best to get it for them. When there was an old person close to death, we (women) made sure that we always had a new clean caribou skin at hand when we travelled. Later, when we could get cloth, we took it along in place of the skin.

When a person died, it was the women who were the last to touch the body. The closest female relatives would wash the body while the other women would make the immutitsanga. *This was the clothing for the dead. It was wrapped around the body, and we would also make a small white hat to cover the head.*

Before the arrival of the itsigarjuasait *(priests), the* angakok *would say incantations or the* angajuqqaaq *(camp leader) would say words over the body for all to hear. The body was then carried by the men to where there were stones and covered up so that no animals could eat it. The close family would grieve together for a day. We did not grieve for many days; life had to go on.*

"And where will you go when you die, *Anannatsiak* (Grandmother)?" I asked.

Oh, my spirit will go to killak *(heaven), and we will all live in a big beautiful house, and I will never have any more worries and no more sorrow.*

Knowing that Grandmother had been around when the shamans Alariaq and Aliguq were alive, I asked her about the role of the *angakok* in the death of a person during traditional times. She did not want to talk about such things. Sensing that she was tired, I ended the conversation by asking, "How would you like a nice hot bowl of chili con carne, Grandma?" Death was instantly put on the back burner. We made short work of the chili, along with bannock and a big pot of Red Rose tea.

Attachie catching the arrows shot at him during
the battle at Kangisurituq (Andrew Gordon Bay).
Drawing by Napachie Pootoogook.
(courtesy, West Baffin Eskimo Cooperative)

ISLAND OF THE DEAD

I met Pudlat Pootoogook in Cape Dorset in the spring of 1975. Pudlat was one of five sons of Pootoogook. Pudlat's daughter Pia, a lovely young woman whom I had met several years earlier, was my first interpreter. The weather at the time was unsettled, and as I could not find a travelling companion, I chose to remain in the settlement until travel was safe. Rather than loll about, I met with Pia and asked her to ask her father if we could get together some afternoon. I wasn't sure what I had to learn from Pudlat, except I was aware that he knew the Sikusiilaq area like the back of his hand.

For some reason, Pudlat and I liked each other upon our first meeting. With Pia interpreting, Pudlat began by describing the landscape around Ikirasak, which was his father's camp on the east side of Kangisurituq (Andrew Gordon Bay), as well his and his brothers' spring, summer, and winter camps. Realizing that he was eager to talk about all the places he knew, I asked if we could get together the following day, when I'd bring along my topographic map 36B Edition 1, 1963, of the Foxe Peninsula. Pudlat enthusiastically agreed.

The following day, Pudlat looked over my "nameless imitation of the Earth," as he called it, and revealed from memory the names of more than one hundred islands and places in Kangisurituq. One particular place that interested me, and that I would later visit in 1998, was a remote island, the last in a chain of islands called Iluvirqtuq, which refers to a place of graves. At the time, I assumed this was an ancient burial site, though I was puzzled by why it was so remote. It was difficult to imagine why the deceased would have been transported from the mainland to be buried there.

When I inquired about the number of graves at Iluvirqtuq, Pudlat told me that no graves were there, only bones and broken skulls.

I learned much later from Kananginak Pootoogook that Iluvirqtuq was where the bodies of about thirty men had been dumped after a battle between Attachie's and Kinarnaq's camps. The battle intrigued me, though I had difficulty finding a surviving elder who had been alive at the time and could provide details of the tragic event. Napachie Pootoogook, Eegyvudluk's wife, made a small drawing representing Attachie (Atachiealuk) fending off a blizzard of arrows from Kinarnaq's men, but she died before we could talk about the battle. I turned to Kananginak for what few details I could get. This is what Kananginak could recall of what his father, Pootoogook, told him when he was a young man.

As you know, Inuit everywhere have games each year. These are games of strength and skill. Sometimes the prize is the adoration of a young woman, but often it's to show who are the strongest, fastest, and best with shooting bows

Death at Iluvirqtuq.

AN INTIMATE WILDERNESS

and arrows, as well as throwing a harpoon with accu-
racy. The games were often between the men of different
camps along the coast. However, sometimes the hunters
from Kangiqsualujjuaq (Wakem Bay) or Ivujivik and Sal-
luit would come across to Sikusiilaq when it was safe to
travel. It was then that we would have a big feast where
everyone from the camps along the coast would join in.

There was always some rivalry between Attachie and
Kinarnaq, as well as between our people and their people,
even though many of us were related to one another. It
seems that our side was winning most of the games, which
made Kinarnaq and his men short-tempered. Besides the
anger that was growing, there was a nasty woman in
his camp who spread evil rumours about cheating and
other bad things she said were going on. As you know,
gossips can be very dangerous. Kinarnaq finally became
enraged and challenged Attachie and all his followers to a
battle. He knew Attachie had a bad eye and walked with a
limp, so he probably could easily kill him. They agreed to
fight each other on the sea ice where every one would be
in the open. They chose the place for battle near a small
island far out in Kangisurituq.

At this point, Kananginak's memory of what his father had
told him about the actual battle thinned out, except when he
recounted the following.

Arrows were falling everywhere, and one of Kinarnaq's
men had a gun (rifle) which he was shooting everywhere.
Attachie had fallen down, and the man with the gun
ran up to him to kill him. Attachie, with a gun pointing
right at his face, said "I have never seen such a thing.
After it makes fire it has such a strange smell. Before
you kill me, let me smell it!" The man with the gun
pointed the barrel of the gun so that it touched old
Attachie's nose, whereupon Attachie seized the barrel,
moving so fast that the gunman was killed by his own

The ghostly stone figures at Itiliardjuk.

gun before he knew what happened. Every last man from the other side, including Kinarnaq, was killed. Everyone! It was decided that their bodies would not be left on the ice but should be dumped on the shore of a nearby island, and so they were like so much garbage.

As I would later learn, the bodies were never buried. Their bleached white bones could be seen on the island of death for many years after the fateful battle. Mikkigak, one of my travelling companions, said Qiatsuq once told him, "For each man killed, we made an inuksuk, such was our remorse."

None of my travelling companions was eager to take me to the site, but as fate would have it, I was able to fly over the site in a helicopter in 2000. There were no bones or signs of the tragedy — just a pile of rocks and a little wooden cross under an ominous dark sky. I was told that the small group of worshippers from the Pentecostal Church in Cape Dorset had gathered up the remains of the tragedy and buried them under the cross of Jesus.

JAYKO AND THE RENDERING VAT

During traditional times, the custom, I was told, was to bury men under stones facing the sea and women facing the land. Children were sometimes buried facing the rising sun. I never studied the orientation of graves during my travels. I have on occasion come across human remains simply scattered about on the tundra. Being a superstitious person, I would avoid them, often whistling as Simeonie Quppapik advised me to do under such circumstances. Better safe than sorry.

But I knew about an unusual "burial" that had taken place several years ago close to Itiliarjuk. Old Jayko had died suddenly while hunting in Kanglsurituq, in the Andrew Gordon Bay area. The land was frozen solid, making it impossible for his companions to bury him. If they had left Jayko's body out on the land, it would have been ravished by polar bears, wolves, foxes, and ravens.

Apparently one of Jayko's companions had an idea about how to save old Jayko from such a fate. Many years before, the whaling ship *Polar Star* had left large iron rendering vats on the shore. The men placed Jayko on their sled, took him to the site, and lowered him into one of the iron rendering vats. A stone was placed over the opening to keep out any nasty *niqituinnainaaq* (meat eater).

The subsequent years were kind to old Jayko. Hot and cold extremes in the vat that had once held whale oil mummified him, thus preserving him for years until the day his sanctuary was deliberately breached. It so happened that several years after Jayko's death, a small group of people in Cape Dorset who sincerely believed in the importance of a Christian burial removed Jayko from the vat. They took him to the side of a nearby hill, where they gave him a Christian burial beneath a pile of stones mounted by a newly fashioned cross.

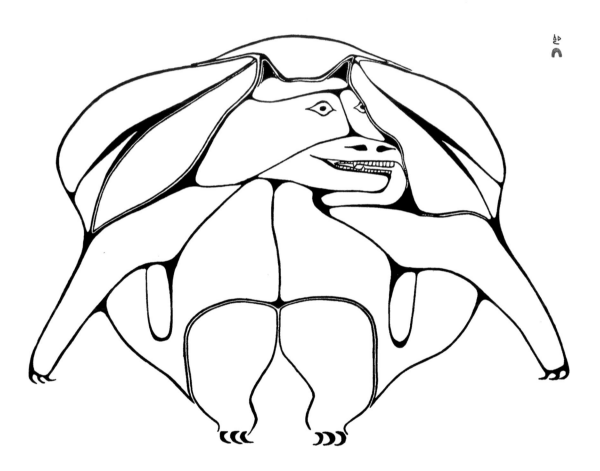

AN INTIMATE WILDERNESS

THE OLD WOMAN WHO
WAS CARRIED OFF BY WOLVES

After I had told the story of Jayko to a couple I met in Rankin Inlet, they, in turn, told me of a strange event in which they were involved. As the woman recounted, "My *adsagek* (mother's sister) had a deep respect for wolves and told us many stories about them. Maybe she believed in *tuurngait*, some of which were wolf spirits. When my aunt could no longer look after herself, she came to live with us. We looked after her until her dying time. Her last words to my husband and to me were, 'When I am dead, do not put me under the stones. Take my body to the hill behind our camp and leave me there uncovered.' We did as she asked. That night we heard sniffing near our *tupik* (tent) and then low growling in the distance. We stayed in our *tupik* until morning. My husband went up to the hill where we had placed her, but there was nothing there except the footprints of wolves."

Amarok, the wolf, was an animal despised by several hunters I knew in south Baffin. Ohito Ashoona told me that some hunters would pursue a wolf over great distances in order to kill it and remove that menace to the caribou. Sam Metcalfe, my Inuk friend from Labrador, told me that in his part of the North, people once had feared wolves above all other animals.

My most memorable encounter with a pack of Arctic wolves occurred in central Baffin in 2002. The region between Piling and Wordie Bay includes a place known to the Inuit as *Amaroktalik*, "a place of wolves." The increase in caribou in the grasslands that summer attracted wolves. On one occasion, we saw three young and apparently healthy wolves stalking a lone caribou. They were so intent that the noise of the helicopter approximately 275 metres away neither frightened them nor broke their fixed attention.

On another day, in the Flint Lake region, I saw a hunting party consisting of seven mature wolves. They were not scattered but were rather in a Y formation. The two wolves at the head of the hunting party were spread apart to form a pincer, the next three were in a line about forty metres behind the pincer, and just behind them were two wolves flanking the line. At the bottom end of this Y formation was a single wolf moving at the same speed as the others, but some thirty metres back. They moved with utmost ease across a rugged field of boulders as if they were a single animal. We rounded a bend in the river and there were the intended prey — a small heard of about twenty caribou, upwind, contentedly grazing by the bank of the river, completely unaware of the drama that was about to unfold.

A COWBOY SONG FOR MIKKIGAK

Several years ago, I had returned to Cape Dorset from Itiliardjuk, my favourite place up the coast. I was planning to stay in town for a few days before heading out to fish for Arctic char. One of the pleasant rituals some of us older folk enjoyed was going to the print shop at the West Baffin Eskimo Co-operative a few minutes before 10 a.m. to mooch a cup of coffee and sit together at the large window facing the centre of town. The window gazers often included Jimmy Manning, Ashevak, Itulu Itlidlouie, Kellypalik, Aoudla, Paulassie Pootoogook, Apirsuqti, and Pee Mikkigak. But this time, Pee Mikkigak was not at the window. He was at home in bed, dying.

Jimmy called me that same afternoon and said that we should go to Pee's house and show ourselves to him, as he was expected to live for only a few more hours. I agreed. I went to the small freezer in the home where I stayed and took out five bags of frozen stew I had made weeks earlier. We entered Pee's house and were met by many of the older women who had gathered there to comfort his wife. We simply nodded to one another as I gave them the frozen stew. I knew the food would be welcome after their long vigil.

Jimmy and I went into Pee's bedroom. Standing at his side was his grief-stricken wife. Pee was lying under a thin sheet, his eyes closed, hardly drawing any breath. Jimmy left the room for a moment while I sat on the bed at Pee's side. I put my hand on his knee and softly sang him the words to an old Irish melody "The Streets of Laredo." Later that day, Pee died. Jimmy and I gathered up his bedsheets and bedclothes and took them to the nursing station. Jimmy and I parted without saying a word.

The author, Joannassie Salamonie (centre) and Namonie Ashoona (right), 1973.

AN INTIMATE WILDERNESS

LAMENT FOR AN OLD FRIEND

I was anxious to return to Cape Dorset in the spring of 1999 because my close friend Joanassie Salamonie was dying. I knew I wouldn't see him if I waited until summer. Joanassie had gone through much suffering in his lifetime. But instead of being hardened by his travails, he was imbued with sensitivity and compassion. He was one of the most respected welfare workers in the eastern Arctic.

Being a grandson of Pootoogook attached Joanassie to one of the most prominent families in southwest Baffin. Joanassie was a critical link between the generation of people who had lived all their lives on the land in the traditional manner and those who had been obliged to leave it behind forever. He had much knowledge about traditional perceptions of life. Though careful how he shared that knowledge, Joanassie was generous with those whom he trusted.

A short time before I was to leave for Cape Dorset, he phoned, asking me to hurry up. "It's beautiful here, lots of snow, soon the eider ducks will be flying in and we will go by dogsled down the coast to Kiaktuq and talk about the old days."

"Yeah, but who will look after two old geezers like you and me?" I asked.

Joanassie said something I couldn't make out, and then I heard giggling in the background. "Where the hell are you?" I asked.

"In heaven," he replied. "I'm in bed with my dear Kanajuq."

We laughed together and said our goodbyes. Joanassie died just before I arrived in Cape Dorset. I still remember Kanajuq softly crying as I held her in my arms.

Top: The great ceremonial site at Igaqjuaq (Qujaligiaqtubic) in summer.

Bottom: A frozen Igaqjuaq (Qujaligiaqtubic) in early spring.

AN INTIMATE WILDERNESS

TRANSFORMATIONS IN TIME

An everyday experience as simple as observing the melting of ice may reveal an event of epic proportions. A slight breeze, an intense reflection of sunlight, then a sudden "whoosh." A slab of ice collapses from the edge of a glacier. The earth below receives its first sunlight in a hundred thousand years.

Somewhere on another island, a young man searches for the remains of ancient alligators that lived here during that split second in geological time — between the comings and goings of the ice ages. These cosmic seasons varied in duration from sixty thousand to one hundred thousand years. The very islands upon which I stand are moving upward. Imperceptibly, they continue to rise from the bottom of the sea, free of the great burden of ice that reshaped this part of the world.

Not in one hundred thousand years but in about one hundred days, from the first week of August, ice that left our shores only at the beginning of July will start to form in the bays and inlets of the High Arctic. Under certain conditions, it may form with astonishing speed and eventually extend up to eighty kilometres from land.

Tuvaliuti, the moon that shines when the sea ice begins to form, signals the return of winter conditions. The land and the sea are in transformation. Rivers, ponds, and lakes that make up nine percent of the world's fresh water begin to freeze. They become solidly attached to the landscape by the same forces that alter the profile of the entire Arctic coastline. Each day, the ice grows thicker, reaching outward as it resurfaces this part of the world. Islands become joined by the frozen sea. Northern Greenland can now be reached by sled from Ellesmere Island.

We may travel on sea ice over one metre thick, and in some places it will have rafted, broken, and piled up slab upon slab, becoming several metres thick.

Yet there is danger. In places, powerful sea currents prevent the formation of ice, or ice is too thin to bear a person's weight. Years of travelling on the ice may end in a single moment, as happened for my friend Quvianaqtuliak Parr when the ice broke beneath him. Death may take its time in coming to a hunter drifting further and further into the Arctic Ocean on an ice floe.

There was a time when people lived on or near the ice from November until the middle of June. Accounts worth repeating of violent death, epic journeys, and miraculous survival often related to life on the ice. They could be heard better at night by the light of the *kudlik*, while one lay naked between friends and caribou skins on the sleeping platform. "Have you heard the story of Taktillitak," I'm asked, "the man who survived being swept out to sea on an ice floe?"

"Yes," I reply. Pingwartuk had shown me the island Taktillitak had managed to reach. I was told that certain he would die there, he made his own grave. A few days after, a seal crawled up on some ice attached to the island and Taktillitak was able to kill it. Later, he managed to kill two more seals. He skinned them from their mouths making skin bags which he blew up making two floats. He then made crude paddles from their scapulas. He waited for the tide moving toward the mainland, took his life in his hands and paddled on his sealskin floats toward the mainland. Ping pointed on my map where Taktillitak landed. I've heard that story from several people in Dorset with one slight addition. It was said that when he appeared in his village he scared the *anaq* out of the people who thought he was a ghost. "What about the three guys who were drifting out in the Foxe Basin last year?" I asked.

"Helicopter got 'em," my companion replies.

The sea currents along the entire stretch of coastline of southwest Baffin become particularly strong during *tirilluliuti*, the April moon, so you must approach the floe edge with great caution in many places. This is a good time to hunt seals, the big square flippers called *udjuk,* and hunt inland for caribou. This is the time of year when the sunlight can be dazzling, when shadows have razor-sharp edges and echoes are no longer muted by drifting veils of snow. A time when you feel the urge to hunt, to travel and visit friends in distant places, or simply to be alone, talking loudly with friendly spirits or conversing with a fragile mountain.

It's okay to be a little mad from time to time but never, ever, to be careless.

One of Pudlo Pudlat's mystical landscapes drawn for this book.

AN INTIMATE WILDERNESS

ADRIFT

I had few conversations with Pudlo Pudlat. He was a rather stern and aloof man who would just as soon tell any *qallunaq* who had come to see him to "Go away!" One day, however, he invited me to his house.

"Why are you are always talking to my brothers Simeonie and Oshutsiak and not to me?" he asked.

I had no polite answer, so I simply replied, "*Achoo*, why don't we talk now?" I said, "You have done many beautiful drawings of the land. Talk to me about being out on the land, *Angak* (Uncle)."

Pudlat walked to the window, stared out, came back to the kitchen table, and picked up a pencil. He placed the pencil back into an old enamelled mug and began to speak.

Many years ago, I went to the other side of Aupaluqtuq with my young nephew to hunt at the floe edge. He was a good boy without experience, obedient and deserving of my attention. He would learn from me as I learned from my uncle. We set up our camp well back from the floe edge because it was a full moon. The wind was still and the sky was full of stars. I showed my nephew the stars which tell you where the mainland is and the ones on the eastern horizon, used for telling the time. It was beautiful and clear; you could see stars having a shit from time to time (meteoric showers). We were overcome by sleep beneath the moon, unprepared for what was about to happen.

Sometime during the deepest part of my sleep, a light snow had fallen and a wind came up when the tide was at its greatest strength. I heard the sharp sound of a crack,

*but for all my experience I did not rise up immediately —
how careless! I finally jumped up, ran outside, and saw
that we were being separated from the main ice. I yelled
to my nephew to leave everything and run behind me
toward the small island nearby. It was still possible to
jump the gap which was widening between us and the
landfast ice. In his confusion he waited too long. The
gap widened, and I heard him cry out, "Uncle! Uncle!" All
I could do was cry out to him. My nephew, the dogs, and
all our belongings were being carried out to sea. What a
pitiful sight! I had a small telescope tied to a cord inside
my parka for which I traded some fox skins a few years
before. That's all I had. I watched my nephew drift toward
Itiliardjuk, where the currents are treacherous. There was
a sickness in my heart as he disappeared. What a terrible
thing it is to lose someone who is in your care.*

*I figured that there would be other hunters between
where I was and Itiliardjuk, so I decided to go along the
coast in the direction which my nephew disappeared. Many
things were going on in my head. I didn't even notice a
small black thing moving on the ice way in the distance.
What was it? I looked at it with my telescope and still
couldn't see what it was, but it was moving. I walked
in the direction of a high hill further down the coast.
The tide had changed and so had the direction of the
wind. Still I had seen no hunters and knew that I couldn't
keep walking down the coast forever. I climbed to the top
of the hill and through the telescope watched my dear
nephew waving his hands. What a joyful sight! The tide
had returned him to me.*

Taima (I have finished speaking to you).

TEA TIME ON AN ICE FLOE

Itulu Itidlouie and I had been seal hunting for many hours. The weather was good and there was a fair amount of ice all around us, carried in from the Hudson Strait. But I was getting cold, and my enthusiasm for spotting seals was fading in proportion to my discomfort. I desperately wanted to get out of the wind and out of the canoe to stretch my legs and have something to eat.

I became more sullen as we sailed further and further away from land, bumping and grinding among huge pieces of floating ice. I could see three icebergs in the distance and more ice appeared to be drifting toward us. The entire scene had a kind of menacing beauty, and I said to Itulu, "Isn't it dangerous to be so far from land drifting among the ice floes?"

I had distracted him. He put down his rifle, snorted, and said, "Tea time!"

He ran the canoe toward a very large piece of ice, where we landed with a bone- jarring bump. On this little floating island of frozen water, I was about to learn properties of ice I had never known.

Our ice island was at least four years old. *Aujak* (summer) had freed it to move about, propelled by wind and tide. After we landed, Itulu found a sheltered place and set up the battered Coleman stove as I brought up the grub box to use as a table. He took the tea kettle and, after carefully examining various places, began to fill it with ice he had chipped away with his knife. I learned that water collected this way is potable. Setting the kettle back on the stove, he took off again and returned with a two-metre- long stem from a kelp plant as thick as my wrist, which he dangled suggestively between his legs, causing us both to laugh until tears rolled down our cheeks.

So there we were, enjoying tea time as we sat suspended between the sea and the sky on a sheet of drifting ice. We used that ice to make water for our tea. We sat on it in comfort, sheltered from the wind behind a ridge, and chewed on a nutritious piece of kelp that had been tossed here during a storm.

"You know," he said, "ice can be a great friend when you are out at sea. It can be dangerous if you are careless, and it can be dangerous if you are without it."

I was puzzled by the danger of being without ice until he explained further. "In the old days when one travelled by kayak and *umiak*, the great killer at sea was the wind. Everyone feared the storm wind at sea. Everyone who hunted at sea knew its dangers. My father told me that whenever they set out on long sea trips, it was important to have the presence of ice nearby. Should a great storm arise unexpectedly, there was safety on the ice. As you can see, it's like being on an island. Its presence is reassuring."

Year after year, a huge field of ice shrinks and expands, depending on the season. It is in constant motion, moved about by the forces of tide and wind. Between the moving icefield and the shore lies the landfast ice, which in some places can stretch several kilometres out to sea. This landfast ice is like a great white shelf about two and a half metres thick and stretching along the entire coast. In a sense, it's a temporary and reoccurring coastal highway, often providing the shortest, easiest, and safest route between distant places. The falling tide causes the ice to shear along the shore, in some places revealing gleaming white cliffs that appear and disappear with the rise and fall of the tide. Travelling from the shore toward the sea, you eventually arrive at the outer edge of the landfast ice, known as the "floe edge." From that edge, hunters went out to sea in pursuit of walrus, whales, and seals.

Ice was the transcendental part of the world that lay between the land and the open sea and between different hunting techniques. In traditional times, hunting on the tundra and hunting at sea or at the floe edge also required different spiritual observances and precautions. In traditional times, the flesh of land animals was never brought onto the ice for fear of offending *Aglulik*, the guardian spirit of seal holes. I was told that this *tiriguhunginiq*, this observing of an ancient tradition, was once practiced throughout the Arctic. It was believed that one of more than forty spirits delivered the seal to respectful humans. In return, as a sign of respect, the hunter or his wife would melt some ice in his or her mouth and give it to the dead seal who had thirsted for fresh water.

Abandoned Hudson's Bay Post at Amadjuak (Qarmaarjuak), near Kimmirut, south Baffin.

THE PEOPLE WITH
THE POINTED SHOES

Until the very end of his life, Simeonie Quppapik possessed a remarkable memory. He could still sing the songs he had learned many years before when he lived in skin tents and snow houses while growing up at Qarmaarjuak (Amadjuak), the land of the ancient sod houses. His *inuuviga*, his birthplace, remained like an island at the centre of his heart.

During one of my last visits with him, Simeonie described the time his family, with nine others, travelled to Qarmaarjuak from their camps along the coast to trade skins with the *qallunaat*, white men:

> The qallunaat *had come great distances bringing tea, needles, and all kinds of wonderful things to trade for meat, skins, and information about stones they said had great value. We called these people* ujaranniaqtiit *(those who look for stones). Time passed, we were happy to have them in our midst, and then one day a great umiak arrived and it was time to say goodbye to those who leave and to say "I must go" to those who stay. I remember very clearly the last treat. It was a little, tastes-so-good thing called "cake," upon which danced a little blue fire.* (Simeonie was referring to fruitcake that had rum poured over the top and was then lit.)
>
> We never knew if the stones which could bring much wealth were ever found, and then some years later another great umiak arrived with an unbelievable cargo called "reindeer"! We were told that they were not the same as a tuktu, a caribou, and they came from far away. A boat

full of reindeer, imagine that! There were not only reindeer, there were some people we had never heard of. They were something like us but not quite. We knew they were different from the qallunaat *by the way they could relate to the animals, and they seemed at home in our place. We called them the* nubukqulait *(people with the pointed shoes).*

Simeonie was referring to the Sami herders from the Sápmi region of northern Europe. The Hudson's Bay Company had had the idea that reindeer could survive in southwest Baffin and be developed into large herds, which would be a renewable food supply close to the Hudson's Bay trading post. In 1921, more than six hundred reindeer with twenty Sami herders and their wives, children, and dogs arrived at Qarmaarjuak aboard the Hudson's Bay Company supply ship *Nascopie*. The experiment was a failure, and most of the Sami returned to their homeland within the year.

Simeonie talked at length and in detail about the people with the pointed shoes. He dug out some drawings he had made, along with notes for a short story about the time when they had all lived together, when the reindeer could be "taught to pull sleds and be ridden, if you could imagine that!"

Yet who could imagine that, a few years later, I would be in Jokimukka, Lapland, presenting a copy of Simeonie's manuscript to a member of the Samic Museum. He accepted this unadorned small gift with respect and solemnity. Sadly, the book was never finished, but it preserved in memory that many years ago, some men had come from far across the sea wearing pointed shoes and had taken a herd of reindeer to Qarmaarjuak.

TWO TATTOOS

In your imagination, come with me on a journey I took several years ago to Qaqqaq Ashoona's camp. Our travelling companion is Charles Gimpel, an interesting fellow and a highly respected art dealer from Paris. He's joining us because he is fascinated with Qaqqaq's carvings, which are in great demand in some of the most prestigious galleries in Europe. Despite his genuine enthusiasm about being here, he seems out of place here. I shudder each time he takes out his grimy handkerchief and grinds it into the lens of his Leica to remove bits of snow and any other debris picked up along the trail.

Travelling on sleds, our journey takes us east along the coast in the hopes of reaching Qaqqaq's camp before complete darkness overtakes us. The landscape is shrouded in semi-darkness and looks forbidding. There are no shadows. We see only grey on grey. Distant hills look like jagged pieces of old paper stuck one upon the other. No depth perception exists. We move through this great, silent void. The cold comes upon us, starting at our fingers and then moving to our feet. We jump off the sled and run alongside to warm up, careful not to perspire, then jump on the sled again.

Time seems to have slowed down. In the gloom, each hill looks like the other. With darkness approaching, we see far in the distance the faint profile of Itiliardjuk. The sight lifts our spirits, for Qaqqaq's camp is now within easy reach. At that moment, my sled hits a sharp ridge of ice and I'm thrown off, landing on my shoulder with such force that I'm disoriented. I see the sleds disappearing into the oncoming darkness. How long will it be before the others know I have been left behind? How long can I bear the cold? I can barely make out their sled tracks, but I try to follow them nonetheless, forcing each step along the way.

I pray that no wind will rise to obliterate this faint pathway. *Keep moving, keep moving. They'll come back looking for you. Don't think of what is happening, forget the cold, think of Janet my college sweetheart, think of Christmas, think of anything except the present, just keep moving.* They do come back and pick me up. They think this is the funniest thing to have happened since the time that other qallunaq, Max Whatshisname, fell out the side door of an airplane, which fortunately was on the tarmac.

We arrive at Qaqqaq's camp just before darkness. Qaqqaq has also just returned to his camp, his sled laden with blocks of ice chipped from the frozen freshwater lake about a kilometre to the north. We shake the snow from our parkas and kick it off from our boots and follow him into the cabin, a little bit larger than my garage back home. Though Qaqqaq offers no greeting, at least the women are pleased to see us. His wife, Majuriaq, brings us mugs of tea and chunks of bannock, which we devour with great relish. It's amazing how some fried flour, salt, water, and a gob of lard can taste so good when the belly is empty.

The inside of the cabin is simple: some shelves, benches made from scraps of wood, a small table, a bed and a mattress on the floor, an oil stove, a Coleman stove, and, of course, a *kudlik*, the traditional blubber lamp. Above our heads, on lines, hang three frozen white foxes, casting their eerie shadows upon the walls. When the foxes have thawed, Majuriaq will carefully skin them and take them to the Hudson's Bay Company in Cape Dorset. They will be sold to buy the scant necessities required at the camp.

Despite Paul's smiles, friendly gestures, and modest gift of biscuits, sweets, and tea, Qaqqaq seems distant toward him. As we begin to feel the wonderful warmth, we remove the second layer of our clothing and roll up our sleeves. Qaqqaq notices marks on Paul's arm.

"What is the meaning of that *uluaruti*?" he asks. The *uluaruti*, or *tunniq*, as it is known in Cape Dorset, is a small tattoo that some elders had on their arms or fingers. It might have signified a bond with another person, penance, or perhaps an event that had changed one's life. But what was the meaning of the marks on Paul's arm?

There are no words, expressions, or even concepts in Qaqqaq's language to describe a concentration camp, Jews, Gypsies, or genocide. There is no word for millions, to tell him how many people were killed by other people. All we can explain is that Paul bears the marks of a very great suffering, when many of his people were killed. This Qaqqaq could understand, and clearly he is affected by this story as he puts his arm upon Paul's shoulder. Paul is to be given the name "Udjuk," meaning a bearded seal, so named for his bristly whiskers.

Many years later, I visited Qaqqaq at his camp. The cabin was almost completely buried in snow. I had to enter by a passageway chopped through a snowbank. Everything was as I had remembered it. We drank tea, and ate boiled caribou and chunks of bannock slathered with strawberry jam. Qaqqaq mentioned the names of several people who had visited him; he seemed to be reminiscing as if they were in the room with us. He then asked unexpectedly, "Is Udjuk still alive?"

"No," I answered. "Udjuk died quietly far, far away from here."

I left Qaqqaq, never to see him again. He died the following year.

In the shadows, under the stones.

DARK SHADOWS

I walked with Akula (not her real name) down the road chatting about the days when many of the elders were still alive. On this grey afternoon, I expressed a sense of melancholy. I felt that the days of discovery, insights, childlike wonder, and forging of new friendships were swiftly coming to an end. I felt a great longing for my dear and departed friends who had given me so much. Even the smouldering sunsets at Mallik now seemed to evoke a sense of yesterday rather than a promise of tomorrow.

Rather than commiserate, Akula rebuked me. She began by reminding me that I had never written down the things told to me about the dark side of life. I replied that I had not done so to avoid offending the very people whose trust I had earned over many years. "I'm a *qallunaq*," I said, plaintively. "Who the hell am I to write about such things, and why should I?"

Akula answered simply, "For us. There are those of us who have been abused in every way. When we became teenagers, we got into booze, drugs, and other terrible things. Some committed suicide. Others began to abuse their own kids, just as they were abused. Yet we were always told that life in the camps was good. We were told that people were happy and kind to one another and that we became the lost generation. Well, many of us don't believe that everyone had a life that was perfect in traditional times. Why don't you ask some elders if there was abuse in some of the camps?"

I was very reluctant to pursue the subject. I recalled a statement by a colleague, Nelson Graburn from University of California, Berkeley: "Ironically, when I was writing and later delivered a paper on Inuit child abuse observed during my field research in 1959–68, I was condemned publicly by my non-Inuit colleagues for broadcasting negative aspects of Inuit behaviour when 'they and their public image have suffered enough already'. Yet I was thanked by a number of Inuit for looking into an aspect of their more traditional child-rearing that they thought might throw some light on chronic outbreaks of abuse that had later occurred."

Akula persisted, and in my heart, I knew she was right. It occurred to me that at times, a bit of cowardliness is the source of political correctness. With Akula's help and encouragement, I sought guidance from Inaktak (not his real name), as to whether or not the subject should be looked into and, if so, how to go about gathering the information. It was decided that I would begin with Inaktak.

(I am using pseudonyms for Akula and Inaktak to avoid future misgivings they might have for talking to me about abuse. My friend Kananginak once said, "To openly talk about hurtful things may at first relieve a burden of the one who suffered them, but later, such talk may spread the hurt to others and so people kept quiet.") The following is Inaktak's choice of words and expressions.

There were times when some of us suffered. Sometimes wives were beaten, but eventually the man was forgiven. There was no such thing as separation in traditional times. Yet, there were instances when a poor woman who was abused constantly would flee to another camp only to be brought back by her husband. When we were growing up, we experienced both love and terrible fear. If I did something wrong, I was told of a fearful thing that could overtake me. There were worse times. There were times when cold words were hurled at me. They were terrifying to any child. Words such as, "We will leave you behind; the people in this camp can do with you as they wish." It makes me tearful to think of such expressions. It was a terrible threat to be cut away from your family.

There were eliaqjugijait *(orphans) who were often abused. There were kids known as* iiqsaniku; *they were not orphans but unfortunate children of the same family who were abused. Such children were easy to recognize. Their clothes were tattered; they were dirty and smelly. They would have hidden bite marks, bruises, cuts, and welts. They often had big bellies. If ever they found food, they'd gorge themselves. They were pitiful. Families who saw others abusing kids did not interfere, mainly because it would only bring more abuse upon the poor child.*

Though our elders often spoke of the old days with fond memories, life was hard. Sometimes food was very scarce. Tensions were always close by. Anger and finally harm might be done to another person. Violence and abuse went around in a circle. Abused children later in life would often become the abusers. Sometimes they sought revenge on their own families. The word for physical abuse is sukuziaq, *verbal abuse is* suagujuq, *and sexual abuse is* akunniluktuk. *There is another word you should write in your book; the word is* pigulangmigavinai, *meaning hope. I remember the times my older brothers saw only my lack of competence, my disabilities. I hoped to be as good as them, and so I went out for a long time with three of my close friends who taught me the necessities of life. I grew up, became stronger, and a good hunter; as my brothers grew older and weaker, they came upon their own disabilities. Now I share my food with them.*

The discussion concerning abuse in some camps during traditional times ran much deeper than this. In addition to Inaktak, I spoke to others, including a middle-aged woman who, in a quiet voice, provided a horrifying account of her life in a residential school in the Western Arctic. The emergence of healing circles in various communities is an important step toward repairing the lives of the abused and the abusers. Despite the comment that in the past one family did not interfere with abuse in another, there are echoes of what we might term "healing circles." There were times when things weighed heavily on a person, said Inaktak. If the burden got too heavy, the only way to get rid of it was to publicly repent.

Inaktak added: *Evil things of today are the same evil things of the past. The way we got rid of them was to repent in front of the whole camp. It was often an annual event. Less serious matters such as stealing or cheating were dealt with in this manner. The thief or cheater would step forth into the middle of the circle and say out loud, "Whoever stole something, step forward!" Of course, anyone who was bothered would do so. There might be several people, young and old, in the circle. Someone might have stolen a knife, another person a couple of fish from a neighbour's cache, another who "found" a piece of valuable equipment, and so forth. Everyone in the circle would start repenting, trying to outdo one another, and soon the whole scene became a great amusement for the onlookers. "Everyone knows the nature of my trouble and now I have been relieved of my burden" was the expressed feeling of the confessor.*

If the situation was that certain families were growing hostile toward one another, the camp might decide to attiqtut, *to split up. A family that found itself continuously picked on would often separate from a camp. A family certain that living in another place would be much better may also decide to split from a camp. The decision taken by a family to separate on its own is called* qimatigtuq.

If the tension that arose in a camp was very serious, there would be a meeting of the whole camp. The decision makers would try to reason with the offender or offenders. Physical conflict was to be avoided whenever possible. In cases of a killing, revenge was to be avoided because revenge had no end. Yes, there was violence among certain people in certain camps. A violent person might be driven out from a camp and, in rare cases, killed. Sometimes a violent person may flee from a camp and try to survive on his own, living in constant fear. Sometimes the people in the camp would take pity on him and try to lure him back. Forgiveness was natural to us; such was life on the land.

Hanging around the camps was for old people and those who were too sick, crippled, or too lazy to hunt. Sometimes tensions would arise in a camp. They may be caused by tigutujuq, *people who steal things. In some camps there was an* angakok *(shaman). If there was a bad situation in such a camp, one would fear the person who was creating the badness because they could see him or her doing it. But because you never knew what the angakok was up to, there could be additional fear there too. Because the most competent people were away, the tensions could grow into serious situations, even murder. It was very important to deal with all tensions and conflicts that arose in a camp.*

One of the most dangerous things to occur in a camp was minaraniqluktii, *the spreading of malicious gossip. It was like poison. It was evil gossip and jealousy that started much killing at Iluvirqtuq.*

Inatak was referring to the same battle between two camps that Kananginak spoke of previously. On a visit in 1997, I observed the bleached bones of the dead that lay scattered about the small island.

The omen.

THREAT AND RECONCILIATION

On a beautiful July morning, two young ornithologists were preparing to set out to locate gyrfalcons reported to be nesting about a day's trip by boat east of Cape Dorset. They asked if I would come along, as they were new to the area and spoke no Inuktitut. I enthusiastically agreed. Their guide, Quvianaqtuliak (Kov) Parr, was a competent hunter and a person of considerable stature in the community.

Early in the morning the day before our departure, I went down to the beach, threw my gear into Kov's canoe, and stepped in. Kov was tending his motor and then turned toward me. His expression grew dark. He said in a guttural tone reserved for subjugating dogs, "Who gave you permission to get into my canoe? Get out, *qallunaq*!" There was a steely anger in those few words hurled at me and contempt on Kov's face. Startled and confused, I grabbed my gear and got out of his boat.

Kov's nephew Nuna said in a low voice, "The old man is pissed off. You should have asked his permission to get into the canoe." I told Nuna to tell his uncle to go to hell and began to walk back up the beach, muttering obscenities to myself. "Come back," Nuna shouted. For a moment, I wondered if I had further offended Kov by departing without his permission, but I yielded and returned to the canoe. Nuna said that Kov would allow me to accompany the other *qallunaat* as long I apologized in their presence. Fortunately, the ornithologists did not understand what was going on.

This was just the beginning of a journey I would never forget — an experience that had layer upon layer of meaning. I would learn the meaning of hostility, verbal abuse, racism, and, eventually, respect.

Our first landing was near Itiliardjuk on the way to Kangiqsuqjuaq. This was Xangajuq Shaa's outpost camp. The tide was out, forcing us to walk about 180 metres across gooey mud flats. Nuna and Kov wore hip waders, the two ornithologists rubber boots, and I a new pair of ankle-high hiking boots. I was puzzled as to why Kov had not landed a little further down the coast, where we could have avoided the clinging mud. Several people I knew were at the camp, and as I was about to make the round of shaking hands, Kov snarled "Go away, you're not welcome!"

No one looked at me. I shouted, "No goddammit!" No one said a word.

Kov turned away and began talking with the others as if nothing had occurred, as if no one other than they were there. I did not exist.

The following day we headed to Kangisurituq (Andrew Gordon Bay) and into a storm. My well-worn rain gear did little to protect me from the numbing cold spray. I sought the little bit of shelter at the bow of the canoe, remembering the frightening effect of having suffered hypothermia a few years ago in such a storm. After some time, Nuna stuck his head into the cubbyhole at the bow and shouted, "Kov says show your face! C'mon, show you face!"

I peered out and saw Kov leering at me from the stern of the canoe. He was drenched to the skin. He shouted above the wind, "Me, the cold doesn't hurt me. Look at you... you hide from the cold like an old woman. You are nothing but a weak *qal-lunaq*. Me, I am Inuk! You are useless. I should throw you away!" Fortunately, Nuna did not translate Kov's tirade for fear that the two ornithologists would have been alarmed at the turn of events. Kov continued to mutter threats, and Nuna decided to steer clear of his onslaught of insults.

The next day, the storm had subsided, and we landed far up in Andrew Gordon Bay. As usual, we landed on an extensive mud flat. Nuna and I struggled across the sea of mud, carrying all the equipment on our backs to where we would set up camp. The next day, the ornithologists set out to find the gyrfalcons while I stayed in camp to clean up the gear and do other chores. I had a feeling that sometime during the previous evening, Nuna and Kov had had a discussion about *piungilak uivepok*, "the useless one."

Later the following day, to my surprise, Kov asked Nuna to tell me to come down to the beach and eat some caribou with them. There we were, chewing on chunks of boiled caribou in total silence when Kov looked at my mud-caked boots, shook his head, and smiled. For some reason, this condescending attitude bothered me more than all the threats and insults. I said to Kov, "I'm not the one who is stupid, you are. I was going to give you these new boots after our trip as a gift, and you have done everything to ruin them. You say I'm useless. You have insulted me in front of others. You can't even remember my name. I will give these boots to someone in Cape Dorset who deserves them." I got up, threw my remaining piece of caribou into the pot, and walked back to my tent.

Kov and Nuna said nothing. For the next few days and during the journey back to Cape Dorset, Kov made no threats and no sarcastic comments. Because of high head winds, we arrived in Cape Dorset late in the day. The tide was out, exposing the extensive mud flat in front of the community. I was about to jump out of the boat when Kov shouted, *"Ahgaa!"* No! He came up to me and commanded that I get on his back. I was embarrassed. *"Ati, ati"* he growled. "Move it!" I did as I was told and climbed on. He then proceeded to carry me to the beach. For some reason that I cannot explain, I found myself gently waving to the puzzled people watching us from the shore.

I held on to the boots until the day of my departure for the South. Kov was at the airport, probably waiting for the arrival of a relative. I walked over to him and, without exchanging any words, gave him the boots.

Each time I returned to Cape Dorset, I would visit Kov and his family. We drank tea, ate fresh bannock, and exchanged news about our respective families. I often performed a little magic trick for the kids, who would squeal with delight or step backward a little frightened by the fake spider that had jumped out of my pocket. It seemed that our small talk was never too small. The one subject we never talked about was that horrible journey to Kangiqsuqjuaq.

On a visit some years later, I was shocked to see Kov using a walker, trying to make his way to his canoe down at the beach. He had had a stroke. As we stood at the beach looking toward Mallik Island, he said, "Those boots you gave me were warm, and every time I wore them I was lucky. I always managed to get a seal or caribou." He paused for a moment, then looked at me and said quietly, "I can't wear them any more."

Despite his crippling affliction, Kov would not give up going out on the land. He often made his way to the beach and worked on his canoe or mended some broken item. Then one summer when I went to his house, his wife, Ikkuma, with tears in her eyes, told me that "Quvianaqtuliak is dead." The words shocked me so that, for a moment, I could not believe what I had heard. I was to learn that in the spring, before my arrival in Cape Dorset, Kov had managed to get himself onto his snowmobile and had headed out on the sea ice to the floe edge. He had travelled the same route he and others had taken for generations. Having reached the floe edge he would have been taken aboard one of the canoes and joined his friends in the spring seal hunt. But he never made it to the floe edge. He had broken through the ice and drowned. I was told that hunters returning from the hunt had found him frozen still clinging to the broken edge of ice.

THE LAST TRADITIONAL INUIT TRIAL IN SIKUSIILAQ

In the early spring of 1990, I was in Cape Dorset attempting to reach Inuksugalait, the highly revered place of many inuksuit. All my previous attempts to reach this site had been thwarted because of heavy seas, bad weather, and other forms of disappointment. A succession of violent spring storms also thwarted what I thought would be my final attempt.

During one of those spring storms, two children vanished from the community. Upon returning from a second day of searching, Niviaqsiaq, who had been at my side pretending to look for the missing children, was handcuffed and flown out of the community. I was told that the bodies of two children who had been strangled had been found stuffed into a hockey bag in Niviaqsiaq's house. The bags, too, were hastily removed from the community for autopsies to be performed on the bodies. The only thing left was an all pervasive sense of grief and helplessness. "In the old days" an elder said, "we would have dealt with such a killing in a way that it would never be forgotten."

At the time, I wasn't sure what he meant. I had no idea that later I would be shown where trials once had been conducted and that I would learn about the last traditional trial to be held in southwest Baffin Island. The idea of a "trial," in fact, contradicted the prevailing notion that Inuit had no formal system of exercising justice in traditional times. *The American Heritage Book of Indians* claimed, "There were no tribal governments, no real village governments and consequently no war and no law other than the observance of custom and taboo. A murderer was punished by the victim's relatives, if they felt up to it." This point of view is consistent with other writings.

Pitaloosie Saila's drawing from memory of Akitsiraqvik.

Just before returning to the South, I had tea and bannock with Pauta and Pitaloosie Saila. Pauta Saila commanded a strong presence. He stood tall, looked you straight in the eye, and assumed the dominant position. A master carver whose works are in major collections throughout the world, Pauta believed he was born in 1916 near Nurrata. Now deserted, it was one of the oldest permanent camps on southwest Baffin Island. His father, Saila, was a powerful camp boss. It was said Saila could kill a walrus with a single thrust of a harpoon. While Pauta might not have inherited his father's powers, he did possess a passionate reverence for the land. In the evening, when we were all in the tent, he would often sit by the entrance with hands folded and a faint smile on his face. Then, unexpectedly, he would softly sing to himself some ancient song.

Sensing my disappointment at being unable to travel to Inuksugalait, Pauta hinted that if I returned the next summer, he might take me there. After thinking for a moment, he added, "And maybe I will be able to show you something even more important."

272　　　　　　　　AN INTIMATE WILDERNESS

Slowly and carefully, he went on to describe a place where, "there is a stone structure unlike any other, a place of great power and significance."

Seeing that I was fascinated by this revelation, Pauta's wife, Pitaloosie, made a detailed drawing of the site for me. Her skilled hand revealed a great circle of upright stones unlike anything I had seen in the Arctic. Knowing the importance of names to the Inuit, I asked, "What is the circle called?" Pauta had to search far back in his memory but was able to recall the name that he had learned from his mother. "It is called Akitsiraqvik."

Pauta spoke about the place and what had happened there, and I was careful not to interrupt or to introduce notions of my own. He described the place as "a kind of Parliament where judges — powerful men like high priests — sat in judgment of the most serious matters."

The next summer, I returned to Cape Dorset and, true to his word, Pauta, along with Pitaloosie and other members of his family, took me first to the legendary Inuksugalait and then on to Akitsiraqvik.

On a bright and windy day, all nine of us piled into an open twenty-two-foot freighter canoe powered by a ninety-horse-power motor and headed out to sea. By twilight, we had reached Inuksugalait. That evening, I walked quietly among ancient stone figures silhouetted against a deepening sky. Far in the distance, an iceberg drifted into the path of the sun's last rays and for a moment became incandescent. The next day we took down our camp, loaded the canoe, and once more headed out to sea. It was a sullen day with fitful winds and a biting cold. We had to stay well out to sea because of the countless jagged shoals that could tear any ship apart, let alone our wisp of a canoe. As the wind grew stronger, frightening moments ensued when the mounting waves might have ended our journey. We pressed on not because we had a sense of daring but because we had no choice.

When we entered the stretch of water known as Surbiluit, I became unabashedly afraid. About two hundred metres off our portside, huge white-capped waves rose straight up from the sea. An equally frightening roar could now be heard above the wind.

Pauta skillfully guided the canoe until the wind made any head-way impossible and dangerous. Sensing the critical moment, he turned the canoe around, and we made a dash for a tiny cove where he had found shelter many years before. That night we all fell into a deep sleep. On the third day, the sky brightened, the wind and tide were still strong and favourable, and once more we struck out to sea.

We travelled for several hours along the coast, ever watchful for shoals lurking just below the surface. We were now in walrus hunting territory. The sea was dotted with islands upon which roosted countless gulls that took to the air upon our approach. The motion of the canoe , the hours at sea, and the endless panorama of a distant shore set me adrift on a daydream. Then it all came to an end.

"Taika!" yelled Pitaloosie. Look, over there! We were heading straight for shore. I saw nothing unusual. "Over there!" she gestured. I saw what appeared to be a jumble of rocks in the distance and was overcome by a deep sense of disappointment. We had travelled so far on rough seas in threatening weather — was this all there was? I felt reluctant to go further, believing that my disappointment would be confirmed. We unloaded the canoe and, with a sense of reluctance, I climbed up the rock strewn slope toward the small plateau.

The very moment I stepped upon it, I was astonished. What had looked from a distance, at sea level, like a pile of rocks was in fact a great circle of upright stones. My companions set up camp; Pauta's young son Davidee and a helper went caribou hunting; and the kids were told to leave me alone.

I walked slowly about the great circle, looking quietly and carefully at each immense stone. As shadows gave way to encroaching darkness, I reluctantly returned to our tent and was greeted by the delicious aroma of caribou stew. Pauta stopped singing a song, looked up at me, and asked with a faint smile, "Are you happy?" I simply couldn't find the words to express how unbearably happy I was. The next day I set out with all my equipment to photograph and measure the great circle, and to make notes on its details. I needed to work very quickly, for Pauta and his family were anxious to get back to Cape Dorset.

Having returned to the site, I took in as many of the details as possible. I stood on a vast, flat sheet of rock about the size of a playing field. At its centre lay a circle constructed of huge, thick granite slabs standing on their ends. The naturally formed slabs range from half to one metres high, were half a metre thick, and weighed up to one tonne each. Seventeen in all, they formed a near-perfect circle 6.7 metres in diameter.

At one end of the circle stood a single, massive, upright stone 177 centimetres tall, about the height of an average person. Directly opposite stood an even greater stone reaching more than two metres high. Within the circle were stone slabs forming a seating arrangement. At the base of the tallest stone was a seat suggesting the place where the most important person had sat during meetings and sessions held here in ancient times. The reddish granite had a patina of black lichen that gave the great circle a sombre appearance. On the periphery of the circle were naturally formed ledges creating a large, semicircular seating arrangement — an amphitheatre.

I stood there awed not only by what I saw but also by the thought that sometime in the distant past, someone as mortal as I had caused this great structure to rise from a field of broken rock.

I looked up and saw Pauta, Pitaloosie, and all the kids heading toward me. Pauta came into the circle and purposefully placed himself where the most powerful person once had sat. Pitaloosie joined us to convey what Pauta wished to tell me. Pauta carefully looked about as if absorbing something still lingering there. Finally he turned to me and, choosing each word with great care, he began to speak. This had been an ancient place for as long as anyone could remember, he began. People came from all along the coast to this place, but they never lived here. From the earliest times, this was where people had held celebrations, where games of strength and skill were played. On special occasions camp bosses would meet to deal with matters of great importance affecting all who lived in Sikusiilaq (the Inuit name for the Foxe Peninsula).

Pauta paused, as if taking a moment to decide whether or not to go on. Then, moving his arm in a circle to describe where we sat, he went on to explain that this was also the place of their

"Parliament, where judges who were powerful men, like high priests, sat in judgment of the most serious matters." Pitaloosie carefully chose the words to explain exactly what Pauta was saying. Right before me was a contradiction of the widely held belief that all Inuit had no traditional system of justice. The depth of revelation awaited me still.

Late that evening, I returned to the great circle alone, approaching it from the landward side. I beheld it silhouetted against the darkening sea, enchanted by what I saw. The perception of a circle was no more, its image now the likeness of a ship sailing northward. I sat alone among the stones and listened to the northwest wind. The image of Pauta sitting at the head of the circle came to mind, as did an illustration from a reference book. It depicted a great stone circle much like the one before me. It too was a Parliament where justice had been rendered, and sitting at the head of the circle on a stone bench was the "chief justice." Surrounding him were other powerful men — Vikings who had sailed the Arctic seas.

The distant sound of children's voices suddenly broke my reverie. Pitaloosie had sent the kids from the camp to be with me on our last evening at Akitsiraqvik. They approached laughing and clasped my hands. We formed a line and danced joyfully round and round the great circle. The next day we took down our camp, loaded the canoe, and, before leaving shore, said *nakomek* (thank you) to the land. Reluctantly, we headed for home.

Upon our return to Cape Dorset, I was told that Osuitok Ipeelie, my old mentor, wished to speak to me. So Osuitok, my dear friend Annie Manning, and I gathered together for a hearty meal and an evening's conversation. Osuitok knew I had gone for several days up the west coast with Pauta and his family. Looking me straight in the eye, he asked me what I had seen during our journey. I faced a troubling dilemma, for I had promised Pauta not to reveal that he had taken me to Akitsiraqvik. Pauta did not want an archaeologist to find its location and dig up the site.

On the other hand, Osuitok had been my mentor for more than forty years. Over time I had earned his trust, and so he divulged many things to me that he had never shared with any outsider. Would I sidestep his simple question? I decided to tell

Osuitok that I was caught between telling the truth to him and honouring my promise to Pauta. I admitted I had been taken to Akitsiraqvik. "I know," he said. "Now I have something else to tell you. It's about the old way of justice."

On a calm, clear day in August 1924, Osuitok began, a bullet had extinguished a hunter's life. He lay buried just behind the hill from where we sat. The fate of the victim's hunting companion — a hunter known as Lukta, (not to be confused with Qiatsuq's son whose name was also Lukta) had fired the fatal bullet. His fate was to be decided at Parketuk, about nine kilometres northeast of Cape Dorset.

At the time, at least fifty camps spread along the coast from Nuvudjuak, at the northern tip of the Baffin Peninsula, to Markham Bay, some 480 kilometres to the south. Some camps had as few as two families, while others had five or more. It was not unusual for camps to grow or shrink with the seasonal availability of food. Each camp had its boss, whose leadership was based on demonstrated ability. He was kept informed of everything going on in the camp and in the surrounding area. He had the final word about anything that really mattered, including the location and timing of hunting, the division of food, procedure for marriages, membership in or departure from the camp, and the nature of tasks and any punishments. Lines of authority and indications of respect were clear from the servants, or camp slaves, all the way up to the camp boss.

Certain camp bosses and shamans achieved a higher status than other leaders because they were acknowledged to be the best thinkers, speakers, and achievers in the region. They were the *tapananitiit*, the powerful ones who merited the highest respect. They could choose words with great skill and arrange them in amazing ways. Collectively, these men who formed a power elite exerted a great influence throughout southwest Baffin Island in traditional times. Though the *tapananitiit* lived in various camps throughout the region, they came together on certain occasions — when they needed to discuss thoughtfully and consider what action to take about such matters as murder, pestilence, impending starvation, and difficulties associated with the arrival of the *qallunaat*.

The Great Council, as they were regarded, met in various locations as required by events and prevailing conditions. One place, however, was favoured above all others as an enduring symbol of the Council's power: Akitsiraqvik. The name Akitsiraqvik, Osuitok explained, is so old that its exact meaning has been forgotten, but it suggests "to strike out, to render justice." Akitsiraqvik was a court where the Council sat, questioned the accused and witnesses, heard confessions, listened to pleas, resolved conflicts, and decided punishments. Unlike any court we know today, it was also a centre for celebrations, games, and feasts at various times of year.

In 1924, the Council gathered at Parketuk so as to be close to the place where the great *umiak* — the supply ship *Nascopie* — would arrive with tea, tobacco, needles, beads, pots, and all kinds of other useful things. The Council was also to render judgment on Lukta (not the Lukta I knew personally), who claimed that his shooting of his hunting companion, "O," had been an accident.

The unfortunate event might have been endured with quiet resignation except for two factors: First, the victim's family argued that their son had been murdered and great tension thus continued between them and the family of the accused. Second, both the victim's natural father and his acquired father (he had been adopted while a child) insisted that the accused be summoned to account before the Council. It happened that these two men were powerful members of the Council. Understandably, a general feeling prevailed that the accused would be found guilty and quickly put to death.

Some members of the Council had been taken to the place where the victim had fallen. They had examined the area where the accused had taken his position to shoot birds; they had considered the weather, the time of day, and the myriad of details familiar to hunters. Then they met to reach a decision.

Only the accused and his parents were permitted to appear before the Council. The accused gave his testimony and answered questions. Having been required to stand throughout the proceedings, he became very tired and lost his balance but recovered. Then, resigned to dying, he said, "If you decide to kill me, take me away from this place and shoot me where I will bleed to death slowly and if that punishment doesn't satisfy you, then take my child and do the same."

The Council remained silent for a long time. Then Osuitok's father and Pootoogook, a powerful camp boss, whispered back and forth. Finally Pootoogook exclaimed, "Whoever kills this man removes my will to live!"

His penetrating words struck at the thoughts of everyone on the Council, and they decided to spare Lukta. But there was a condition: Should the accused ever be involved in another person's death in any way, at any time, his own death would swiftly follow.

The decision prescribed a standard of conduct for Lukta to follow for the rest of his life. He would be vulnerable whether he was in the presence of friends or strangers, yet to live apart was inconceivable. His fate become known throughout southwest Baffin. To him it meant *inuugiaqarnirama*, or "My time to die is not yet come, my life is fated to continue." So Lukta's life continued without incident.

The timeless expression, *ajurnarmat*, or "it cannot be otherwise," had a particular meaning for Lukta. With the arrival of the great *umian* from the South came many desirable and wonderful things. Also with it came different beliefs and practices that altered the traditional way of life and erased, at least in this part of the Arctic, the Inuit way of dispensing justice.

I shared the site description with eminent Arctic archaeologists William Taylor Jr. and Charles Arnold, both of whom stated they had never seen such a structure as Akitsiraqvik, nor were they aware of any account of an Inuit system of justice. My friend Robert Jarvis, a lawyer in Toronto, suggested that I send a copy of my notes on "The Last Trial" to his colleague Professor Alan Grant of Osgoode Hall Law School. Professor Grant reviewed the material from an investigative and prosecutorial/defence perspective. Grant, who was formerly Chief Inspector, New Scotland Yard, had several interesting things to say. What follows is a brief account of his analysis of the trial.

The defendant did not appear to seek to address the main issue of whether the killing was intentional or accidental. In addressing the Council, the accused seemed to take for granted that fact that he would be convicted. Further, he eschewed making a speech in mitigation of punishment. Rather, he appeared to encourage an increase rather than a decrease in punishment meted out. Slow and painful death was being advocated over a swift and painless one. Thus the defendant, on the surface at least, turned his back on the classic advocate's approach of denying responsibility, and if that fails, seeking the least possible sanction.

However this accused must be taken to have known the culture from which he came and his lack of legal training served him well because he was nevertheless able to persuade the key member of the Council not to favour the death penalty. Obviously, the accused used the technique of persuasion most suited to his situation in that particular culture. That it would have won no prizes in a southern Canadian or American law school exercise in trial practice is dwarfed to insignificance by its success in Baffin Island where his life — rather than his formal legal skill — was literally on the line.

An aboriginal court thus acted upon a basis that would have been totally unpersuasive to a non-aboriginal tribunal. But if the outcome was "just" in that community, one can understand the increasing interest in Canadian aboriginal communities in having their own justice systems re-established.

When Grant reviewed the part dealing with the Council, who were in fact the judges, he noted:

It shows the Council as triers of fact familiarizing themselves with the scene, rather like a modern jury "taking a view," as it is called, when they go to the scene of some very important event in a case. This is very seldom done in criminal cases now, but is still possible.

The incredible megalithic structure at Akitsiraqvik.

In fact, in early English legal history, the jury was not picked from those with no knowledge of the case, but from those who had express knowledge of the case. Witnesses were then called to support the reputation for veracity of different members of the jury. It was only much later that a jury was chosen from those with no connection with the events to be tried.

On January 14, 1992, I was informed that the former Honourable Chief Justice Antonio Lamer of the Supreme Court of Canada had circulated a copy of the Last Trial paper to his colleagues and then had it deposited in the Supreme Court Library for future reference.

Why Pauta and Osuitok decided to reveal this place and such an important event to me is a mystery — and no less mysterious than the ancient tales of circles of power and things that resembled sea monsters once believed to have travelled in these Arctic waters.

Remains of Thule semi subterranean houses near Nurrata, southwest Baffin.

AN INTIMATE WILDERNESS

THE MYSTERIOUS TUNIIT

A short distance from Cape Dorset is Pudlat Inlet. The inlet is a favourite stopover for seals, beluga whales, and, occasionally, bowhead whales. Inland, caribou feed on an abundance of lichens while freshwater ponds attract flocks of geese. This entire area is indeed an *inigijuminaqtuq*, a favoured location. Evidence of early human habitation, usually small stone shelters, attests to hunters having been active here in the past as they are to this day. One particular place at Pudlat Inlet is a wonderful sight to behold. Its name is Igluakjuak, the Place of Big Houses. It is a site I visited many times, usually on the way up the coast toward Itiliardjuk. Here at Igluakjuak lies the evidence of a fascinating series of events that unfolded some eight thousand years ago.

In geological terms, the story began when the Laurentide ice sheet that once covered most of North America retreated to the High Arctic. With the great weight of ice gone, the entire south-west coast of Baffin Island began to rise and the land around Pudlat Inlet and the islands emerged. About five thousand years ago, colonies of plant life existed, land mammals fed on the tundra, and sea mammals thrived within a well-established food chain.

Around four thousand years ago, a small group of hunters arrived who were descendants of ancestors that had left Alayeksa (Alaska) on their great trek east. They found a land with a good supply of food and decided to stay. Near the coast they constructed a few small shelters ringed with stones and covered with skin roofs. These people are now known to scholars as Paleoeskimos. They not only survived in the eastern Arctic but also expanded their hunting range along the coast and inland and, by 600 BCE, we believe that they had developed what we now call the Dorset Culture, complete with an intricate belief system of a world inhabited by spirits.

Tent ring in a 4,000 year old paleoeskimo site near Mingo Lake, southwest Baffin.

Then, around 1200 CE, a group of hunters arrived at Pudlat Inlet. They had dogs, sleds, large skin boats, and, most important, the equipment and techniques to hunt large sea creatures, including walrus, beluga, and bowhead whales. (Dorset people had been hunting walrus and beluga for centuries before the Thule.) Although having arrived in the Canadian Arctic at the end of a warm period, they had the ability to adapt to their environment as it changed to a cold period during the 15-18th centuries, known as the Little Ice Age. In many cases, they simply took over the site of those who had come before them, likely killing individuals who resisted but keeping a few young women as camp slaves. They set to work building semi-subterranean dwellings of large stones with roof rafters of whale ribs covered by skins and sod. These were to become their permanent winter dwellings. In the process of construction, they tossed aside the artifacts of the original inhabitants and, like practically all other cultures, built upon the remains of those who had come before them. Here on the sandy slope of Pudlat Inlet, the people we call the Thule

AN INTIMATE WILDERNESS

created a small permanent village called Igluakjuak, the Place of the Big Houses. The Inuit we know today are their direct descendants, and they call their ancestors the Tuniit.

When visiting Igluakjuak, you land on a shore covered with well-worn shattered rock and smoothed outcrops of granite and then climb a steep hill of sand covered with an overburden of various plant life. Astonishingly, the beach rises to about fifteen metres above sea level, indicating extreme uplift and tilt.

Near the top of the hill, you come upon a curious site, a patch of exposed sand no larger than a dining room table. On this little patch are scattered thousands of small bird bones, many broken, suggesting that the marrow has been sucked out. You look closer and discover tiny flakes of grey-brown chert scattered among the bones. Still examining the site, you are drawn to points of light emanating from the debris; the sunlight reflects off the flakes of quartz crystals. Eventually you are rewarded with the sight of a minuscule arrowhead no larger than your fingernail.

When I visited the site with Itulu Itidlouie, he seemed amused by my avid interest, since he had seen many such sites in his travels. "Tuniit," he said. I counted seventeen partially buried houses in the area, averaging about five metres in diameter with sunken rock walls about one metre in height. Inside were the remains of whale ribs that once held up the sod roofs. Itulu explained that these were the winter houses of the Tuniit.

Almost unnoticed, tucked away in the lee of a hill, was another dwelling smaller and more oval than the larger dwellings we had seen. Growth virtually covered its walls. No whale bones were to be seen. Itulu also referred to this hint of a dwelling as a Tuniit house.

I was struck by the dizzying time travel that I'd experienced since climbing the slope from the shore to this place. The scattering of bird bones and small chert artifacts were remains of a Paleoeskimo site approximately 3,500 years old. Close by was a small dwelling dated from the Dorset Culture some two thousand years ago. We then encountered the larger Thule Culture dwellings, easily five hundred years old. Still evident were whale ribs that served as roof rafters and other small pieces of whale bone laid in some of the dwellings. All had a cold trap, the ingenious invention that required people entering the dwelling to use a short tunnel in which they first crawled downward and then upward into the house.

That's not all: One of the Thule Culture dwellings had a section of wall higher than the rest. At the base of the wall were several recently spent shotgun shells. Hunters from Kinngait still came to this site year after year to hunt geese. They had repurposed one of the Thule dwellings into a large and comfortable hunting blind from which they hunted geese that arrived at the rain ponds each spring and fall. Turning toward the slope facing the sea, we saw a strange sight attesting to sheer genius. The hunters had removed the wings of the geese they had killed and placed them on the slope. Each breeze would cause the wings to flutter as if alive, inviting geese that flew overhead to land. In a metaphorical sense, the fluttering of wings and the midden of tiny bird bones illustrated an almost 4,000 year span of time that we traversed in a mere 150 footsteps.

These range from Paleoeskimos 2500–600 BCE; Dorset 600 BCE–1300 CE; Thule 1200–1700 CE. Allowing for a hundred years of overlap between Dorset and Thule. We don't have much information about overlap between Pre-Dorset PE and Dorset because there is a culture/period know as "Intermediate, Independence II, or Groswater" depending on whether you are in Central Canadian Arctic, Greenland, or Labrador dating ca. 1000 BCE to 200 BCE. This is a period when Pre-Dorset subsistence continues with the gradual addition of Dorset types of technology and housing. All of this is not worth mentioning except to maybe coordinate the end dates of Pre-Dorset and beginning of Dorset at the same time, ca. 1000–600 BCE.

The Kinngnarmiut (the people of the Cape Dorset area) referred to the Paleoeskimos, the earliest inhabitants of the Arctic, as Tuniit and described them as Inuit *sivulliit tamaanigiagnaliqtillugit*, "the earliest humans." They regarded the Tuniit as a distinct people. These "earliest humans" probably arrived in the Foxe Peninsula area, a unique place, about 3,500 years ago. A combination of weather patterns, sea floor topography, ocean currents, and freshwater supplies offered greater biodiversity than could be found in most other northern locations. The prevailing conditions meant a year round renewable food supply accessible even in the dead of winter, allowing the Tuniit to stay. Over time, they developed and modified hunting techniques and specialized equipment, giving rise to a material culture perfectly adapted to their environment. Embedded in their hunting culture were magical motifs such as charms, fetishes, and shaman's paraphernalia, including masks, wolf-like ivory teeth, and amulets.

I struggled with how best to describe periods of time so that I could better place the events, stories, and oral histories in a general time frame familiar to the elders. Pia Pootoogook, my first interpreter, visited several elders and presented me with a time frame that would prove to be invaluable:

Before there were humans:
   Suli inutagalautinagu silaqjuaq
The time of the earliest humans:
   Inuit sivulliit tamaanigiagnaliqtillugit
The time of the Tuniit:
   Tuniqtaqaliqtillugu
The time of our earliest ancestors:
   Sivuliriagnavut tamaaniliqtillugit
The time when we lived on the land:
   Inulimaat nunaqaqatatillugit nunaliralagnulutik
The time when most Inuit moved into settlements:
   Ilunagalatik Inuit nuumata nuna

The use of the term *Tuniit* to identify the creators of virtually every ancient artifact and site intrigued me, and I was determined to record the Kinngnarmiut's beliefs about these mysterious people.

My first exposure to tales of the Tuniit began in 1960 atop a windy hill in Kinngait. I was visiting a fine old man by the name of Kingwatsiuk. His dear wife, Peoliaq, was no longer alive, and he was living alone in a tattered old tent on the prominent hill near the old Anglican Mission. I didn't have his favourite food — boiled seal head — to bring, instead offering a tin of ham, a brick of Red Rose Tea, and a two-dollar orange that came all the way from Florida. At the time, my understanding of Inuktitut was practically non-existent, yet we managed to struggle along with simple gestures, smiles, and nods of confirmation. At one point, Kingwatsiuk reached under his bed and drew out an old wooden box that reminded me of a seaman's chest. He opened it, took out a round black object, and snapped it on the edge of the bed. To my astonishment, it turned into a well-worn top hat. He then reached in and took out another, smaller object, wrapped in toilet paper, which turned out to be a medal from Aberdeen, Scotland. Kingwatsiuk rattled on while I politely added *"eee,"* meaning yes, hoping it was uttered at the right times. I finally said goodbye to that lovely old man.

That evening while visiting some friends, I told them of the magic show in Kingwatsiuk's tent. I would learn that it was a not magic show but rather a fascinating slice of life. Kingwatsiuk's age could be measured in the context of a major event of the period — the time of "the men who arrive in spring," the seafarers from Dundee who hunted whales from Sikusiilaq all the way to Salliq (Southampton Island) and far beyond. Kingwatsiuk was very knowledgeable about where Tuniit had once lived and, like his father, Atsiaq, was intimately familiar with vast stretches of the coast, its tides, shoals, and the places from which the Tuniit *arvaniaqtiit*, the Tuniit whale hunters, set out to sea. You can still see remains of their semi-subterranean dwellings and the whale skulls placed at the entrance of each in many spots along the Sikusiilaq coast.

Some time later, Mannumi Davidee would fill in the blanks:

Atsiak, who was Kingwatsiuk's father, is still remembered, though he died a long time ago. He was a respected hunter and a man who travelled great distances. He was respectful of strange places and very careful in everything he did. It is said by the old people that Atsiak's footsteps are everywhere. He was an Inuk who was driven by something that made him look for places where no other person has been. He could read the signs that told of a change about to happen in the weather. He could travel by the stars and understood the behaviour of living creatures. He was an Inummarik, *a real Inuk, and he was curious about new and different things.*

In the old days, qallunaat *came here to hunt the big whales. It was at that time that Atsiak, his son Kingwatsiuk, and Anigmiuk went on a whaling ship to Salliq. According to one elder, "The whalers were pretty good people, they were hunters like us and we learned new things from them." It was not unusual for an entire family to travel with them for the summer. It was at Salliq that they believed the people they saw were the Tuniit.*

"Yes, we saw Tuniit," said Kingwatsiuk to his hunting companions. "They were not Inuit like us. They were a different people. They didn't speak our language. They spoke a language which was like baby talk to us. We struggled to understand some of the things they said, but it was difficult. They were smelly people. They had long hair that was tied up into a big knot on the top of their head. They were very, very strong. You could see their strength by looking at the size of the stones that they moved to make their homes and their inuksuit."

I pursued my inquiry about the mysterious Tuniit with other elders, including Oshutsiak, Simeonie, Mannumi, Ikkuma, Sheojuk, and Osuitok. Curiously, they spoke about the Tuniit as if they had existed up to the time of the elders' immediate ancestors, whom they remembered. Osuitok recounted:

We could never move stones that big. Their clothing was different from ours; it was made in a different way. I have heard it said that long ago, the men had parkas that were long enough to touch the ground. They used to spread out the bottom of their parkas around them like a tupik *(tent) and light a small* kudlik *(oil lamp) inside their parkas to keep themselves warm when waiting for a seal.*

These people made everything from stone, bone, wood, and ivory. They had no iron tools. We feared them because they were strangers living in our land and living in stories told to frighten us when we were children. We envied them because we were told that they possessed strength greater than our own and, more important, they were great hunters who could make weapons from anything. If you both fear and envy a person, it can make you want to harm or even kill them.

This has happened so many times. These people, the Tuniit, were killed in small numbers over a long period of time. Some Tuniit managed to escape from the Inuit and fled to Kalaallit Nunaat (Greenland). I am sorry to tell you this, but some were even tortured, so great was the fear and envy of the Inuit toward the Tuniit. The few families that Atsiak saw at Salliq died of a sickness they got from the arvaniaqtuiqqaaniqpaaminiit, *the early whalers.*

Mannumi then recounted a story about a family of Tuniit who had escaped from being killed:

A long time ago, some Inuit hunters came upon a camp of Tuniit who were living on the east side of Baffin Island. The hunters were surprised and frightened at seeing this small camp and hid themselves behind rocks. They asked each other what they should do. Some wanted to leave the place unseen, while a few of the others wanted to attack the camp and kill the Tuniit. To kill a formidable enemy was to gain prestige in your own camp. In those days you could wear your pride on your nose. (It was a custom to have a single line tattooed across the bridge of the nose upon the killing of a powerful adversary.)

The hunters who wanted to kill the Tuniit talked the hunters who didn't into joining them, and they attacked the camp. One family in the camp was preparing to go down the coast to hunt and so, by accident, was able to flee while others were being killed. The hunters were like drunk men after they killed the remaining people in the camp. They did not want a single Tuniit to be alive, and so they decided to chase that poor family and kill all of them as well.

The hunters chased the family for days and days, going northward along the coast. Their hunger to kill was greater than the hunger in their bellies. Then a strange thing happened.

The Tuniit family turned their dogs away from the coast and drove their komatik toward the sea. It was during the coldest time of the year, and the sea was frozen for many miles. But the hunters kept chasing them because they knew that the family could not turn back now, and eventually they would come to the open water between Qikiqtaaluk (Baffin Island) and Kalaallit Nunaat (Greenland). The hunters got closer and closer to the family. Even the dogs now got excited. It would be very soon when the final killing would take place.

Then another strange thing happened. The Tuniit family stopped fleeing. The old man who protected them turned to face the hunters with only his dog whip in his hand. He drew the whip back, and with all his strength, whipped it toward the sky. There was a very loud crack. Then, like an echo, there was an even louder crack that grew into a terrifying sound. The ice between the family and the hunters split with a great noise and water rushed upwards.

The old man with the whip shouted words to the hunters which, though they could not understand, they knew from the tone to be a powerful curse. Those who know of this thing say that the family did get to Kalaallit Nunaat. As for the hunters, they were despised. They still are, even as they now live only in stories many of us know.

The reason for collecting the stories and accounts of
the elders is to give them to those who have never heard them.

CULTURAL THREADS

In 1990, with the indispensable aid of Jeannie Manning, I listened to Osuitok Ipeelie, Abraham Etungat, Munamee Sarko, Paulassie Pootoogook, Mannumi Davidee, Sheojuk Toonoo, Oqsuralik, Ottochie, and Simeonie Quppapik. I set up a series of afternoon tea and cookies sessions to make my friends comfortable and videotaped while listening to each person talk about the Tuniit and other topics. (Through the years, I would collect more than twenty-three hours of videotaped conversations.) What impressed me was the thoughtfulness of everyone I visited on what each one considered to be a special occasion. Often the house had been tidied, the linoleum floor washed, the plastic tablecloth cleaned, and the kids told to pick up their stuff and stay off the sofa. The widowers' houses might not have been as tidy, but somehow the old boys always managed to dress in clean shirts and spot-free pants. This could be a bit embarrassing when I appeared in a grungy sweatshirt and with a big toe poking out of an old sock. At one point Issuhungituk, by offering to mend my clothes, delicately hinted that I should look a little nicer when visiting the elders.

What did I learn from the elders about the Tuniit? For one, when they came upon an old site or found an artifact different in style from the familiar ones, the elders referred to it as having been left by the Tuniit. Archaeologists, on the other hand, would identify certain artifacts as originating with the Paleoeskimos, Dorset Culture Eskimos, or Thule Culture Eskimos (from whom today's Inuit are direct descendants). But the elders I knew did not distinguish among these three cultures; all were simply regarded as Tuniit.

How contemporary Inuit acquired such a rich and descriptive history of a people that they apparently had met only through artifacts was puzzling. The only answer I managed to get from the elders was that their ancestors had encountered the Tuniit, some even taking Tuniit women as their wives. Stories and accounts of the Tuniit were handed down from generation to generation. Not surprisingly, then, the elders whom I met repeated to me various stories I had encountered in earlier years, offering a measure of consistency to their narrative.

When the elders I knew were children, they had lived on the land and travelled about the coast of Sikusiilaq according to the seasons and the availability of game. Though they rarely, if ever, had camped on a Tuniit site, they often had camped nearby. Most traditional camps along the southwest Baffin coast that were occupied as late as the early 1950s have a Tuniit site in the vicinity, attesting to their strategic locations. Sheokjuk said the sites were visited by children who scampered among the ruins looking for things with which to play. Small stones and bones could be turned into anything the imagination would allow for, but the real treasure was to find a little *inunnguaq*, a child's doll, made of driftwood or antler.

Mannumi Davidee and Simeonie Quppapik both referred to the Tuniit as if they had departed a short time ago. They spoke of how the Tuniit, without any metal, had made tools and weapons of ivory, bone, and stone with great skill. Blades of knives were often made of ivory and their handles of antler. They spoke of finding little carvings of seals and humans, a small *kudlik*, and a stone pot where the Tuniit had lived. Those with whom I spoke revealed finding all manner of things, such as needles made from ivory, as well as ivory harpoon heads, thimbles from the soft part of caribou antler, and fish spears almost identical to those made by their fathers. "I'm sure that the Tuniit lived just like us," Mannumi said. "I think that Tuniit and Inuit lived together for a time. I wish that they were still here." He added, "It's strange that you could find all kinds of things where they lived, but why did they leave them? Where did they go? We have never seen their graves."

When I sat down with Osuitok Ipeelie to talk about the Tuniit, he began by apologizing for relating things about the

Tuniit that I had already been told, but nothing was familiar in what he shared during one afternoon visit in July. His gaze drifted toward the window as if he were looking for something, then he would turn his attention to his hands, which he examined carefully as he spoke. Osuitok began his account of the Tuniit by revealing that some Inuit had become mistrustful of the Tuniit and regarded all of them as *angakkuit* (shamans), maybe because they had found so many different magical charms where the Tuniit lived. He said some Inuit had become *iqsitsuni pizilutsaqtuq* (referring to fearful and envious) of the Tuniit and plotted to drive them out of their territory. He confirmed what other elders had stated — that the Inuit had eventually killed the Tuniit in small numbers over several years. In one instance, the Inuit lured a Tuniq leader to their camp, where they grabbed him, tied his hands and feet, and threw him to the ground. Then one of the Inuit brought out his bow drill, placed it between the poor Tuniq's eyebrows, and began to drill a hole into his head. I was told that the victim's eyes were open as he pleaded, but as the drill went deeper, he said, "My eyes will never open again." This terrible event became widely known among several Inuit who lived in Sikusiilaq.

Osuitok said that the Tuniit were more skillful than the Inuit and that the Inuit who had lived at the same time learned many things from the Tuniit: new ways to hunt birds, seals, and walrus and how to make the best points for their harpoons and arrows using the rib from a bearded seal. Osuitok used the term *angakkuit uqausingt, sakagusingit ilitaminiit tunirnik*, shamanic words that Inuit *angakkuit* had learned from the Tuniit shamans. He said the most powerful words and incantations known to the Inuit *angakkuit* had their origins in the Tuniit shamans' language.

I was surprised when Osuitok mentioned that the Inuit took some Tuniit women as second wives. "It would be stupid to waste a good woman," he said. I asked Osuitok to explain what constituted a "good woman" whereupon he described the virtues of a woman who did everything well. She could make fine *kammiks* (boots) and scrape, stretch, and make skin clothing that a man would be proud to wear; would be the first to rise in the morning and light the *kudlik* (seal oil lamp); and would do everything the first wife told her to. Osuitok used the word *Tunirnagajuit*, the half-Tuniit, referring to the first generation of children of an Inuk father and a Tuniq mother.

I should not have been surprised. Several years earlier, Ikkuma had told me that when the Adlait (Indians, likely Cree) had raided Inuit camps in Nunavik (Arctic Quebec), they would take desirable Inuit women either for second wives or camp slaves. The children they bore who were part Inuk and part Adla were referred to as *Allangajuk*.

WORDS: THE VANISHING ARTIFACTS

My pursuit of the meanings of words and expressions was a constant throughout my many years in the North. It shaped the nature of the questions I asked, and influenced how I observed and perceived the material objects around me.

I learned an early lesson in the power of words and observing the invisible on a trip to a significant site. I was not aware that we had arrived at an *aglirnaqtuq*, a place where strict Inuit customs were once observed. All I could see was a relatively clear space with a scattering of a few boulders. Nothing seemed noteworthy. Yet when I was taken from where I stood to a new vantage point, the scattering of boulders no longer appeared random but suggested a formal setting. And when I was given the *taijaujait* — the names of things — a revered place and all its objects of veneration appeared before my very eyes. It seemed reasonable to assume, then, that the *taijaujait* words might prove to be non-material artifacts of considerable value to inquisitive people.

Over time, the gathering of names, words, and expressions became the real medium of exchange through sharing of information and insights with elders in various communities throughout the Arctic. A good example of this occurred in 1995, when I was collecting information about the Tuniit during a trip to Cape Dorset. I had asked the seemingly simple question, "Why were the Tuniit called Tuniit by the Inummariit (the ancestors of the elders with whom I spoke)? Why weren't the Tuniit considered to be a different people and given a name, perhaps related to their appearance, behaviour, or the nature of the places where they once had lived?"

That simple question evoked much discussion. A common thread appeared to run through the numerous stories I gathered about the Tuniit: The elders claimed that their ancestors had learned how to make superior implements and hunting instruments directly from the Tuniit. They said artifacts from Tuniit sites were often collected and carefully examined. I learned that these artifacts were called *tunirtasajait* and that flint was known as *tunirijaq*. Several words that express "giving" and "receiving" have as their root *tuniq*. One of the most revered spiritual sites revealed to me several years ago was Tunillarvik. The name of the place, its central revered object, and the events that occurred there in the past are all related to the act of giving and receiving favours. Our discussion led us to the conclusion that the Tuniit were known as "the givers." As Pingwartuk explained to me many years ago, the Tuniit "were those who prepared the land for our ancestors".

It is not uncommon to see early Paleoeskimo, Dorset, Thule, and contemporary artifacts along the southwest coast of the Foxe Peninsula on south Baffin Island, suggesting a relatively abundant food supply over a very long period. The location of main and seasonal camps, meeting places, ceremonial and religious centres, travel routes, and the disposition of inuksuit, stone traps and food caches were directly linked to where food, in its variety of forms, could be taken. Between these life support centres were the *uumajurniavissagalaaluit*, places feared, revered, or beheld as benign by the elders. They make up more than what we would call "a sacred landscape," for they included places that could be both life-threatening and spiritually uplifting.

The shades between reverence for and fear of a particular place were, for me, often imperceptible. Gathering the names, meanings, and characteristics of places considered to be important to the elders provided source information upon which further lines of inquiry could be drawn. Going into considerable detail about the nature of the use of a given site and the purpose of the principal objects found there was possible. It was pleasing to be able to compare the dominant features of the major "spiritual" site on Sentry Island (near Arviat), where Luke Suluk had taken me, with similar features at an ancient "spiritual" site near Cape Dorset more than one thousand kilometres away. This comparison was not simply visual but also involved the names given to the objects displayed at these two great *aglirnaqtuil*, places where strict adherence to custom and tradition had to be observed. With only slight differences between the two dialects, the meanings given to all the entities to be respected at both places were essentially the same.

Many of the words and expressions I was taught were very old and could be considered by some to be archaic. Inuktitut itself is composed of many distinct dialects; pronunciation differs, and often words used in one community vary with those used in another. For these reasons, I got tripped up more than once. When I attended a feast in Kugluktuk (formerly Coppermine), in the Kitikmeot region of Nunavut, I found myself seated with two young women. In an effort to make small talk, I asked in Inuktitut if square-flipper seals were abundant in the area. Both women exploded in laughter. Tears streaming down their cheeks, they asked me to repeat what I had said to several other people nearby. I did as I was asked and met with snorts and gales of good-natured laughter. Somewhat indignantly, I asked what was so funny. Using the southwest Baffin term *udjuk* for a square-flipper seal, I had simply asked if they were abundant in the area. My pronunciation of the term was *oodjook*; but the women had heard *ooyook*, so to their ears I had asked if there were many big penises in the area.

On another occasion, I was in Kugaaruk (formerly Pelly Bay) giving a presentation to the elders that consisted of images and accounts of the many ancient sites of Sikusiilaq. During the presentation, I used several terms that I had learned from Oshutsiak, Simeonie, Pauta, Osuitok, and other elders. About a quarter of the way into the presentation, the young interpreter quietly whispered, "Speak English and I'll translate. Some of the words you are using are *tusliminaittut uqausiit* — strange, different, or so old that people don't understand what you mean."

For the Inuit, words are carriers of culture, and their loss is profound. Speaking to the Inuit Language Commission in 1984, artist Davidee Niviaxie said, "The most urgent thing where action must be taken immediately is to save our disappearing language." He added, "I have made a list of all the tools and household implements men used to make and there are 103 of them. These days, only about four items are made. There were sixty-seven items women used to make, and only five of those items are now occasionally made. We will have to record the names of all those items. There were 1,034 words which are no longer used here in Inukjuak. Those words have disappeared from the everyday language of the people. It must be the same in every community."

All the elders I knew from my early days in the Arctic are no longer alive. Gone with them are many words and experiences that shaped their perception of reality; no instruments, deductive processes, or linguistic endeavours can adequately recreate those words. In that sense, the most valuable cultural artifacts are the most perishable.

They are the words and thoughts that shaped my *taututtara avatinniituq*, my reality, how I experienced everything around me.

MEMORIES AND VISIONS

Osuitok's knowledge of the history and traditional values of the Sikusiilarmiut was truly outstanding. I am indebted more to him than to any other single person I have known in the Arctic. Visiting him and listening to his tales was always a highlight on my trips to Cape Dorset.

Two years after having first talked to me about how the Inuit hunted, tortured, and killed the Tuniit, Osuitok picked up on our conversation about how Inuit shamans had in fact "kept alive" ancient words spoken by Tuniit shamans. He carefully suggested what other elders have said to me, namely that the missionaries did not erase the existence of shamans or shamanism. He said, "Real shamans never die. As long as there are people in the world, someone will believe in them. They are listening as we speak."

During that same conversation, Osuitok spoke about life in the early days before the arrival of guns and missionaries:

These were times when seals, walruses, caribou, and all kinds of birds were plentiful. They didn't fear us. We could get food close to where we lived. These were times when strange creatures could be encountered in the sea and on the land. There were qalupaliit *(malevolent creatures) living in the Kangisuqitaulup area.*

All this began to change as quickly as guns and missionaries came here. The guns scared off the animals and uqammun *(he who talks much, or the first missionaries) scared off the strange animals by his presence, or maybe it was just that we couldn't see them any more. It was after* uqammun's *arrival that some of our people began to believe that they could acquire a power that would allow them to fly like angels or run as swiftly as any caribou. This special power is called* ipiqisimajuq.

Osuitok switched course and began discussing a subject he had never mentioned during the thirty or more years I had known him. He talked about how the magnetic north pole is constantly shifting its position; he assured me that he was quite aware the Earth had shifted on its axis and was subject to dramatic climate change. He went on to explain in his terms how climate change could cause famine. (It reminded me that the Inuit had been the most generous donors of all Canadians to the Ethiopian Famine Relief Fund.) Osuitok talked about technology not as an end in itself but as a "force or new ability" for humans to become stronger than ever before. He spoke somewhat casually about instant communication. I asked myself, "What the hell has gotten into him?"

Osuitok paused, looked at his hands, then continued: *It is because of all of these things that we must make peace with nature or we will suffer greatly. Besides, we have nowhere else to go. I don't think that the world will end. It will first die, and life will slowly come back again.*

Osuitok looked straight into my eyes and, for the first time, told me that when he was only a child of five, his grandfather had seen growing in him that which was necessary to become an *angakok*, a shaman.

THERE IS GREAT BEAUTY
IN FOND MEMORIES

Sitting on my dock on Palmerston Lake near Ompah, Ontario, with a glass of Macallan Elegancia, my thoughts turned to memories of my journeys in the Arctic. Each and every one occupies its own place somewhere in my mind. Collectively, they shape the story of the other side of my life in the North where, for a short time, I became the person of my childhood dreams. One memory that I revisit from time to time is of a journey that stands out above all others. That journey began on a bright summer morning in July of 1965.

Itulu Itidlouie bumped into me while I was buying some supplies at the co-op in Cape Dorset and suggested we have a coffee together. He told me that his father, Itidlouie, and mother, Kingmeata, wanted to go out on the land. The entire family had decided to take the old man and his wife out for a few of days, and Itulu was kind enough to ask me if I wanted to come along. Of course I agreed.

The following day we loaded the two canoes with gas, food, tents, rifles, fishnets, two harpoons, and kids. Toward the end of the first day, Itidlouie indicated that we should land at a small bay down the coast and set up camp. We unloaded both canoes, set up Itidlouie's tent first, then our own, and had some boiled caribou and bannock. We then settled in for the night, which was still bright enough for the kids to play in the hills.

Early the following morning, Itidlouie said that he wanted to move further along the coast. We took down the tents, repacked the canoes, and proceeded in the direction of Itiliardjuk. Upon sighting familiar islands, Itidlouie pointed to one and said to Itulu that we were to camp there. So the process of unloading the

Itidlouie who taught me that there is great beauty in fond memories.

canoes, setting up the camp, getting pails of fresh water, as well as performing other chores, began again.

The next morning, while I was attending to business behind a hill, I could hear Itulu calling to me to hurry up. "We're moving again!" he shouted. Once more, we loaded the canoes and travelled further along the coast. As to be expected, Itidlouie signalled a landing site and the chores involved in setting up the camp resumed. The following day, the old man said he wanted to leave. I turned to Itulu's brother, Udjualuk, and asked, "What's wrong with the old man? He's driving us nuts. It's as if he's never satisfied wherever we camp." Udjualuk just shrugged and replied, *"Achoo?"* Who knows? Again we took down the camp, loaded the canoes, and continued along the coast.

Though the days remained sunny, we always noticed a chill when travelling on the water. Itidlouie took note of my discomfort and whispered to Kingmeata, "He's getting cold," whereupon she unrolled a caribou skin and carefully wrapped it around my legs. I was touched by her maternal gesture and Itidlouie's fatherly concern. I could no longer find reason in my heart to grumble

One of my dear "aunts" Kingmeata Itidlouie who made sure I was warm at sea.

over the setting up and tearing down of camps, which continued until the day we reached Sapujjuaq. This was a traditional gathering place, where many families set up their tents when the fish began their river run. The place was alive with children, men setting fishnets in the river, mothers feeding babies, and the younger women filleting the fish, which they hung on lines strung between figures that resembled little inuksuit called *nappariat*.

That evening I walked over to Itidlouie's tent to thank him and Kingmeata, whom out of respect I now called *Anannatsiak*, Grandmother and *Atatasiak*, Grandfather. When I opened the tent flap, Itidlouie, with Grandmother in his arms, was lying comfortably on a nice Serta mattress. A Coleman lantern was brightly hissing away while a brand-new kerosene stove filled the tent with warmth. As I left them, I could not help but think of what I had just experienced. Itidlouie and Kingmeata, who had spent practically all their lives on the land in skin tents and temporary snow houses, enduring the hardship of winter with only the faint glow of a seal oil lamp, were now happy and snug while out on the land in what must have seemed like paradise.

Toward the end of the following day, after we had set the nets, I took a walk along the riverside and happened to see the silhouettes of three small figures on the high, steep hill behind our camp. I assumed that some teenagers had climbed up there and thought no more of them until I approached the bottom of the hill, which I intended to climb to scan the horizon. The figures I had seen from a distance were not three teenagers but three old men cautiously picking their way down the steep hillside, with Itidlouie in the lead. In good time, they reached the camp-site and sat beside one another, on a large flat rock facing the sea. Shortly, four young girls arrived and gave each elder a mug of tea and large piece of bannock before running back to their tents. The men just sat there looking at something in the great beyond until the sun dropped below the hill.

The following year, Itidlouie died, and the others followed shortly. I met Grandmother, Kingmeata, in the co-op store. Without the need for words, I embraced her. We both sat on the floor as others, without a glance, carefully stepped around us, picking up their supplies to go out on the land on their way to Sapujjuaq. The journey we had made together the previous year now became clear. The setting up and tearing down of camps each day was because before he died, Itidlouie had wished to visit all the places he loved dearly.

There is a saying in Inuktitut that means, "There is great beauty in fond memories."

To you dear Issuhungituk Qiatsuq Pootoogook, Oshutsiak Pudlat, Pudlo Pudlat, Quvianaqtuliak (Kov) Parr, Ikkuma Parr, Pauta Saila, Pitaloosie Saila, Eegyvudluk Pootoogook, Kanaginak Pootoogook, Pudlat Pootoogook, Paulassie Pootoogook, Joanassie Salamonie, Kiawak Ashoona, Pitseolak Ashoona, Qaqqaq Ashoona, Majuriaq Ashoona, Kenojuak Ashevak, Pingwartuk, Ottochie Ottochie, Itidlouie Itidlouie, Kingmeata Itidlouie, Lukta Qiatsuq, Mannumi Davidee, Munamee Sarko, Kingwatsiuk, Simeonie Quppapik and Osuitok Ipeelie — to all of you who enriched my life, I have now kept the promise.

Taima.

EPILOGUE

There came a time when the elders no longer handed down tales, songs, customs, and mysteries. Instead, catechism and schooling were to shape the Inuit child's knowledge and future.

But the interest in traditional times remains strong. It is not unusual for a young Inuk to ask about a grandparent or other family member they never knew. I remember when a young lady asked me about her uncle Osuitok Ipeelie. She had grown up in a community far from Cape Dorset and had only occasionally heard family members refer to her uncle. As she grew older and Osuitok rose to prominence in the Inuit art world, her curiosity grew.

We eventually met one day in Kanata, a suburb on the western side of Ottawa. On a pleasant summer afternoon, we sat in a small plaza surrounded by boutiques and sparrows looking for crumbs on the pavement. I asked her why she was so interested in knowing about a distant uncle she had never met. She said that her family members were reluctant to talk about him, yet she felt a persistent desire to know more. So I began by giving her a broad description of Osuitok:

Your uncle was a remarkable person. He told me that he was born in 1923 and that he was very curious. His grandfather noted that even at the age of five, Osuitok possessed the mind that could be developed into an angakok but your uncle chose otherwise. He became one of the most skilled Inuit sculptors in the entire Arctic. His long, delicate fingers could fashion a caribou out of stone so fine that you were afraid to touch it. His sculptures are the pride of museums and galleries throughout the world.

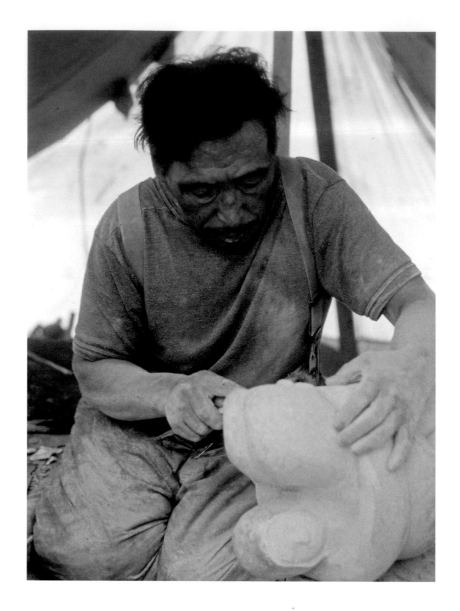

My dear Osuitok though its late, there are still a vast
number of stories to be told, but who will tell them?

I've been out on the land with him as he searched for
the perfect piece of stone. The search involved a long
process of tapping, banging, and smashing stone after
stone until he found that rare, flawless piece of rock that
would become an object of exquisite beauty in his hands.

Out of respect, I referred to Osuitok as my uncle.
Practically everything of any importance I know about
the Arctic had its beginnings in some conversation with

him. He provided far more than just information. He gave me insight essential to take on that long journey into the realm of thought and wonder. He taught me how to observe things and admonished me by saying, "Even if you can't find the answer, try to know why things are the way they are."

Your uncle was not only a great artist and a deep thinker. I saw a spiritual quality in him. He seemed to be able to disconnect himself from the noise and activity around him and become totally absorbed in transforming a rough piece of stone into an exquisite work of art.

At this point, Osuitok's niece became very interested. She asked how I knew her uncle had had a spiritual side. I shared that Osuitok often had talked to me about the *angakkuit* and how one should respect the land and especially certain places that the elders had believed to be very powerful. He reminded me that even though some of the old men went to church, they still carried the old beliefs with them when they went out onto the land. I told her, briefly, about some of Osuitok's hardships, about the death of his daughter Pishukti, who drowned in a metre of water in Yellowknife. I recounted the time when he was invited to Moscow and beguiled the staff at the State Museum by casually describing the names and functions of several ancient artifacts which, until his visit, had puzzled the curators.

I spoke to Osuitok's niece for the better part of the afternoon. She thanked me profusely and left me thinking about what had just happened. In talking at length about her uncle, I had been talking also about a way of life she had never known. She and her generation were born in or near a nursing station, grew up in a settlement, went to school, and no longer needed to rely on traditional knowledge in order to survive. Some would spend a few days on the land with their parents, but knowledge of the necessities of life for surviving on the land had vanished.

Many children just like Osuitok's niece have asked me similar questions: What were my grandfather and grandmother like? What was it like being out on the land with them? What kinds of stories did they tell? Have you ever seen a ghost? Have you ever seen someone do magical things? Did you ever get lost, or were you ever chased by a polar bear? Surprisingly, these questions are similar to those asked by schoolchildren I met in the Orkney Islands of Scotland years ago. Many had grandfathers or uncles who had sailed across the sea to work in the Arctic as "Hudson Bay Boys." Like the Inuit children, the Scottish ones hungered for stories that would connect them to missing pieces of their past. When I was growing up, many first generation immigrant children were admonished to "be like the English". We didn't learn about our eastern European heritage. We heard a few stories from relatives who sat around a table talking about the past. Unfortunately, we didn't hear many stories from grandparents or uncles of what life was like. Connections to our heritage were never made.

Then one day, when I was twenty-two years old, I met a remarkable man who cast a light on a landscape I had never known. His name was Benny Korda (not to be confused with Buby Bulan or Benny Korda the musician). Benny was highly educated and tempered by extraordinary experiences. He had been a Polish cavalryman, one of those wonderful madmen who mounted a charge against a battalion of well-armed but badly exposed German infantry during the early invasion of Poland in the Second World War. Like several of his comrades, Benny had been captured and imprisoned by the Germans. Rather than being released by the advancing Russians, he found himself packed into a cattle car with other prisoners headed for prison camps in Siberia. Benny did not speak about the harrowing experience of his second escape nor describe how he wound up in a responsible position in the Canadian government.

We met because he brought a collection of his fascinating photographs to my office when I was employed at the National Film Board of Canada. During lunch, Benny asked me the origin of my family name. I explained that I didn't know, though both sides of my family were from Bukovina. "Have you ever returned to the Old Country for a visit?" he asked.

"No," I replied. "I had no reason to search out my heritage." And I added, in an attempt at self-deprecating humour, "since I'm sure I'm a descendant of an ancient tribe of peasants."

"Well," Benny said, "let me tell you a little bit about the heritage of which you know nothing."

Among the fascinating things Benny revealed was that Bukovina had been populated since at least 4500 BCE. My ancestors must have belonged to a tribal group that lived either on the rolling plains, perhaps near the Black Sea, or on the slopes of the Carpathian Mountains in what is now the territory stretching from Ukraine and Moldavia to Romania. Some of my neolithic ancestors would have lived in large settlements, while others would have chosen a nomadic life similar to that of their relatives in Siberia.

I assumed that this ancient place of my ancestors would have been populated solely by Slavs. Benny said, on the contrary, the place of my ancestors had been populated by Ukrainians, Poles, Romanians, Hungarians, Armenians, and Germans, all of whom shared a common experience: that of being ruled by various empires at different times in their turbulent history.

My Polish cavalryman friend told me that some of my ancestors had probably been among the finest and most daring horsemen in all of central Europe. They had gone on raiding parties as far as the Black Sea. "You Bukovinians," Benny said, "had an amazing talent for winding up as very influential advisers in the various Royal Courts of central and eastern Europe. Your people were not all peasants as you may have thought."

I sat quietly for most of the afternoon listening to a man I hardly knew connect me to the origins of my culture. It was not a history lesson but a story that was a bridge to my past.

The stories within *An Intimate Wilderness* are accounts of life on the land by a remarkable people who lived at the edge of the world. Having no written text, they kept their entire history in their collective memory, passing it from one generation to the next through the power of words.

ACKNOWLEDGEMENTS

The many people who helped me *(* denotes deceased)*:

Baker Lake — Qamani'tuaq (64°19'05"N 096°01'03"W)
Martha Tiktaq Anautalik
Myra Kukiijaut Arngna'naaq
Norman Atangala
John Killalark
Lucy Kownak
Margaret Narkjangerk
John Nukik
Barnabus Perjoar
Hugh Tuluqtuq
Elizabeth Tunnuq

Belcher Islands — Sanikiluaq (56°20'N 79°30'W)
Lucassie Arragutainaq

Cape Dorset — Kinngait (64°13'54"N 076°32'25"W)
Kenojuak Ashevak*
Kiawak Ashoona*
Majuriaq Ashoona
Ohito Ashoona
Pitseolak Ashoona*
Qaqqaq Ashoona*
Mannumi Davidee*
Osuitok Ipeelie*
Itidlouie Itidlouie*
Itulu Itidlouie
Kingmeata Itidlouie*
Kingwatsiuk*
Jimmy Manning
Oqsuralik*
Ottochie Ottochie*
Quvianaqtuliak (Kov) Parr*
Ikkuma Parr*
Pingwartuk*

Eegyvudluk Pootoogook*
Issuhungituk Qiatsuq Pootoogook*
Kananginak Pootoogook*
Napachie Pootoogook*
Paulassie Pootoogook*
Pudlat Pootoogook*
Pudlo Pudlat*
Oshutsiak Pudlat*
Lukta Qiatsuq*
Simeonie Quppapik*
Pauta Saila*
Pitaloosie Saila
Joanassie Salamonie*
Munamee Sarko*
Pauloosie Tulugaq*

Eskimo Point — Arviat (61°06′29″N 094°03′25″W)
Margaret Aniksak*
Peter Aningaat
John Arnalugjuaq
Henry Ishuanik
Elizabeth Issakiak
Mark Kalluak*
James Konek
Andy Mumgark
Luke Suluk
Peter Suwaksiork
Leo Ulayok
Silas Ulinaumi

Holman Island — Uluksaqtuuq (70°44′11″N 117°46′05″W)
Wallace Goose*

Pangnirtung — Pangniqtuuq (66°08′52″N 065°41′58″W)
Jim Killabuck*

Pelly Bay — Aqvilikjuaq (68°31′59″N 089°49′36″W)
Three very old hunters*

Pond Inlet — Mittimatalik (72°41′57″N 077°57′33″W)
Simon Akpaleeapik*

Povungnituk — Puvirnituq (60°02′0″N 77°16′0″W)
Taamusi Qumaq*

Rankin Inlet — Kangiqliniq (62°48′38″N 092°06′53″W)
Rev. Armand Tagoona*

Specialists who provided assistance:

GUIDES:
Arviat (61°06′ 29″N 094°03′25″W)
Phillip Tasseor

Baker Lake — Qamanituaq (64°19′05″N 096°01′03″W)
John Nukik

Cape Dorset — Kinngait (64°13′54″N 076°32′25″W)
Timmun & Kristiina Alariaq
Itulu Itlolouie
Jimmy Manning
Pingwortuk*
Peter Pitseolak*
Lukta Qiatsuq

Rankin Inlet — Kangiqliniq
Henry Kablalik

ILLUSTRATORS:
Baker Lake — Qamanituaq
Ruth Qaulluarjuk

Cape Dorset — Kinngait
Osutsiak Pudlat*
Pudlo Pudlat*
Simeonie Quppapik*

INTERPRETERS:
Cape Dorset — Kinngait
Pallaya Ezekiel
Salomonie Jaw
Annie Manning
Jeannie Manning
Nina Manning
Mukshowya Niviaqsi
Leetia Parr
Mark Pitseolaq
Pia Pootoogook

Pelly Bay — Aqvilikjuaq
Dolorosa Nartok

LINGUISTICS:
Igloolik/Ottawa
Deborah Evaluarjuk

REFERENCES:
Arviat
Eric Andee
Peter Komak
Donald Suluk
Aniksarauyak

Povungnituk — Puvirniqtuuq
Tammusi Qumaq*

RESEARCHERS:
Arviat
Luke Suluk

Baker Lake/Ottawa
Sally Qimmiu'arq-Webster

Ottawa
Jared Buchmayer
Diana Cousens Hallendy
Deanna MacDonald

Toronto
Linda Morita

USA
Carolyn Wyland

AN EXPRESSION OF THANKS

My longtime friend Alan Morantz has been invaluable, turning my wandering thoughts into a beautiful narrative through brilliant editing. Robert Hoselton, one of Canada's finest graphic artists, designed this book. Without the skill of Sharon Kirsch as my copy editor, my syntax, grammar, and consistency in the use of names would have been chaotic.

Dr. Denis St-Onge made it possible to obtain help from the Polar Continental Shelf Project and supported my work throughout the years. In addition, he convinced his son, the highly respected geologist Dr. Marc St-Onge, to invite me to join his team in the field, thus making it possible for me to map many ancient sites throughout the entire Foxe Peninsula as well as across central Baffin Island. The helicopter pilots, Terry Halton and Jamie Boles, were a great help in locating unusual features and traces of past human occupation. Paul Budkewitsch provided exquisite satellite images and maps prior to my departure north. I thank First Air and Tom Koelbel publisher and editor of First Air's well-read magazine *Above & Beyond* for their ongoing help. I am grateful to Dave Maloley, formerly with the Polar Continental Shelf Project, not only for his generous help, but for being at the other end of the line in case of need. Polar Continental Shelf Project and the staff made it possible to explore remote and important areas with my elders.

My thanks to professors William Cowan and Thomas Fotiou for introducing me to the importance of semantics; to Charles Martijn for his undivided interest; to Drs. William Fitzhugh and Stephen Loring for their support and encouragement over the years; and to the late Dr. William Taylor Jr. for his unequivocal support when it was most needed.

The Kinngait Cooperative and the Hamlet of Cape Dorset welcomed me each time I travelled north and supported my work throughout the years. I am indebted to Terry Ryan for his assistance, northern hospitality, and unwavering friendship. Patricia Ryan looked after me graciously whenever I was in Dorset in the early years. Timmun and Kristiina Alariaq remain among my closest friends in Cape Dorset; they operate one of the finest tour companies in the Eastern Arctic. I cannot omit mention of Bryan Pearson, an original Arctic scallywag whom I greatly admire.

I am most grateful to Diana Cousens Hallendy, who keeps "the farm" running and some semblance of order in my life, wherever I may be.

What a wonderful thing
it was to know you

Anirnik

Napachie and Eegyvudluk Pootoogook

Jamassie Teevee

Issuhungituk and Arnaqalaq

Anna Kingatsiak

Eleeshushee Parr

Enoosik Aningmiuq

Ineak Pingwatok

AN INTIMATE WILDERNESS

Axangajuk Shaw

Johniebo and Kenojuak

Innukjuakju Pudlat

Kakulu Sagiatuk

Kiawak Ashoona

Mary and Ezekiel Ashevak

Koomwartuk Ashoona

Mangitak

Kooyoo Ottochie

Ningeooga

Pitaloosie and Pauta Saila

Pudlo Pudlat

Lissie and Saggiak

Parr

Osuitok, Pishukti and Nipisha Ipeelie

Nee and Timothy Ottochie

Milia Jaw

Lucy Qinnuayuak

INDEX

Akaunaarutiniapiga *(my great fortune)* 29

Akianimiut *(what the Sikusiilarmuit called their relatives in Arctic Quebec — refers to "those of the other side")* 55, 221

Aksarneq *(the northern lights in Sikusiilaq; ghostly phenomenon refers to "sky dwellers playing a game of Kick ball with the skull of a walrus"; also spirits of children)* 122

Ajurnarmat *("it cannot be otherwise")* 279

Alariaq *(name of person and name of an island)* 54, 69, 190, 225, 231, 315, 318

Alga 93

Amarok *(the wolf; Amaroktalik "a place of wolves")* 239, 240

Amauti *(Amaut a woman's parka hood)* 44, 45, 122, 213, 228

Ancient camps 55, 68, 117, 164

Andrew Gordon Bay 139, *232*, 233, 237, 268

Angaituq *(a specialist)* 45

Angak *(Uncle)* 50, 203, 204, 249

Angakkuit *(Angaquiit (pl.) — shamans)* 54, 57, 212, 215, 217, 224, 225, 295, 309

Angakok (sing.) *(angakoq — shaman)* 50, 112, 167, 168, 170, 203, 204, 209, 212, 216, 217, 221, 222, 224, 225, 227, 231, 265, 302, 307

Angakuluk *(the respected one — one of Norman's names)* 27

Angusuitug *(a good hunter, a very competent person)* 47

Anthropomorphize 119

Apirsuqti *(the Inquisitive one — one of Norman's names)* 29, 185, 204, 241

Apumik inunguaqutilik *(a figure created to destroy human souls)* 128, 224

Arctic butterfly 94

Arctic char 41, 65, 73, 115, 241

Arctic fox 116

Arctic landscape 40, 75, 170

Arctic legends 122

Arctic natural phenomena 121-124, 135, 136

Arctic Ocean 67, 246

Arluk *(killer whale)* 84

Arnainnarnut qaujimajaujuq *(retreats known only to women)* 76, 139

Arvaniaqtuiqqaaniqpaaminiit *(the early whalers)* 289

Arviat *(formerly Eskimo Point)* 75, 123, 204, 211, 213, 229, 314, 315, 316

Arviat elder 80

Ashevak, Kenojuak *(artist)* 9, 308, 313, *321*

Ashoona, Kiawak (Kiugak) *(master carver)* 9, 22, 73, 102, 105, 129, 215, 306, 313, *321*

Ashoona, Majuriaq *(wife of Qaqqaq Ashoona)* 9, 140, 141, 230, 258, 306, 313

Ashoona, Namonie *(Ohito's uncle, brother of Qaqqaq and Kiawak)* 101, 242

Ashoona, Ohito *(artist)* 101–105, 239, 313

Ashoona, Pitseolak (Pitseolaq) *(famous artist, Grandmother of Ohito)* 9, 101 306, 313

Ashoona, Qaqqaq *(master carver)* 9, 140, 141, 257–259, *259*, 306, 313

Atatasiak *(Grandfather)* 53, 305

Aujak *(summer)* 251

Aulaqquit *(inuksuit acting as scarecrows or bogeymen; term from Nunavik)* 91

Aurora borealis *(the northern lights)* 35, 121

Ausuittup Qikiqtanga *(Ellesmere Island)* 40, 245

Azalujuk *(painful dislocation of joints also expression used when the runners of a sled start to splay outward)* 45

Baffin Island *(Qikiiqttaaluk)* *38*, 42, 53, 55, 57, 76, 78, 116, 122, 169, 190, 221, 271, 272, 277, 280, 283, 290, 298, 317

Bannock *(unleavened bread made primarily of lard, flour, baking soda, salt, cold water)* 29, 69, 138, 161, 217–220, 231, 258, 259, 269, 272, 303, 306

Beechey (Captain) Frederick William 77

Beluga whales 69, 73, 83, 111, 155, 283, 284

Bill Barrow *(ornithologist)* 116

Black soapstone *(preferred material to make Kudliit)* 117

Bowhead whales 83-85

Bukovina *(a region in central Europe)* *30*, 31, 310, 311

Caches 45, 65, 70, 88, 91, 111, 117, 173, 265, 298

Cape Dorset *(Kinngait; refers to high mountains or hills)* 8, 22, 29, 41–43, 49, 51, 53, 55, 57, *60–62*, 64, 68–70, 76, 78, 87, 95, 101, 102, 104, 107–109, 115, 117, 124, 126, 140, 153, 159, 183, 185, *188*, 189, 205, 207, 219–222, 224, 225, 230, 233, 236, 237, 241, 243, 258, 267, 269–271, 273, 274, 276, 277, 283, 286, 297, 299, 301, 303, 307, 313, 315, 318

Caribou 23, 27, 28, 42, 44–47, 69–71, 73, 74, 76, 80, 84, 91, 92, 97–99, 105, 108–113, 115, 116, 118, 119, 123, 127, 128, 138, 140, 148, 149, 167, 169–171, 174, 175, 181, 184, 186, 191, 192, 199, 200, 205–207, 209, 217–219, 222, 225, 230, 239, 240, 246, 247, 255, 259, 269, 270, 274, 283, 294, 301–304, 307

Caribou, ascending 127

Ceilidh 119

AN INTIMATE WILDERNESS

Chinese astrologers 121
Cognitive maps 51, 75
Column of light illuminating the clouds 130
Community Council of Cape Dorset 64
Cooking 151, 164
Cooperative hunting
    Inuit 84, 85; wolves 239
Country food 58, 74

Davidee, Mannumi
    9, 159, 215, 224, 288–290, 293, 294, 306, 313
Department of Northern Affairs 41
Dogs 43, 47, 58, 83, 116, 118, 119, 123, 127, 128,
    159, 167, 168, 181, 191, 199, 200, 215, 221,
    222, 250, 256, 267, 284, 290, 291
    destruction of 58

Eider duck eggs 74, 116
Ellesmere Island 40, 245
Ephemeral landscape 75

Fish 43, 65, 70, 71, 73, 76, 78, 79, 98, 99, 107, 110,
    115, 133, 140, 148, 170, 186, 241, 264, 294,
    305
Flaherty, Robert (American filmmaker,
    Inuit name - White Swan) 53
Foxe Basin 67, 117, 246
Foxe Channel 67
Foxe Peninsula
    43, 55, 67, 68, 75, 76, 80, 106–108, 110, 111,
    139, 233, 275, 286, 298, 317
Foxe, Luke 67
Fungus 93, 94

Geese 27, 35, 68, 76, 79, 83, 111, 158, 186, 222,
    229, 283, 286
Geographical terms in Sikusiilaq 22, 75
Geography of shallows 46, 76
Geological Survey of Canada 101, 108
Ghost 122, 124, 127, 128, 169, 203, 208, 211, 228,
    236, 246, 309
"Glass" found in some rocks (clear quartz)
    84, 285
Glass Nose (White Swan's girlfriend) 54
Graves 63, 88, 117, 122 173–175, 203, 228, 233,
    234, 237, 246, 294
Great Plain of the Koukdjuak 68, 111, 158
Greek and Roman philosophers 121

Hakamuktak (a large inuksuk built so it can be seen
    from a distance built along the coast and
    inland where caribou are taken or where
    something like food has been left Haningayok
    — back river place, Kivalliq area) 99
Hare 39, 105
Helicopter trips
    64, 107, 108, 110, 111, 236, 239, 246
Hooks made from polar bear claws 85
Hudson Bay 40, 211
Hudson Bay (Amadjuak Trading Post) 79
Hudson Strait 50, 51, 132, 170, 221, 251
Hudson's Bay Company 42, 55, 58, 83, 189, 223
Huish, Robert (author who wrote about
    Captain Beechey's travels of the Bering Strait
    Human effigies) 77
Hunting blinds 112, 128, 286
Hunting equipment 43, 88, 286, 298

Icebergs 39, 40, 50, 251, 273
Iga (fire place) 74
Igaqjuaq (described as "the overturned kettle";
    the name implies a great fireplace;
    archaic name is Oujaligiaqtubic)
    76, 154, 170, 171, 174, 244
Igloolik 22, 47, 67, 172, 315
Igloolikmiut (people from Igloolik) 47
Igloos 28, 128, 181, 191, 192, 209, 210
Ijarovaujakpok (when one sees the great shimmering)
    103, 104
Ijirait (the caribou spirits) 127, 169, 198, 199
Ikahimaluk ("attached to one another" inuksuit
    — some are windows or sight-lines) 99
Ikaniigiik (map of the shallows) 46
Ikirasaq or Ikirasak (camp where Kananginak
    Pootoogook was raised)
    43, 58, 124, 233
Ilisaqtaulaurpunga innarnut (their student)
    29
Ilunagalatik Inuit nuumata nuna
    (when most inuit moved into settlements)
    287
Iniqijuminaqtuq (the place you favour above all others)
    158, 283
Innupak ("Big Foot" — one of Norman's names)
    29
Inua (the life force) 39, 175, 210, 229
Inugaruvligak (dwarf) 99
Inuit ("the people")
    7, 23, 27–29, 41–43, 49, 50, 53, 54, 57, 58,
    61–63, 67, 73–75, 77, 83, 87, 88, 102, 119,
    136, 137, 140, 167, 170, 171, 174, 196,
    201–203, 205, 234, 239, 261, 262, 271, 273,
    275, 276, 279, 284, 286, 287, 289, 290,
    293–297, 299, 301, 302, 307, 310
Inuit cooperatives (formerly Eskimo cooperatives)
    41, 198, 238, 318
Inummarik (a real Inuk; someone who could live
    on the land) 288
Inuit sivulliit tamaanigiagnaliqtillugit
    (the time of "the earliest humans")
    284, 285
Inuksugalait or Inuksugalalait
    (Inukso Point, the major inuksuk site located
    on the west coast of the peninsula)
    92, 100–104, 107, 109, 271–273
Inuksuit made of hard packed snow 184
Inuksuit tuktunnutiit (inuksuit placed to frighten
    caribou toward the waiting hunters) 91
Inuksuk (s.), inuksuit (pl.)
    (objects that act in the capacity of a human)
    22, 29, 51, 65, 68, 69, 76, 79, 86–99, 98, 101,
    103–105, 107–110, 112, 113, 115, 117, 128,
    131, 140, 180, 181, 182, 201, 202, 222, 236,
    271, 289, 298, 305
Inuksuk upigijaugialik
    (an inuksuk that should be venerated) 93
Inuksuksiuqti (the "One who seeks out inuksuit"
    — one of Norman's names) 29
Inuksullarik (referring to a very important inuksuk)
    89
Inuksummarik or an inuksukjuaq
    (a large dominant inuksuk to be seen from a
    distance; act as major coordination points;
    often constructed to serve as important
    direction markers) 89, 90
Inuktitut (the language of the Inuit)
    22, 23, 75, 87, 88, 109, 113, 118, 137, 170,
    204, 218, 267, 287, 299, 306

Inulimaat nunaqaqatatillugit nunaliralagnulutik *(the time when we lived on the land)* 287

Inunnguait *(pl.) (human-like figures, mistakenly referred to as inuksuit)* 113, 182

Inunnguaq *(s.) (a stone figure in a human-like form mistakenly referred to as an inuksuk; a human-like form, a doll or effigy)* 90, 101, 182, 187, *214*, 227, 228, 294

Inuquti *(camp slave, the polite term is servant)* 62

Inuruqqajuq *(as if it were alive for a moment)* 95

Inutsuliutuinnaqtuq *(inuksuit that are created to shorten the time while one waits)* 113

Inuugiaqarnirama *(which means "my time to die is not yet come")* 279

Inuvik *(a town in the western Arctic)* 40

Ipeelie, Osuitok (Usuittuq Ipilli) *(a master carver, my guide, mentor and very close friend)* 8, 9, 61, 103, 126, 138, *152*, 153, 155, 159, 162, 163, 165, 167, 170, 209, 210, 215, 216, 224, 227–229, 276–279, 281, 289, 293–295, 299, 301, 302, 306–309, *308*, 313, *323*

Iqaluit *(formerly Frobisher Bay)* 40, 55, 127, 213

Iqniqanitusiutut *(the pull of the moon; its affect on tides, springs and on the behaviour of people and animals)* 126

Iqniqanitut *(when the tides are their highest and the currents strongest)* 126

Irniq *(diminutive name for a son, name of my close friend)* 7, 116

Issuhungituk Qiatsuq Pootoogook *(daughter of Qiatsuq (Qiatsuk) and wife of Paulassie Pootoogook)* 9, *48*, 219–221, 223, 225, 227, 293, 306, 316

Itidlouie, Itidlouie 9, 303–306, *304*, 313

Itidlouie, Itulu *(Itidlouie, Itidlouie's son)* 69–71, 170, 218, 241, 251, 285, 303, 304, 313, 315

Itidlouie, Kingmeata *(Itidlouie Itidlouie's wife)* 9, 303–306, *305*, 313

Itidlouie, Leetia *(one of my early interpreters)* 71

Itiliardjuk *(the point of land between the mainland and Alariaq Island, my favourite place)* 22, 54, 69, 98, 122, 130, 140, 209, 217, *236*, 241, 250, 257, *259*, 268, 283, 303

Ittutiavak *("Respected elder" — one of Norman's names)* 29

Kalaallit Nunaat *(Greenland)* 289–291

Kingwatsiuk, Iyola *(son of Kingwatsiuk, Kingwatsiuk)* 118

Kangia or Kungia *(place)* 79

Kangisurituq *(Andrew Gordon Bay)* 43, 78, 139, *232*, 233, 235, 237, 268

Katittarvit sinaani nunaqpagiarnialiqtunut *(gathering places on the shore in preparation of going inland)* 45

Kattaq *(an entrance also an entrance to a place to be respected)* 109

Kayaks 57, 67, 83, 131, 186, 221, 222, 252

Keewatin *(region in Nunavut)* 79, 215

Killabuck, Jimmy 83, 314

Kingwatsiuk, Kingwatsiuk 9, 287–289, 306, 313

Kinngait *(Cape Dorset; refers to high mountains or hills)* 8, 22, 41, 53, 55, 58, *60*, 68, 153, 170, 171, 185, *188*, 215, 286, 287, 313, 315, 318

Kinngnarmiut *(present day people now living in Cape Dorset; whatever they were called before changed when they settled in Kinngait (Cape Dorset))* 54, 55, 286, 287

Koukdjuak *(means a Great River; connects Nettilling Lake to the sea, mid Baffin Island)* 68

Kudliit *(pl.) (seal oil lamps)* 117

Laumajurniavissagalaaluit *(areas that support life)* 75

Leituriaraluit *(voracious mosquitoes)* 42

Lichen 27, 51, 69, 70, 81, 94, 96, 140, 157, 275, 283

Lukta *(son of Qiatsuq a shaman)* 9, 48, 51, 225–227, 277–279, 306, 314, 315

Maktaaq *(edible skin of a Beluga whale)* 74

Manning, Annie *(interpreter)* 22, 62, 276, 315

Manning, Jeannie *(interpreter)* 22, 54, 62, 293, 315

Manning, Nina *(interpreter)* 22, 62, 315

Map(s) 36, 43, 50, 51, 54, 55, 75–79, 101, 107, 108, 117, 169, 171, 233, 246, 317

Map *(cognitive)* 46, 51, 54, 75–77, 129

Markham Bay 117, 277

Matta *(person's name)* 116

Microclimate 93

Migration route, caribou 110

Mosquitoes 42, 71, 111, 116

Muskeg 109, 112

Najuratsaungittuq *(places forbidden to ordinary human beings, places where evil things were practiced)* 75

Nalliit *(caribou crossings)* 108, 170

Nalunaikkutaq *(inuksuk known as a deconfuser, usually a single upright stone)* 76

Nanuk (Nanuq) *(polar bear)* 115–117

Nappariat *(small inuksuk like figures to which lines are attached to dry fish and caribou)* 65, 99, 115, 305

Narwhals 83

NASA astronauts 121

Natsilik *(Nettilling Lake — a huge freshwater lake in central Baffin)* 46, 47

Nikkisuitok *(the Pole star also known as Tuktujuaq "The great Caribou")* 81

Niungvaliruluit *(inuksuit constructed with a window; often acted as sightline to important places)* 89, 91

Niviaksiak *(a virgin, a person's name)* 115

North American Native peoples 36, 119,121

Northern folklore 121

Nuna *(the land)* 29, 287

Nuna *(nephew of Kov)* 267–269

Nunaliriniq *(when we are at one with the land)* 103

Nunannguait *(pl.) ("imitations of the earth" — maps)* 54, 77, 78

Nunannguaq *(map)* 75, 78, 79, 81

Nunarrak *(the land, sea and sky)* 39

Nunatiavaluk *(a very fine land rich in food and beautiful to behold)* 39

Nunatsiaq *(the beautiful land)* 39

Nunavik *(Arctic Quebec)* 37, 55, 91, 132, 133, 221, 230, 296

Nurattamiut *(people of Nurrata)* 55

Nurrata *(implies where the land and the sea appear as one in winter a place NW of Cape Dorset)* 45, 55, 68, 75, 173, 272, *282*

AN INTIMATE WILDERNESS

Nuvudjuak *(the furthest camp (abandoned) NW of Cape Dorset)* 45, 68, 154, 277

Ojibwa 36

Ottochie, Ottochie 9, *188*, 189, 293, 306, 313

Paleoeskimo site *284–286*, 293, 298

Panar *(snow knife often made from the rib of a whale)* 84, 85

Pangnirtung *(Pangnituuq refers to "place of fat caribou")* 38, 85, 314

Paris 55, 257

Parr, Ikkuma *(Leetia's mother)* 132, 133, 143, 145, 146, 149, 151, 215, 270, 289, 296, 306, 313

Parr, Leetia *(interpreter)* 22, 62, 71, 159, 163, 165, 315

Parr, Quvianaqtuliak (Kov) *(Leetia's father)* 9, 215, 246, 267–270, 306, 313

Pingo *(a large dome formed by an up thrust of ice)* 110, 126

Pingwartuk, Pingwartuk (Ping) *(the first person to take me out on the land)* 9, 49, 246, 298, 306, 313

Pitseolaq, Mark *(often my travelling companion and early interpreter)* 108, 315

Polar bear 39, 80, 81, 85, 103, 115–118, 171, 174, 183, 224, 237, 310

Polar Continental Shelf Program 108, 317

Pollen 94

Pootoogook camp 57, 78

Pootoogook, Eegyvudluk *(son of Josephie, Pootoogook)* 9, 234, 306, 314

Pootoogook, Kananginak *(elder, artist and son of Josephie Pootoogook who was the most respected man throughout Baffin Island region)* 9, 42, 43, 57, 77, 78, 157, 222, 234, 255, 262, 265, 314

Pootoogook, Paulassie *(son of Josephie, Pootoogook)* 9, 107–112, 115, 171, 217, 219, 228, 241, 293, 306, 314

Pootoogook, Pia *(interpreter, daughter of Eegyvudluk Pootoogook)* 22, 62, 233, 287, 315

Pootoogook, Pudlat *(son of Josephie, Pootoogook)* 9, 233, 234, 306, 314

Portugee *(Cape Dorset term used to refer to black-skinned people)* 49

Propitiating a spirit 112

Ptarmigans 73, 74

Pudlat, Osutsiak *(artist, elder and friend)* 198, 315

Pudlat, Pudlo 9, *248*, 249, 306, 314, 315, *322*

Puikkatuq *(a mirage)* 128, 135, 208

Qajaq *(s.)*, qajait *(pl.) (kayak(s))* 83, 84, 186, 187

Qallunaat *(pl.) (white people; Caucasians)* 42, 49, 54, 57–59, 61, 62, 67, 73, 108, 201, 203, 255, 256, 267, 277, 288

Qallunaq *(s.) (white person)* 74, 107, 138, 196, 197, 215, 249, 258, 261, 267, 268

Qamani'tuaq *(Baker Lake)* 79, 313

Qarmaaqjummiut *("People of the sod houses")* 54

Qarmaarjuak *(Amadjuak - Ammaarjuak, a place between Kimmirut (Lake Harbour) and Kinngait (Cape Dorset); also refers to land of the ancient sod houses)* 53, 54, 78, 79, 97, 255, 256

Qaulluaryak, Ruth *(artist from Baker Lake)* 77, 79–81

Qaumainnasuuqmiut *(regional group; means the People of where the land is bright; later known by other Baffin islanders as Sikusiilarmiut; also known by their relatives in Nunavik, Arctic Quebec as "the People of the other half")* 55

Qaumarvik *(the land that is in brightness; included the ancient camp of Nuvujuaq and several small camps whose people were known as Nuvujjuaqmmiut)* 55, 75

Qaummaqquti *(the white stone placed upon a grave to focus the life force skyward; refers to "light")* 122

Qimmuksiujait *(phantom dog teams)* 128

Qugalugaki *(the imp who lives beneath the bed)* 65

Qujaligiaqtubic *(or "the place from which one returns to earth refreshed" the ancient name for the place Igaqjuaq, the "Great Fire place")* 76, 171, 174, 244

Qulliq *(also kudlik) (soapstone lamp)* 44

Qupirqurqtuuq *(the lake where the water is empty of fish but filled with "crawly things"; also refers to "crawly things" themselves)* 107, 110

Quppapik, Simeonie *(one of my dear friends and mentors)* 9, *52–55*, 61, 63, 66, 77, 78, 92, 95, 97, 157, 170, 199, 215, 217, 218, 222, 228, 237, 249, 255, 256, 289, 293, 294, 299, 306, 314, 315

Raven, repertoire of sounds, pecking order, antics 97, 102, 104, *114*, 115, 117–119, 141, 159, 175, 204, 205, 211, 218, 237

RCMP 57

Sacred or ceremonial sites 79, 128, 169, 172, 174, *244*, 298

Saila, Davidee *(son of Pauta and Pitaloosie Saila)* 130, 131, 138

Saila, Pauta *(master carver)* 9, 55, 131, 132, 135, 139, 169–171, 215, 272–277, 281, 299, 306, 314, *322*

Saila, Pitaloosie *(my little "sister" a fine artist, wife of Pauta)* 9, *60*-62, 131, 139, 140, 142, *155*, *166*, *194*, *238*, *272*-276, 306, 314, *322*

Salamonie, Joanassie *(dear friend, son of Salamonie, grandson of Josephie Pootoogook)* 9, 74, 124, 128, 211, 228, 243, 306, 314

Salliit Qikiqtanga *(also Shugliaq and Salliq — Southampton Island)* 101

Sami *(Laplanders — reindeer herders "People with the pointed shoes")* 79, 121, 256

Sapujjuaq *(a traditional fishing place)* 305, 306

Sargarittukuurgunga *(a word that suggests travels across a land of vast horizons)* 27

Sarko (Sarkuq) *(refers to the "armpit"; a camp on a Alariaq Island, near Itiliardjuk)* 69, 71

Sarko, (Shaqu) Munamee *(a fine sculptor)* 9, 169, 293, 306, 314

Saw *(clear quartz set into piece of caribou bone or ivory handle; used to etch, make holes, grooves and decorations)* 84

Schkoodayodabah *((Ojibwa) "great fire sleigh" or railway train)* 36

Seal 42, 44, 46, 47, 49, 57, 58, 67, 69, 73, 78, 99,
      102, 111, 116–118, 128, 130, 131, 137, 145,
      146, 149, 155, 174, 186, 190, 191, 195, 206,
      207, 208, 213, 216, 217, 219–222, 224, 246,
      251, 252, 253, 259, 270, 283, 287, 289, 294,
      295, 299, 301, 305

Sekkinek *(the sun)* 27

Siiliitut *(a festival celebrating human fertility)* 76

Sikusiilaq *(southwest Baffin Island area; means
      where there is open water in winter)*
      22, 23, 29, 42, 47, 51, 54, 57, 61, 64, 67, 75, 76,
      92, 101, 102, 107, 117, 122, 139, 167, 168, 172,
      225, 233, 235, 271, 275, 288, 294, 295, 299

Sikusiilarmiut *(people of the southwest Baffin)*
      54, 55, 117, 301

Sila *(the weather, also intelligence, wisdom)*
      50, 104, 105

Silent Messengers *(the book)* 10, 113

Snow machine 57, 102, 103, 125, 175, 204

Southampton Island *(known to Inuit as Salliit
      or Shugliaq)* 67, 76, 101, 117, 224, 288

Southwest Baffin 22, 42, 54, 55, 57, 58, 64, 76, 78,
      87, 92, 97, 101, 112, 116, 117, 122, 125, 157,
      168, 169, 205, 221, 243, 246, 256, 271, 272,
      279, *282, 284,* 294, 299

Spiritual landscape 75, 203

Starvation 80, 170, 191, 192, 224, 277

Story telling 65

Sugba *(a huge inlet of very turbulent water
      west of Cape Dorset)*
      45, 107, 111, 115, 117, 225

Suluk, Luke *(respected elder in Arviat)*
      123, 211, 300, 314, 316

Syzygy *(Russian term referring to when the sun,
      moon, and Earth lie in a straight line)* 126

Taimagiakaman *(the great necessity of staying alive)*
      88

Tapananitiit *(the powerful men)* 277

Tapestry 79–81

Tautouquaq *("lightening in the ice")* 123, 124

Tautugaqarviuqattaqtuq *(where one may have
      visions)* 123

Tauuunguatitsiniq *(creating a picture of a thing
      in another person's mind or the act
      of conveying images onto another person's
      consciousness)* 46, 92

Tent rings 65, 117, 138, 173, *284*

The Bay *(Hudson's Bay Company)* 58

Tides 50, 51, 67, 71, 75, 103, 126, 132, 139, 164,
      170, 187, 205, 206, 246, 249–252, 268, 269,
      274, 290

Tikiraaqjuk *(the Great Finger; the peninsula
      pointing to Southampton Island)* 45, 75, 139

Tikkuuti *(pointers of different sizes and shapes)* 90

Tikotit *(s.) (pointer)* 99

Tiriguhunginiq *(observing an ancient tradition)*
      252, 253

Torngatalik *(the haunted hills where spirits inhabit)*
      107

Traditional knowledge, loss of 59, 88, 309

Travelling by dogsled 57, 127, 202, 243

Tukiliit: The Stone People who Live in the Wind
      (the book) 113

Tukilik *(a major inuksuk site far inland in
      the middle of the Foxe peninsula;
      "a thing which has meaning")*
      92, 106, 107, 110–113

Tukipkota *(small inuksuit indicating a place
      where there is lots of fish)* 100

Tulugaq, Pauloosie 204–209, *206, 207,* 314

Tulugaq *(a raven)* 118, 119, 218

"Tulugaq-tulugaq-turaarit-tuttuit-mitsaanut"
      (incantation) 119, 218

Tuniit *(regarded as those who prepared the land
      for the Inuit. The "Ancient ones")*
      79, 283–291, 293–298, 301

Tunillarvik or angaku'habvik *(where shamans
      were initiated)* 91, 298

Tunirrutiit *(little stones representing gifts
      often left at ancient inuksuit)* 95

Tunirnagajuit *(the "half Tuniit")* 296

Tunnilie, Quvianaqtuliak (Kov)
      *(carver, hunter one of the last to live
      on the land)* 105

Tupqujak *(a shaman's entrance or doorway
      into the spirit world)* 79, 109, 112

Turaaq *(an inuksuk acting as a pointer
      indicating the best route home)* 89

Tuttunik utaqqiurvik
      *(the place where hunters would gather
      to wait for the arrival of the caribou)* 113

Tuurngait *(the spirits)*
      39, 133, 167–169, 212, 215, 216, 223, 239

Udjualuk *(a friend's name who I have known
      for many years)* 69, 304

Udjuk *(bearded or square flipper seal)*
      44, 146, 190, 247, 259, 299

Ukpirijaujut *(things which are believed)* 65, 228

Ulu *(women's knife)* 44, 143, 149, 204

Umiak *(s.),* umian *(pl.) (large skin boat(s))*
      83, 221, 252, 255, 278, 279

UNESCO 55

Unganatuq nuna *(an overwhelming attachment
      to the land often expressed in spiritual terms)*
      28, 95, 174

Uqausitsapuq *(the "Word collector" —
      one of Norman's names)* 29

Utirnigiit *(referring to traces of coming and going)*
      88

Uujurumiaq *(when the earth appears to tremble
      because of heat rising from the stones)*
      123

Viking navigators 121, 276

Visible landscape 76

Walrus 66, 67, 70, 73, 85, 122, 155, 171, 173, 177,
      204, 216, 272, 274, 295

Weather 41, 49, 50, 53, 69, 75, 103, 104, 128, 129,
      164, 167, 173, 186, 187, 191, 207, 208, 222,
      233, 251, 271, 274, 278, 286, 288; flat light:
      129; whiteouts: 129; "time of magic light":
      129

White Swan *(Flaherty's Inuit name)* 53

Wolves 35, 105, 111, 181, 237, 239, 240

Xanthoria 94